Ben Graff was born in Aldershot in 1975.
He read law at Bristol University.
Find Another Place is his first book.

Find
Another Place

Ben Graff

Matador
9 Priory Business Park,
Wistow Road, Kibworth Beauchamp,
Leicestershire LE8 0RX
Tel: 0116 279 2299
Email: books@troubador.co.uk
Web: www.troubador.co.uk/matador
Twitter: @matadorbooks

ISBN 978 1788034 548

British Library Cataloguing in Publication Data.
A catalogue record for this book is available from the British Library.

Printed and bound by CPI Group (UK) Ltd, Croydon, CR0 4YY
Typeset in 11pt Minion Pro by Troubador Publishing Ltd, Leicester, UK

Matador is an imprint of Troubador Publishing Ltd

For all of them

'The past is a foreign country: they do things differently there.'
L.P. Hartley, *The Go-Between*, 1953

'Do not ask your children to strive for extraordinary lives. Such striving may seem admirable, but it is the way of foolishness. Help them instead to find the wonder and the marvel of an ordinary life. Show them the joy of tasting tomatoes, apples and pears. Show them how to cry when pets and people die. Show them the infinite pleasure in the touch of a hand. And make the ordinary come alive for them. The extraordinary will take care of itself.'
William Martin, *The Parent's Tao te Ching: Ancient Advice for Modern Parents*, 1999

'In my youth I was determined to become a writer. I tried to write stories about spies and criminals, a world of which I had no experience. Little did I realise that the family I have just described provided the material for any number of novels. By the time I did realise it, it was too late.'
Holmes Family History – As remembered by Martin Holmes, 2000

Dear Girls (special)
11/11/04
'Just a few bits & pieces for you both. The velvet trousers will look adorable on you, Annabelle, & the pink outfit is for you, Madeleine. Give my love to Mum and Dad. Will be seeing you all at Xmas. Until then, kiss, kiss, kiss.'
Grandma Theresa

Contents

2014 Part 3

Foreword

"Families are their stories," said my grandfather Martin that late autumn day in 2001, as he placed a clear plastic folder containing his journal into my hands. His fingers felt cold on mine as they brushed briefly, the copper wrist bracelet he wore to help with his arthritis seeming to hang a little more loosely than before. The remaining hair on his head was the same natural black it had always been, the grey moustache neatly trimmed as ever, but he walked cautiously and weighed his words carefully, just as the writer he had always wanted to be might have done. He both was and was not quite the way I remembered him.

In the summer you would be able to hear the shouts of children playing at the sailing school across the creek, but they were long gone now, and other than the clank of the car ferry unloading, no sounds carried across the water. Over the years, I had spent many hours watching from the shingle of Fishbourne beach, and from the deck of family boats, as the ferries went about their work. I had crossed this stretch of water at the beginning and end of family holidays, and listened to their low rumble in the quiet of the night, which was still just audible even from Martin's house in Ryde.

We stood alone and it would be years before I saw that this moment too was also part of a story that could be re-told, made sense of or not, that had meant something once and might do so again. He had nodded proprietorially and told me that his story was complete and, if older and wiser, I might have seen something almost mystical, sacred even, in that moment, but I was not and I did not.

Now as I write this in 2017, his use of the word complete is what I think to most, and I can see that day again when we stood together outside the Fishbourne Inn on the Isle of Wight, with a breeze from the Solent gently blowing dying leaves off the trees and into the mud of the near-empty beer garden. There were no other patrons outside, nor any sign that there had been any. No beer that had been reduced to a layer of foam in lipstick-marked glasses, no cigarettes smouldering to nothing in abandoned ashtrays, no nearly empty plates yet to be removed by the waiting staff. After eating we had only come outside to get some air, and the meal had not been a complete success. He seemed distracted, perhaps thinking to what he was going to share, but it might have been that he was tired. I had lost at chess the previous night and kept drifting back to why I had pushed the pawn when playing the knight would have been so much better, unable to separate myself fully from the disappointment. He had fiddled nervously with the folder while we ate, but he did not mention it until now, when he handed me his story.

I did not ask whether he meant to say his journal was complete, or if he thought something more fundamental was drawing to a close. Perhaps I already knew. He had finished his writing and his life as good as, while at twenty-four my own was only just beginning to inch toward any form of definition, and my writing would not have overly employed whoever had printed and wrapped in plastic the copies of his journal.

I had met Katharine and she was pregnant, but we were closer to being married and further away from being parents than we thought. I was two years into a job that I did not much like but feared to leave, while Martin's much more protracted career was long since over. Instead of the novelist he had wanted to be, he had spent his working life running shops that sold clothes, then shoes, finally musical instruments; I would later find that the other commercial ventures that were meant to give him a way out were described in his writing as disastrous and best forgotten. My own career had been mainly spent writing policy papers for a large organisation, which generally liked the way they were written, though the pieces were always wrong as somebody more senior either already had, or had not yet, decided what the answer was meant to be. In contrast, Martin's journal was much more substantive, a last piece of work, a final project. As a matter of chronology, everything else he had done had led up to its creation.

If you don't find a way to write things down it all gets lost in the end, or at least I think it does, he had said as we stood there. He told me that he had wanted to do this, to share the things about him that nobody else could know. His journal contained stories about him during the Second World War taking pot shots at planes from his bedroom window, an unrequited romance, boarding school in the 1920s, and difficulties with his father. It seemed that problems with fathers was a pattern that followed in our family just as regularly as white has the first move in a game of chess. This troubled me even on first reading, another potential warning sign, as being a father moved from being an aspiration, to something that had gone wrong, to finally a reality for me. I did not really understand what he had given me, or appreciate that his story was part of my own and that both of us were part of a tapestry of events that were larger and more complex still. I was subsequently to lose his neatly typed reflections and not think of them again for many years.

However, by 2016 much had been lost and much had changed. Many of those who had shaped the first part of my life were no longer alive and others had not so much taken their place in the family as created their own. Martin had been dead for fourteen years, my grandmother, his wife Anna, for twenty-two. My grandparents on my father's side were gone too: Dave in the months before Martin, and Theresa in 2009. If there is a sense of following the natural order in losing grandparents, three of whom were in their eighties, the same does not apply for parents, even if theoretically you might think it should, particularly when both deaths are seen as untimely, both funerals peopled by many already older than either of them would ever get to be.

My mother Mary had died in 2008 at the age of sixty-one when I was thirty-two and my father Colin at sixty-eight when I was thirty-nine. One death shockingly sudden, the other expected, although I was surprised to hear it described as such. I always felt that the second half of my own life began on the day of her death; that things had started to turn and that while they would keep moving, they would not go back. The years that followed with my father after my mother's death were not always easy, and then they too were gone. He was both more and less himself after her, and while we had more physical proximity during that time, it made our relationship more complicated, rather than closer.

But this is not all about deaths; there were new lives too. We had four children: Annabelle, Madeleine, Francesca and Gabriella. My brother Matthew and his wife Rachel had two, Reuben and Evie. I had become a parent and lost my parents. Everything was changing and, in amongst the business and the hustle, I wanted to pause to look not only backwards but also to the future. I wanted to remember some of the things that we did as children that had seemed to matter, while I still could. Remember, too, some of the things my parents had done. I missed them and wanted to talk to them again. I wanted to think about what it all meant for me, not just as the child I had been back then but also as the parent I am today.

I regretted that there were not obvious ways to reach them both afterwards. So much in my memory and in the memories of other people too, but nowhere else. Even the house they shared ultimately had to be sold. My regrets turned out to be only partially founded; there was more remaining than I thought, once I started to look for it. I found Martin's journal again and it was to be the first of a number of discoveries. There were letters between my parents in a desk drawer from before their marriage, although in truth I did know about these. A handful, all carefully preserved in their original envelopes, even if on many the postmarks had faded. They were not in exact sequence but answered each other at a deeper level. They had been mainly posted from Bristol and the Isle of Wight by her, and from London by him, as she started out as a teacher and him a junior scientist. Finally they were stored in the two houses they were to own together in the course of their lives, the first in Aldershot, the second outside a small village in Herefordshire called Bosbury.

As we cleared out what had once been their house, I came across still more papers, in garaged boxes and the loft, in amongst broken bits of Hoovers, an old fireguard and several headboards. Some of the paper had a dusty smell from having been there for so long, but it was all dry and perfectly preserved. Fragments of other diaries, work records and poems, in amongst the more mundane insurance documents, old telephone bills and the various pointless pieces of print that accompany all of our lives, leading up to that final paperwork which is for others to complete on our behalf. We are all destined to get at least one certificate, my father once said.

From a vantage point in my own life I wanted to try and understand all of them better, when I was older than they were in some, if not all, of the moments that the following chapters explore. A chance for them to speak one last time, here on the page, and for me, perhaps, to speak for the first time.

As the family has evolved, births have followed deaths, the generations have intermixed and then separated out again, and the world has changed; while in some ways that matter less, it has stayed the same. For now, I remain as a witness to some of this, but only for now. Living and dying has a force of its own, everything has a time, everything a season, the saying goes. There was a sense of this in my mother's poems, which centre on Bosbury Church through the four seasons. A summer bride, an autumn harvest, all part of cycles that we can share in but will one day go on without us. I wanted them to live on in some way and I needed to find a different way to live myself.

I also wanted to write. If it was not for that, I might just have re-read Martin's journal and my parents' letters and the other miscellany and thought about all this and quietly worried about how best to parent and the generational challenges I had begun to notice. Yet my not writing was part of why I felt incomplete, and losing all of them had served only to accentuate my sense of loss. I did not want somebody in the future to say of me that I had wanted to write but did not; for even this memory to slip away, like the final ferry of the evening, the lights of which can be seen from the shore for a while, before all goes dark.

In the end I realised it did not have to be this way. The family had left so much paper for me, so many other memories and questions as their final gift, that sitting down to write was more joining a conversation than beginning one.

I had spent so many years trying to write, only for my efforts to go wrong, just as things often seemed to go wrong between me and my father; we would start out alright, only to get lost in a fog of misunderstanding that mutual good intentions did not always salvage. My first attempt at a novel was the dark and obscure *Bleeding*. I was twenty-two and it was about self-harm, my only experience of the subject a short story I had read. I did not believe in structure or other devices that might give the reader much of a clue as to what was happening (character names a sense of progression; a feel for time or season). I created a voice that was not my own, to tell a story that was not mine to tell. All cloaked in what I thought was literary language, but which rather than making *Bleeding* beautiful, made it as difficult to read as my father was, with far less reason for anyone to want to try.

There were other pieces from around the same time, including a short story about a man in hospital who spent his time staring at a patch of damp on the ceiling. An old lady who visited him I described as wearing the sort of cardigan that people wore while they were waiting to die. My characters were passive watchers, much as I was, but I did not know any of them and could not make them live.

As my time at Bristol University concluded, I had no sense of what to do, beyond the thought that I would like to be a writer. Hence a creative writing course that I thought might help me on the path to becoming one. A group of us spent the week with Rachel Cusk and David Flusfeder. Philip Henshaw came along for one of the evenings. My father drove me to the station with muttered scepticism and seemed relieved on picking me up to learn that it had not really worked. In amongst the cigarettes and the snooker there were moments, but the tutors wrote publishable books and I did not, which served only to accentuate the difference. I felt further away from where I wanted to be, not closer to it.

You don't have to write the best book in the world, Rachel Cusk had said to me. That makes it too hard. Focus first on writing what you write and see where it takes you. In the end we all have a voice if we can find it, and there are stories all around us. Good advice that I ignored.

I wanted to write the world's best book, and as the chances of fulfilling this aspiration slipped out of reach it became increasingly clear that there would not be another book after *Bleeding*. Not back then. I did not hit it off with my fellow students during the week. They mainly wanted to write about their cats, and my cultural snobbery back then was close to unlimited. I was far closer to them in terms of literary achievement than I was to the real writers, and nobody knew that more than I did.

When, a few months after the writing course, I sent David Flusfeder the final copy of *Bleeding*, he wrote me a letter, which I somehow managed to lose without reading, and he wrote me another one when I told him this, an act of kindness that I will always remember. He was both encouraging and honest, but I was not really ready to deal with the feedback I received from that small number of people who had the misfortune to have *Bleeding* inflicted upon them. Despite my best efforts, *Bleeding* had some nice passages and turns of phrase (albeit they were mostly derivative) but the overall effect was absolutely terrible.

I did not understand my characters. I lacked both the experiences that might have enabled me to sense what they really thought and the technique that could have partially masked this deficiency. My voice was buried under linguistic flourishes which made me sound more like a literary version of the speaking clock than the angst-filled twenty-something woman who self-harmed I was trying to be.

It all depends how much you want these things, and it turned out that I did not want to be a writer enough. I had heard the stories about Iain Banks having six novels rejected before *The Wasp Factory* was accepted, but I lacked that level of resilience. I feared failure and rejection. I think as well, at that time when I had neither experience of being a parent nor of losing one, never had a long-term relationship nor a house nor a life nor a set of things that unfolded that I might watch and relate to, I simply was not ready. Beyond this, my passion for chess which I played competitively and compulsively did not leave much time for anything else.

In *The Chess Artist* the author J.C. Hallman asks the keen chess player Glenn Umstead if he saw himself firstly as a black man or as a chess player, and after some thought Glenn said that being a chess player was more central to his identity. Similarly, I was more chess player than writer (or anything else), no matter that I was nothing special and would sometimes sit at the board thinking that there might be better ways to express myself. The thought was never as strong as the pull of the next game. So whilst the desire to write never went away, the determination to actually do it lay dormant until now, when I finally realised, as Martin had before me, that the things around you are of interest. That the people and the situations you know and have lived with and through are where you should start. At forty, my perspective was different to at twenty. It would be foolish to claim that I was wiser, but I was certainly more experienced and I recognised that if I was finally going to start it needed to be now – here in this moment where my parents would never be able to read whatever it was that I wrote, however heartfelt and whether it touched them or not.

At some level there was also a freedom that came from this, not just in the sense that I was going to be able to write about them and use their letters in a way that would not have been possible if they were still here, there was something else that I recognised, even if I did not feel wholly comfortable with it. Somehow it was easier to do anything, knowing that they would not be able to judge it.

My father always mocked but did not actually read *Bleeding*, and over the years it became something of a one-sided joke that he failed to recognise I did not find funny. When David Kirk, the son of my Uncle Mike's partner, Rona, published his first book, *Child of Vengeance,* to general acclaim, my father's dismissive comment to me that it had been a bit more successful than *Bleeding* was both eminently true and quite hurtful. One of those moments that in some small way epitomised the difficulties we had in trying to hit it off. I remembered the remark but suspect he probably did not.

It was all a long way from where things had started.

Before I became a reader and then briefly a failed writer, I did not like books especially. At one time reading was work. I did not know that books and the people in them could speak to you directly, not until I found Holden Caulfield in *The Catcher in the Rye*, who watched and observed and somehow shared more of himself with you than he thought he had. I secretly feared he might think I was a phony; it transpired that not all books were about the challenges of finding the right marriage in the nineteenth century.

I came to like Salinger's *Franny and Zooey* too and became increasingly intrigued as to why he had written such beautiful books and then just stopped. I wrote a short story about a writer who still wrote but did not publish anymore, which I later came to see as ironic, as by this point my writing had petered away to almost nothing. But I still read lots of books about writers and writing.

Henry Miller in particular, who when he first wrote of having reached thirty-three, the age of Jesus, while achieving precisely nothing, had struck me as really old. Now, in what seemed like a heartbeat, I was older than he had been then, but unlike him I was still yet to commit to paper. Miller wrote about the desire to write, the creative process and how fundamental it was. I liked the crazy, shambolic, itinerant nature of his artistic life, while also knowing that, even if by some miracle I did actually manage to write anything, I would never have been able to live it myself. I recognised the degree of conventionality within myself, which had been meant as a cloak around which a more creative side might flourish but in truth was in danger of suffocating me if I did not try and write something soon.

By the time I was twenty-two I had moved from reluctant reader to devourer of books to would-be writer to failed writer who still read a lot, and stayed there for as long as it takes a newborn baby to become an adult and a little bit longer. There was always a reason not to write. My mother talked to me about some of this perhaps a year or so before she died. Should you not write again? It might be time, she said.

I did not act on her suggestion, in part because I still did not know what it was that I wanted to say.

The day my father died, I waited in the house with my brother Matt for the doctor to come and write his death certificate, and we went through the things that would need to be done to secure the house for its first night without a parent to guard it. There was cash we knew about in the cupboard in the spare room, kept there in case of some unknown emergency. There were keys to find and windows to lock, a bonfire to be built in the orchard to deal with his ruined bed sheets and mattress. In amongst the urgent jobs, I undertook another that was less so but still mattered to me. I found the few remaining manuscript copies of *Bleeding* in the desk drawer of what had been my bedroom and threw them on the bonfire with the rest of his things.

It was time to destroy the evidence of the book that my father had mocked but not actually read. I was finally ready to begin again, both unencumbered by his criticisms and drawn to the memories of him and all the others who were now gone.

This is not a eulogy. All families have their moments. The eulogies have already been given and every word of them was deserved. Now is the time for looking deeper. I finally know what it is that I want to say, even if they are no longer able to hear it. Martin was the first of them to be born, in 1916, and my father was the last of them to die, in 2014, so there are nearly a hundred years, of which I can bear direct witness to, say, thirty-five. I can only ask the questions in relation to my own parenting; they will be for others to answer.

As Martin said, families are their stories. So here it is, our family.

This might not always be easy, but I hope that it is honest. It is written with love. I think, in the end, they did it right.

Prologue – Our 9/11

B lake Morrison wrote that at one point in his life he divided his friends into those who had children and those who did not. Then, not so much later, whether or not his friends' parents were still alive became the truer measure of differentiation.

In those early days of the new millennium, I had no children and my parents were very much alive, but autumn then, as now, spoke to new beginnings and fresh possibility, and Katharine and I were making plans to have children of our own. I doubt we consciously thought back then that through the very workings of time, Blake Morrison's second category would not be avoided forever.

We had returned from Greece the previous day with some inkling, perhaps a little more than that. A notion that something had happened, that our story was moving on.

Much, but not all, from my childhood, was still intact. Two of the grandparents remained, Martin in a convalescence home, writing the journal he would shortly give to me, Theresa still in her Bognor flat in Nyewood Gardens, a year on from Dave's death and thirty-five from that of their then seventeen-year-old daughter, Helen. My mother's mother Anna had been gone for seven years, but my parents Mary and Colin were both still working, her at the Royal National College for the Blind in Hereford, him at the big Ministry of Defence establishment in Malvern, neither even particularly near to their retirements.

The holiday had been alright if a bit basic. A bedroom with no television, floor of tired lino that was never free from sand, and shower which was lukewarm at best. We had jobs but not much money and it had been what we could afford. The lady who cooked on the grill by the pool spoke very little English and her vocabulary appeared to have been gleaned from episodes of *Only Fools and Horses* on UK Gold. "Lovely jubbly!" she would say, over and over, while burning burgers and ramming the meat into white baps. I washed mine down with lager, Katharine drank orange juice. We did not talk about what we were going to do when we got home, as if to speak it into existence might somehow scare it away, but I could not help but think to what might be coming and what fatherhood might entail.

Things were better between me and my father than they had been when I was a teenager, but he still struck me as difficult and hard to get close to. I had heard stories about Martin and his father, Arthur. I even remembered my uncle, Martin's son Mike, telling me at Anna's funeral that he had been closer to Anna than he was to his father.

Perhaps it was a father and son thing? Perhaps it would be easier to have daughters, not that there was a choice about these things. Could it be that parental mistakes were inevitable? That we were all destined to push against the template that our own fathers had set, but in so doing set ourselves up for a whole host of new and different mistakes that might actually make things worse?

In amongst the high-fat food, sun too consistent to be interesting and the lower-league English football that was showing on the television screen above the bar, these were the questions I thought to, even if I did not exactly have any answers. It was not obvious that you could work any of this out in advance; perhaps you just had to hope for the best.

It wasn't that long since we had first talked of this, on the night of the general election in 2001. "Let's have a baby," Katharine had said, while we ate at The Malt Shovel. It did not seem that far on from the time when she had told me that I did not really know her, but things seemed different now. In that moment I had not felt any of the fears that I was to dwell on later. There did not seem to be any reason to say no and there were many to say yes. A family, a new beginning, a purpose, I thought. A move away from the loneliness and lack of definition that had marked the early stages of my adulthood, the time in my life when it had seemed to me that so much was theoretically possible but the reality had never quite lived up to it.

We returned home to watch Hague being annihilated by Blair, who in turn explained why this was a reasoned verdict on New Labour, being based on their record in government, such as it was. (He did not say that last bit, but I had a far greater degree of detachment than a few hours before.) We had agreed to something of much more import, the world was moving away from just being about events that I watched on television. Why not, I had thought as I sipped on my drink and thought to a future I had not previously imagined. It felt more natural than scary, at least whilst I sat at the table that night.

I secretly wanted a daughter, perhaps a subconscious reaction to how fathers and sons had tended to play out in our family; and we flew home from Greece on September 10, sensing that things had happened quickly since the conversation in The Malt Shovel. Katharine went to work the next day. I had holiday to use up and stayed at home. We said we would do the test in the evening.

I spent the morning buying bookcases in Coventry and managing the logistics of getting them home, which was not easy without a car. I still did not drive. I had taken and failed my test on many occasions, baffled by the limitations of my sense of direction, unable to believe that what I could see was really what was there.

Many chess players cannot drive. We are programmed to look deeper, to find some hidden meaning in what is seemingly in front of us, a choice that can only be discerned after considerable contemplation. Useful qualities to have when weighing up a potential pawn sacrifice, less admirable when trying to navigate a roundabout to get onto the A46 with a stream of angry commuters banked up behind you.

An unimpressed taxi driver, not keen to help, was described by the furniture shop owner as ignorant. Finally, he agreed to take the smaller bookcase for an extortionate fee and I wheeled the larger unit up Ball Hill on a trolley the shop had lent me. It was sweaty work, and there were moments when I feared the bookcase might fall off, but no one paid me much attention as I meandered past the pound shops and run-down pubs, back to the first house I had ever owned. A semi-detached in Wyken that I had overpaid for but which was worth it to me.

The house was on the wrong side of town, where property was cheaper and everything was somehow that bit more chaotic. It was difficult to get to and from work on the buses. The next-door neighbours bred ferrets and were too ill to work, but he was often loud and chronically out of time and tune on his return from the pub of a Sunday evening. Their daughter joined the police in then had to leave because of her boyfriend's tendency to steal and sell anything he could lay his hands on, or so it was rumoured. Darren, a fellow Manchester United supporter and work friend, who was to drink himself to death a year or so after my mother died, once asked me if I ever hung out at the block of flats at the end of the road, which I always considered one of the oddest questions anyone had ever posed. I never quizzed him about it then and now it is too late. Was it something he did himself, either more generally or in relation to that particular block?

Mum and Dad had given me five thousand pounds, which was the sum total of the deposit I had put down. I never really appreciated that that was a lot of money for them at that time. They would come up at weekends and he would help me decorate. Trips to Homebase and B&Q, his DIY skills better than mine, which wasn't saying much, but I couldn't afford professionals. Years before, when we moved from Aldershot, he had fallen through the ceiling when we were packing up to leave. He didn't hurt himself, but a shower of plaster scattered like snowflakes and they had to reduce the price. Fortunately, the buyer happened to be a builder.

At the point of exchange, when about to move into the Coventry house, the sellers had tried to pull out, which left Theresa incandescent. "They can't have their cake and eat it," she said, the old legal secretary in her coming to the fore, much as it had saved her in the weeks after Dave had died. Back then she had been sent a letter by some firm saying that he had owed them money and she was liable as next of kin. "We'll see about that," she said with a glint in her eye. She wrote back saying she wasn't paying and what were they going to do if she died too go after some of his distant relatives in Australia? She never heard from them again, but we knew that she had found a way to keep going after Dave.

Move my sellers did, after being read the riot act by their own solicitors. John, my solicitor, a close family friend of my parents, was similarly indignant. The house was bigger than Katharine's in Solihull, albeit it was hers that had the expensive fireplace and elegant drink bottles on the fridge that had so impressed me when I had first been there. She had a glamour and level of sophistication that I could not match, and many had been surprised, including me, when we had first got together. We had moved into our respective houses on the same day, a year or so before we first met. Just a coincidence, perhaps;

lives somehow on parallel tracks that were close to finally twisting, coming together, but still had not.

Katharine had been a Bristol law graduate too, but she was older than me and had finished the year I started the same course. We only met much later when, somewhat ironically, she covered someone's maternity leave at the company where I worked. A mutual friend thought that we might hit it off and invited me on a work night out with the team they were both in.

"So, who are you, then?" she had said and that was pretty much me. When we eventually got together we agreed it made more sense to live in my house in Coventry while we went through the logistics of selling both properties and buying something new. A decision Katharine still winces at today; she never much took to Wyken.

I got the bookcases into place. Loading the shelves, fresh pine scent mixing with the aroma of books, mixing up our collections another sign of where we were and where we were heading. The television news was on in the background, Tony Blair to speak at the TUC Conference, the reassuring comfort of the world unspooling as it was meant to, neatly presented with block heading captions and widescreen angles.

Our books all needed to be properly housed and I was focussed on completing the task before Katharine returned. Perhaps I was instinctively nesting, I don't know. I thought to a work dinner where someone had asked why anyone should bother to keep books that they had already read. Most of them will not be read again, a friend had said. My manager, another reader, sighed. "It's your inner life, is it not? If you don't keep them you might as well throw away your soul." A comment that drew blank looks from the rest of the team, but I knew exactly what she meant. Books said a lot about who you were – the stories that interested you, the places to which your mind had travelled.

I remembered a line from somewhere, to the effect that no one should be allowed to carry a photograph of anyone else without that person's permission. It was too personal, too much theirs, not yours. I used to think the same about anyone seeing your book collection; that to do so was to let them look into you in a way that was deeply personal. It was not something to be taken lightly.

I continued to mixup and house our collections, but the images on the screen stopped making sense even when I turned the volume up. Many things we thought we knew had been changed, first by one plane, then another. Blair heading back to London. Bush talking about the folks who had done this. But still I loaded volumes onto the shelves, unable to tear myself fully from my task; what I was watching simply did not resonate.

Eventually I sat on the floor amongst the novels, just watching. A film that was not a film; the noise and the rubble and the panic were all too real. Years later I watched a replay of 9/11 in real time with our second daughter, Maddie, who had developed an avid interest in the subject. The programme was based on video footage captured on people's phones. Maddie described the twin towers to me as looking like wounded animals, with the smoke that billowed out of them their blood; and now whenever I see the footage again I think to her description.

I was told that our London office closed down early that day, and Katharine returned home from Birmingham early too, at around 4pm. We sat and watched as people who had come into work for a normal day, only hours before, jumped from ledges, a hundred storey up in the sky, sometimes holding hands. There were already extracts of desperate telephone calls being played on the news and it was almost impossible to feel even shock; there was no reference point to make sense of what we were watching.

A radio transcript played of the former world chess champion, the American Bobby Fischer, who claimed that the day was one for celebration. Rejoice, rejoice, he says. What goes around comes around! The USA had this coming.

"Chess players are all crazy, right?" Katharine says to me.

I speak to Martin on the phone and ask him, this compares to everything else he has seen in his life. "It doesn't," he says, but does not elaborate. There are only so many words.

But in our house in Coventry that evening, other things were happening, and while we deferred our plan for an hour or two, the pull of it was too great. We needed to know, and the test confirmed it. A solid blue line; she held the white plastic handle and then gave it to me to look at. Katharine was pregnant.

I was reminded of John Updike's Rabbit books. But there it was, the extraordinary set against the personal. He watched the moon landing, whilst getting divorced. Here a terrorist atrocity was unfolding, while we gained concrete knowledge that a new life had been formed.

Not the best of omens, I thought but did not say. Mum phoned and we did not tell her, but managed to reassure her that it was unlikely that Coventry was going to be the focus of a second wave of attacks, irrespective of what had happened in World War Two.

When things like this happened she always had a way of talking about them as if they were somehow my fault or had something to do with me, which was not her intention but just how she could come across on occasion. I could hear Dad sighing and muttering in the background; things were pretty much as they always were in their house, if not in ours, or in New York or Pennsylvania or Washington, DC. Then Katharine and I watched more of it, curled up together, both with our own thoughts.

I sometimes wondered who else might have been sitting on a sofa at the same time, on that day, reflecting on something similar. Holding a strip with a solid blue line; of course, there must have been many other pregnancies confirmed that day and births and deaths and other ordinary extraordinary things that people would remember, normal life wrapping itself around tragedy like a vine.

They all, Mum, Dad, Martin and Theresa, seemed surprised but pleased when we told them around the ten-week point. It must be safe to do so by now, we thought. Not long after Dave's death, six years after Anna's, and now the first step toward renewal, a generation that would carry us on.

Asking my father for advice would never have

occurred to me. Partly an age thing, also that I felt I was going to have to figure this out for myself, to create a new pattern for how to be a parent, even if this would in turn inevitably prove to be wrong too.

We started to plan at a more practical level, to think about cots and nurseries and baby clothes and where we would spend Christmas, given that the other set of grandparents would then have the first Christmas with our new baby the following year. The permutations were more complex than I had ever really considered; the politics of extended families and the need to keep everybody happy not straightforward.

Then at twelve weeks it all became academic. No sound at the scan. Nothing. No baby anymore. What could they say? There was no reason. No reason why it wouldn't work next time. Everything was normal. "It's part of life," the nurse had said. "Sometimes it is just nature's way." We think it was a boy. The closest I would ever come to a son, who I did not want as much as I wanted a daughter, and who I had somehow let down before he could live long enough for me to disappoint him.

We decided to change our plans and get married first and then see what happened. Then Katharine got pregnant again and we brought the wedding date forward. Mum and Dad were supportive. I think by this point they were never quite sure what we might tell them next.

"You're getting married? OK, son," Dad said, with a tone of approval that I was grateful for. I also heard in him an echo of his father which I hadn't really noticed before.

"You're committed now," said Mum, which was fine.

She went on to say that I hadn't really known Katharine for very long, which was less so, but I told her not to worry.

A week before the wedding we had our twelve-week scan and set out to the hospital with an entirely different mindset, almost assuming that it would all have gone wrong because it was easier to approach it this way. But it hadn't, and we could see what appeared to be a miniature bean leaping around on the ultrasound.

"Would you like to know the sex?" the radiologist asked.

"Well…" I said, and I could tell you that I do not know why I hesitated, except that would not be true and I have promised the truth if nothing else. Partly I was scared that knowing might jinx things. It was more than that though. I assumed it would be a boy and that my first, secret reaction would be one of mild disappointment. Something that would never be admitted to but might colour all that followed.

"Of course we want to know," said Katharine.

"I'm as certain as I can be that it's a girl," said the radiologist.

We married in Coventry, in the local church, where occasionally I would go with Katharine to the short Saturday evening services, at which the neighbouring streets were prayed for on a rota basis. I had tried to show a new interest in religion, as it mattered to Katharine just as it did to my mother, but that was not enough to make it stick. But being in the church on our wedding day felt very natural and Mum did a reading, as did Katharine's mum, Anne.

I still watch the video sometimes, but where once I watched it to look at me and Katharine, I now do so to hear my mother speak. Theresa sat in the front row, the only surviving grandparent on my side, Martin having faded in the December after the miscarriage.

Katharine had three of hers there. Flora in her eighties was the eldest person at the wedding and eventually became the last of her generation within the family to pass on, aged 101. Cliff and Kathleen were there too, Katharine's biological grandparents on her father's side, except years later it would transpire that Cliff wasn't. Rather, David was the product of a brief fling that Kathleen had had years ago with a *Coronation Street* actor.

His sisters had already known for some time, but when Cliff told him it was too late, the actor was already dead, but we did watch an old tape of him in an early episode of *Coronation Street* once.

Cliff and Kathleen are both gone now too. Kathleen's son-in-law cut off his pony tail and put it in Kathleen's hand in her coffin, because she had always wanted him to cut his hair, he told us. No one knew quite what to say to that.

Cliff died a few years later, having been very clear about the arrangements for his family vault and who was going to have which of the remaining berths within it. I remember telling my father this story and we both had the same reaction, which was that we thought this was a Jewish thing. We both liked Joseph Heller's *Good as Gold* with its blazing family arguments over the dinner table as to who might ultimately be buried next to whom. Dad swore that he had been to too many bar mitzvahs when he had been growing up which had been dominated by heated rows on precisely this subject.

"People are people, right?" I said with a smile.

"It is all much madder than I thought," he said. There were photos at Kenilworth Castle in the rain and then in the sun, part of the package deal with the Holiday Inn, the photographs that is, rather than the elements. Dad had wanted to make a speech, but it wasn't what the father of the groom did. It would have been difficult in any event, with Katharine's biological father David and her stepfather Roger, who had married Katharine's mother Anne while Katharine was still little, both there. But I think my saying no disappointed him, just as he was subsequently disappointed for the same reason at my brother Matt's wedding to Rachel, who also had a father and a stepfather. I think back now to whether we could have done something differently, found another setting for him to speak. I know he felt a bit let down by it all, and given that most of the time I wanted him to talk more, it was ironic that at one of the moments when he actually wanted to speak I prevented him.

We were terrified throughout the pregnancy. The antenatal classes felt an unnecessary temptation of fate. Katharine asked more questions than anyone else, as if thoroughness of preparation might act as a guard against anything going wrong. A month out we panic, an emergency scan follows and confirms all is well. Then Katharine's waters break. Two days later, Annabelle is born.

I speak to Mum from the hospital. She said she could

hear her own mother, Anna, in the name we had chosen, a silent affirmation of something that was bigger than all of us, perhaps. A year and six days after 9/11, Annabelle was with us. For all of the horror and the hate we had seen, it was pretty clear that there was one thing in the world that was amazing.

Maddie followed nineteen months after Annabelle, after an all-night wait and a caesarean. There are photos of me in hat and medical gown. The surgeon offered the chance to watch while Katharine was cut open, which I politely declined. Maddie had been breech and the plan was to turn her. As was so often to prove the case, Maddie had ideas of her own and there was not time. She is a formidable child. I remember her, still tiny in a playhouse, confronting a boy who had taken Annabelle's ball. "Give it back, little boy," she said, and brokered no room for debate.

They were all a bit shocked by Francesca, who was conceived whilst Katharine was still on maternity leave with Maddie. "You'll have to stop work now," Katharine's boss said. It was the same pattern. Three weeks early. Before we headed to the hospital I ended up taking Annabelle and Maddie, and a pan of half-cooked pasta, to a neighbour. A story still retold by the children today, even if they do not remember it. So our super sporty one was born. The one who always makes everyone smile.

A new family was taking shape, but the old one remained. There are photographs of Mum, Dad and Theresa with the three girls at varying stages. Baby pictures, complete with glasses of champagne, holiday snaps, and the two images I most associate with Mum during this time: a picture of Annabelle aged four, on Mum's lap, at a Christmas Eve meal in a restaurant. Both smartly dressed, Annabelle sits up straight, her hair blonder then and in a little bob. She holds her book and they smile at each other. Then a later one with Mum, Annabelle and Maddie in St Nicks park, a spring day by the looks of it, but I don't remember the moment. Maddie on reins that Mum gamely holds. It is not entirely clear whether Maddie is under control or not.

"It is really with older children that I'll be able to come into my own," my mother says. But she will not get that chance. There will be presents she has wrapped beautifully for Maddie's fourth birthday that we will open a week or so after her funeral. Tasteful dresses, carefully chosen with love, and there is a temptation just to preserve them for posterity, whatever that is. But ultimately she bought them to be worn, and they fit Maddie perfectly.

Then finally, six and a half years later, Gabriella arrives, but out of Mum, Dad and Theresa, only my father will get to see her. A freezing cold December night, the new house bought in anticipation, at this moment our belongings barely unpacked. The nearly new car frozen on the drive hastily de-iced.

She is the most expensive baby in history and the one who, with her brains and non-flexible negotiating positions, will run the house from here on in. Maddie was not as challenging as we thought, it will turn out. We tell Dad that Gabriella's middle name is Mary. "Mary," he says as he cradles her, whispering in her ear. He smiles. The whisper is not just for her.

Three years later he will be gone and the move from one generation to the next will be complete. The join between them will not be as deep as any of us would have wanted, and I will doubt, whilst not wanting to, the memories the children will claim to have of Colin, Mary and Theresa. But all of it will be something, and I have come by now to better understand the doubts and fears I had that day at the poolside in Greece. How all the questions we have about parenting never go away entirely, and the realisation that they must have been present in my own father in some way, just as they were in both Martin and Arthur and perhaps every other father who has ever been.

I would like to think if we had had a boy it would still have been alright.

Introduction to Martin's Journal

It was years since Martin had first handed me the copy of his journal that I was subsequently to lose. The leaves, which that day had been starting to fall and mix with the mud in the garden of The Fishbourne Inn, were long gone, as were those that belonged to many subsequent seasons, as was Martin himself. I stood on roughly the same spot during the summer when I was writing this, trying to remember if there was more to that moment, if there were things I had forgotten.

Listening to the sounds of a ferry I could not see docking at Fishbourne harbour a few hundred yards away, I wondered if she might have been *Saint Clare*, which had come into service the year of Martin's death and which he had lamented as being too large, bringing too much traffic to the Island. Perhaps it was also her that I had heard but could not see that earlier day; then new now older. I felt older myself as I stood alone, thinking back to that moment between the two of us, that now only I was in a position to remember. It had been years since I had been ill myself, in 2004, after Martin, after Annabelle, before Maddie, before any other deaths.

I scolded myself for thinking of me, rather than him,

but there it was. Was this why things sometimes went wrong in families, that even when we were trying to think of others we thought to ourselves? Did I do this with my own children now? They often said that they would try to talk to me and get nowhere.

"Look at me," Francesca would say, turning my head with her hands, bringing me back to her and a present that I should have been more capable of embracing than was often the case.

There it was. In that instance I started to think about not him but my own health and mortality. Optic neuritis in my left eye. I had first lost the peripheral vision, and then over the course of a few weeks the rest of it. When I eventually went to the doctor it was one of those times when you see a medical professional go very quickly from routine boredom to not being bored at all. Too quickly to realise that it is not a good thing.

Over the next few weeks I struggled to urinate and finally had to admit that I could not, and spent a week in hospital with a catheter, on steroids, having scans of my brain and an excruciating lumber puncture in my back. Over time the symptoms went away and different doctors gave different verdicts. I definitely had MS, or I did not but might develop it in the future, or it was possible too that I had something that was MS-like but not full-blown. The only option, even if it was not very writerly, was to get on with things and never to mention it again to anyone.

It had not come back in the same way, but I could feel the pins and needles sensation in my legs as I stood and thought; this illness or potential illness in me was a difference from the way things had been in 2001. I was the same to look at on the outside and I felt more or less functionally the same on the inside. But everything that had happened served as a reminder that, one way or another, these were early warning signs. I had seen Anna and Martin, Theresa and Dave, Darren and both my parents die. They had all battled illness and health challenges that started innocuously enough, even my mother. In the end it was fairly obvious that things would not be any different for me. I had to take this moment, to use it while I could.

I thought back to what Martin had told me in 2001 when he was being treated for the slow growing cancer on his shoulder. It was a time that had some significance for him; he often spoke of one of his school teachers who had been obsessed by the prospect of the millennium. "Only Homes and Davis have any chance of living long enough to see it," he apparently had said.

I wondered how that teacher would have viewed those early days of the twenty-first century, as the World Trade Center and the Pentagon fell to rubble because hijacked planes had been turned into bombs, seeming in every image to mock the notion that the world was somehow progressing, becoming more civilised and cultured. You could say that the teacher was better off not having lived to see those moments, but if that is really the alternative, what is the choice? The price of living is the need to continue to assimilate the unthinkable, to know that there is nothing that man won't consider doing to man, and then to continue living anyway. Perhaps this is the real reason why all of our life spans are limited. It isn't the physical but rather the emotional side of us that is worn out by all that the world faces us with. Some of our stories simply become too much for us.

I have no idea who Homes and Davis were, or whether they found their way into the twenty-first century to grapple with these questions, but there in its formative period, all was not well for my grandfather, and in truth that day I could sense this, much as some species of animal can smell death on another.

Apparently a number of people had advised against having the treatment, saying that it simply was not worth the risk, but he went ahead anyway. It's a vanity operation really, I heard it said.

It is impossible to know if things could have been different. I asked the same question after Katharine's miscarriage, the deaths of both my parents and that of Darren. When I saw a counsellor after my mother's death she said that you cannot think it different, it will always be this, and as I stood there in the pub garden, that was the one thing I could feel with certainty. It would never change, just as so many other things could never now be changed either.

Martin had a proprietorial air when he handed me his journal, in some ways not so far removed from his more general grandness of manner. Slightly pompous, some might say. I remember a dinner my mother arranged in Bosbury for him with friends of hers from the village. He had opened the conversation by talking about the circles in which he moved, and had lost his audience before he had started. It was sometimes how he was.

There were aspects of the actor in him perhaps, from all those years ago when he was part of an amateur dramatics group during the Second World War, something he wrote about in his journal. There was a certain air he could adopt with people that I now think might have been more about trying to hide his inner sensitivity than projecting any particular impression of grandeur. It is possible not everyone always saw it this way.

Physically weakened as he was by the treatment, a little thinner and more hunched perhaps, there was defiance there too in his mannerisms that day. The journal was his story, and it occurred to me all these years later that he did not really have any hopes for it, beyond the desire to hand out a few copies. He never talked about publishing it more widely or gave any expectation that it would be. There were probably parts of his story that he might have wanted to turn out differently.

I had wanted to find the journal again because I recognised that it was a piece of the story that he had tried to save and I had lost. As time had moved on, my desire to try and go back had grown, just as I wanted to do likewise in relation to my parents. There were final conversations that we were yet to have. Nobody else seemed to be able to find their copy either and I was running out of options when, finally, I stumbled across the original handwritten version, which I did not know I had, in a desk drawer. It was in a blue A5 book that cost £1.50 from Smith's. A number of differently coloured inks used on various sections, all equally unreadable. I was no closer, but I found Kelly Stevens, a handwriting expert, who was able to translate most of it back into typescript, making large parts of it readable once more.

Martin had always wanted to be a writer and this was his longest work. Standing outside the pub, I remembered the initial reaction of polite praise and unspoken disappointment which had greeted its completion. The kind of disappointment that does not need to be voiced to be understood within a family. Something I am sure he picked up on.

He had focussed more on the dead than the living. "You get fewer complaints that way," he had told me with a shrug. I thought perhaps that part of him would have wanted to write more about the living, but he had chosen to play it safe one last time. That said, he was a man of his time, not given to overstatement, quite discreet and, perhaps I have this all wrong and he did not even consider saying more, never thinking to comment on people who were still in a position to read his thoughts. Nobody can know for certain now.

It occurred to me as I re-read his journal that I could go beyond the words on the page in some places, even if this risked making me the phony I had feared Holden Caulfield had seen in me all along. He had been more open in our conversations, often late at night, over the years. Less guarded, I could see that. Hence, where there were places where I was capable of filling in the gaps, going in deeper, I chose to do so. Occasionally I took an informed guess but only where it seemed consistent with what I had heard from him or what I knew from another source.

As I stood outside The Fishbourne Inn, part of me wondered what I had done, but I had made the choice and there was no going back. So it was that years after first reading it, the rescued pages came to form a part of this story. I better recalled the parts that were directly about him than I did the whole host of family members who re-emerged from the dust, alive once again. Here it all was, set against a backdrop of the nineteenth and twentieth centuries, encompassing two world wars, his marriage to Anna and the rise and fall of a number of business ventures. (If we are honest, it was mainly falls and mediocrity really. His son Mike and his nephew Richard were to prove to be the first real businessmen in the family.)

The dramatic and the normal, still a little understated perhaps, but a voice on times and our family that nobody else could replicate, him a bridge beyond where I could go. The image that stays with me now is of him as a meter reader in the war, with a work list that did not always last the day, during those most desperate years in the middle of the twentieth century that would not find an echo until the first year of the twenty-first; the relationship at the heart of it which I think to most was the one with his father, which was difficult and then ultimately better, the family pattern between fathers and sons destined to repeat itself more than once in the generations ahead.

In truth he was the grandparent I was closest to. His storytelling, model railway building and interest in talking through issues were certainly part of that. I think beneath the extrovert most people saw, I could sense a kindred spirit, perhaps slightly more adrift than might be immediately imagined from external appearances.

I remember him telling me once that he had not been the favourite son, but it was still painful to see it written down on paper. I had heard the stories of him having to go into the family business, his brother Hugh being granted more latitude; Hugh was left the house, Martin more shares in the business. The closeness that existed between the brothers was clear for all to see and unaffected by their differing relationships with their father, Arthur.

Hugh was a highly amiable eccentric, who loved hunting with ferrets and drinking, albeit probably not in that order, a colourful presence when we were children. He spent his career racing rich men's boats and falling off the pontoon into Wootton Creek. When he was nineteen he was in a motorcycle accident and was diagnosed with Type 1 diabetes, a condition that would resurface in our family many years later through our daughter Gabriella. We would hear the stories from his daughter Janet, our cousin, of a house with no sugar and one large syringe of insulin a day, to be taken via a gigantic needle every morning. All far removed from the world we have come to know of pumps and Libres, fractional doses and perfect data, even if the underlying challenges remain just as scary as they ever have been, though Hugh's attempts to drive and shoot long after his vision had failed him are things we are hoping not to have to worry about with Gabriella.

So what follows is about meetings, endings and brothers. An old man looking back to a time when he was three and what was set in motion, and the reconciliation that eventually came after his mother's death. I recall Martin's son Mike saying that his relationship with Martin had also improved after the death of Anna. As Mark Twain said, history does not repeat itself but it often rhymes. I am not sure though that I would say the same for my own relationship with my father. It certainly grew deeper as we had to communicate directly with each other rather than through Mary, but that is not quite the same thing.

Just before he was due to start his treatment for cancer we had a meal together at another pub. I think, given I was working, he was disappointed that I did not offer to pay, and we left on a slightly awkward note. For the first time in a long while I remembered that too, with a shiver of embarrassment, as I stood in the breeze of the beer garden.

The week before he died I was encouraged by my mother to phone him but did not, preoccupied with other things, unsure quite what to say. Then finally, I was heading to the bus stop to go to work when Katharine ran after me to tell me that he had died. "Are you coming back home?" she asked, but I did not. I phoned the private room of the convalescence home later that morning and of course the phone just rang.

So there are always some regrets. I cannot re-make that final week and pick up the phone to him as I should have done, but I can try and share some of his stories now.

Martin's Journal –
Meeting My Father

So it is finally time to start telling these stories. I am out of excuses not to and I fear more importantly nearly out of opportunity. But in the more immediate sense, time is paradoxically something that I have a bit of as I sit here now, with my notebook perched on my knees, writing these first few lines. I am going to be in this place, convalescing and receiving treatment for several months. It is not so bad, it is clean and the people are friendly and this is all part of the process of getting better, I would like to think. It has that institutional feel that all such places must have. A routine and a rhythm, the smell of toast, chipped walls and tired furnishings, a sense both of purpose and things somehow on hold.

I have always wanted to write, to try and tell some of my stories, while I still can, and ultimately what else could I need? I have paper, ink and purpose and, of course, my memories such as they are. The family have long encouraged me to write but I am wary of offending, not that any of those who will outlive me have any reason to fear that causing offence might be my intention. Quite the opposite; but in any event the stories I could tell that they are in, they already know about and can do with what they will without me.

No, I think the main focus of these recollections will be to go back further. To try and tell of the times that my beloved Mary and Mike, Colin, Ben, Matthew, James and Francesca (Mike's two children) cannot know of, to at least try and give a window back to days long gone and what things were like for me when I was young. Now I am old I look back on my younger self and think both how different and how similar we both are; I would like to think that that person is still in me, even if there is little trace of him in the mirror.

We all begin with our parents and are destined to look back at much of what follows to us through the prism of our early days. I think that is right. I certainly still reflect on both of my parents now, so many years after their deaths. Albeit, it is my relationship with him that I dwell on more, perhaps because it was sometimes difficult, double-edged even. I should of course begin at the start, with that first encounter which seemed to set the tone for what followed.

When my father Arthur returned from the army in 1919, I met him for the first time in the very Victorian hall of our house, Woodville, in West Street. It had glass cases full of stuffed birds, squirrels and otters in keeping with the fashion of the day, and the whole place had been scrubbed from top to bottom in readiness for this moment. A heightened sense

11

of anticipation had been building throughout the morning as his arrival drew ever nearer.

When I look back it is hard to know what exactly I felt during that wait and whether some of what I write is really based more on looking at all this through the spectrum of my life now ending, rather than the three-year-old I was then. Of course, this must be the case to some extent, all of us can only re-remember things after all, but my predominant recollection of that day was that I could not have been more excited, albeit not by him.

There was a toyshop in St Thomas Square which had a wheelbarrow I had long coveted and my mother had said that I could have it "when Daddy comes home from the war". So my poor father had barely had time to say hello to the assembled family before he and my mother set out for the toyshop, with their son running on ahead. They had only reached the halfway stage when they met me coming back, shouting, "I've got the barrow!" It remained for them to hurry on and pay for it!

Who knows what was set in play in that moment. Whether it irritated him and he formed a perception of me that somehow crystallised. Or perhaps it was simply that you bond differently with a child you first hold as a newborn baby compared to one that you first meet when they are three. Possibly that is just the way it was for him. This would not have been an era in which such questions would have been asked and I am not sure if I even thought to them, at least back then. He was my father, I was his son, we were who we were. But as I sit here so many years later I think to them now.

I wonder in particular what he might have thought about that first return, whether it met his expectations. Somehow, I think it did not. The war for all its horrors perhaps had its share of excitement for him. Even though he probably longed to be home, perhaps the reality fell short. Better to travel than to arrive, as they say. The pressure of developing the business and looking after a son he did not know and his wife, perhaps nagged at him that first day in ways that he could never have shared.

But family life progressed. In 1921 my brother Hugh was born. Somewhat surprising as my mother had been told by doctors she would never have another baby! Doctors do not seem to have had a particularly good record in those days. I would like to say that they have improved a lot since then, but I do not really think this is the case. Certainly a longed for daughter never materialised.

It is often said that the relationships with the most longevity in your life are with your siblings. They come into the world around the same time as you and with good fortune should be with you for most of your days. Whatever was lacking in my relationship with my father was present in my relationship with Hugh. His recent death is another sign for me of all that is being lost; more and more of those I know are passing. If siblings come in with you then I am under no illusions that the opposite must also be true.

What can I tell you as to what my father was really like? Very little, I fear, but I can tell you some things about him. He was a keen footballer, playing for Ryde on numerous occasions; he had the natural sportiness I lacked. He owned a sailing boat, and the first motorbike on the Isle of Wight!

When the First World War broke out he joined the army, being posted to the Royal Engineers. Being a biker he was a natural for the job of motorcycle dispatch rider. This was an adventurous job, carrying dispatches from artillery batteries to the front line. As a dispatch rider he had the automatic rank of corporal. For two years he worked closely with Frank Harrison, his lifelong friend. I sometimes envied their easiness together, but there we are.

Arthur's pay as a corporal was one shilling and six pence a day! Possibly about £20 a week in today's money, a totally inadequate sum for Ada to keep herself and her baby son, me, born March 1916. Those First World War years must have been a struggle for my mother. I never really talked to her about them and it is funny how we often put off what might be most relevant and interesting until it is too late to know.

One other thing I should say about my father was a story I heard through the shop about his uncle, my grandfather's brother. Apparently my grandfather, Alfred, had put him in charge of a shop in Chichester, and shortly after the uncle (I do not even know his name) killed himself. I cannot say what impact this had on either my father Arthur or my grandfather

Alfred, although the Chichester shop was apparently immediately closed down and replaced with one in Shanklin.

I do not know the extent to which my father thought about this after the event, or whether it was symptomatic of a strain of melancholy in the family, a tendency to despair that perhaps resurfaces every few generations. Who can say? Suicide, like so many other things, was a completely taboo subject and this would never have been something I could have raised, even if I would have liked to have understood what he made it of all. I would have liked to have known more about my great uncle so he could be a person to me, not just a whispered fact I picked up from the staff in our shop.

My father and I were never very close, as must be clear from all that I have said of that first meeting and my sense that it defined the contours of all that followed in our relationship. Perhaps it could have been different, but for most of my life I was not equipped to see how.

That said, I am forever thankful that after my mother's death the situation altered considerably. After so many years of awkwardness and quiet misunderstanding, some of this seemed to fall away in his final years. My wife, Anna, had him to church most Sundays (he was always late). He and I were both members of Ryde Rotary Club; I took him around to as many functions as possible, and for the first time in our lives we were as close as I could have believed. In the company of others we somehow found a companionship of our own and I do believe finally that a bond was formed. Perhaps the thing that matters most with family is that you get there in the end, and in some ways we did. It only took the best part of fifty years to recover from our rocky start with the confusion over the wheelbarrow.

The moment I most often think to now again came in the period soon after my mother's death. I had gone away for a short cruise in the boat. When I returned and stepped ashore, he was waiting for me and he said, "Thank God you are back, Martin, I only feel safe when you're around." Believe me, that remark was a revelation, and a very precious memory.

Eventually my father faded away. He died only a week after his last solo trip in his boat; it was not expected. It was only when I had learnt not to have expectations and hopes that we managed to find some form of peace. Even if as I write this I can still think of many unanswered questions that now will never be answered, in some ways I feel that I know enough.

Waiting to be Ripped

In a television documentary Martin Amis described the chess board at the outset as being like a sheet, waiting to be ripped. He said with relish that there was something dirty about chess. Perhaps he meant that the contest always evokes a sense of degradation, that what starts out perfectly symmetrical cannot remain so, that our good intentions as to how things are meant to proceed will often be lost somewhere between the opening and the middle game.

Amis compared chess to other pursuits, noting he had thrown 180 at darts twice in his life, had pulled off pots on the snooker table that would have brought the Crucible to its feet, yet had the same chance of creating anything of beauty on the chess board as a group of monkeys with typewriters had of replicating the complete works of Shakespeare. He said ruefully that he had been unable to beat his chess computer on level one because it was a monster. The same man who wrote *The Information,* with its opening sentence that I could read over and over about cities which contained men who cried in their sleep and then said nothing, thought that creating poetry in chess was beyond him.

What Amis said goes for all of us. In an age where a computer program that can be purchased for £10 is now stronger than the world chess champion (albeit not on level one), to play is to be defeated if creating works of pure beauty is our aim. When we type our supposed masterpieces into the machine's engine after our game is over, many previously unnoticed failings will inevitably come to light, the story will turn out not to be the one we thought it was. Some say there is a case for only allowing computers to analyse your good games; that is soul destroying enough, without asking it to look at the bad ones. Yet chess is ultimately a search for truth, a quest to learn; and what other way is there to improve, beyond asking the all-seeing machine what a truer path might have looked like?

To a point, computers have changed the way we all play. Some opening lines have been put out of business, other endings re-assessed, and yet rather than restricting and constraining the game, in some ways the machines have opened it out. The Grandmaster Daniel King has commented that computers have shown that there are now so many more ways to play, and the machines have unearthed previously unconsidered resources, often of a form that humans would find hard to imagine. Positions that would once have been seen as lost have now been proven as playable.

Perhaps there is some sort of metaphor here for how we live, that other stories away from the board might also be capable of being rescued if we could but bring more analytical power to how we think about them. Perhaps a life computer could have solved the riddle of me and my father, or the generational pattern that impacted Martin and his father, Arthur, amongst others in the family tree; equally the machines might just have confirmed what was already known, found no new ideas, no alternative path that might have been taken.

If you want to be the Champion of the World, you need to have assimilated all aspects of chess theory and to have developed your own ideas on top, to be ahead of the curve; only a handful in any generation ever approach this threshold. The millions of hacks out there like me will not.

Yet increasingly these days when we sit down to play in tournaments, the scoresheets on which moves are recorded will have a carbon underneath them. At the end, we must separate the top sheet from the bottom and hand the story of what has happened into the tournament organisers, who will put the moves into a database where they will be captured forever and be accessible to all. Something has been created that will last for as long as chess is played, should anyone choose to look for it (and all it takes is for somebody to either google your name and add the words chess games, or to type it into one of the more specialist databases, and the story will emerge, your mistakes permanently framed).

I played an appalling move in a game at the British Chess Championships earlier this year, pushing a pawn in such a way that it blocked my knight's only escape square, costing me the piece and ultimately the game. An inexplicable error, and I felt for that poor knight, whose woes have now been frozen forever in the database, my own embarrassment enshrined. It is like a short story that did not really work. The plot was too thin. It was not credible that the pawn would do that to the knight in real life, an editor might say, yet it happened.

All too often an opening goes well and a sense of anticipation grows that this might be it. The greatest game that I have ever played is starting to take shape. I will drift in my thoughts to the congratulatory words my opponent will share with me at the end. I start composing the covering email that will accompany the game's entry into the Leamington and District Chess League game of the year competition. I contemplate whether it will be worth sending it into *British Chess Magazine*, then generally several hours later all such questions have been rendered futile, my very asking of them having played a part in securing my downfall.

Games in chess books often have an inevitability about them which is somehow divorced from the ebb and flow of real match play. You overreach, you miscalculate a line, your opponent's counter punch is a fraction faster than you thought. Most likely, all of the above combine with you drifting into time trouble, while looking for a clean kill that is not there. I have never been mentally equipped to shrug all of this off and to plough on regardless, looking for a less perfect kind of win. The percentage of games I have lost that earlier I had considered as potentially brilliant is depressingly high.

Some of my favourite games I like for reasons other than the actual quality of the moves. In the final round of the Leamington Rapidplay I played my best friend in chess, Adrian Walker. He was on 5/5, me on 4/5 and needing to win so that we would share first place. He had a very good record against me, but I could see that he was nervous when we sat down at the table, waiting to begin. His handshake was wary, almost tentative, and the way he appraised his pieces was as if he sensed that they might somehow let him down. It was he who had everything to lose and, best friend that he was, I was determined to take all from him.

I played in a more circumspect way than normal. Played it long, hoping to prey on his nerves, and finally he cracked. He could still smile at the end, although he did threaten to disinherit me; and we had a cup of tea together while we waited for the prize-giving. Had I been the one to lose I would not have been able to speak to him for at least a week.

For a few years while Adrian lived in Leamington we would often travel to weekend tournaments together. He was roughly the same age as my father and capable of being vaguely cantankerous in ways that occasionally reminded me of him. But he was more open to ideas, to talking about books, poems, the meaning of life, chess of course. The sorts of things I would not really have known how to approach my father on in the main. I always felt more in sympathy with Adrian if truth be told. Once we played in a tournament in Stafford and Adrian felt ill on the way home and we drove to Stafford hospital in the fading light of a Sunday afternoon, arriving at an A&E department that was littered with injured football and rugby players.

"So what sport do you two play?" the nurse had asked.

"We're chess players," we said in unison.

There are three games that stand like separate needles in a haystack for me, where it really did all come together, or at least so it seemed. The strongest player I have ever beaten battered me for six hours (this was in the Four Nations Chess League where games can sometimes go on forever) before suffering a complete rush of blood to the head and launching a wild and unsound lunge that rendered him lost almost immediately. In truth he had beaten himself, but I had clung to life for just long enough to let him do it.

I won the Leamington League game of the year in 2011/12 with a victory against Peter Drury, utilising a bishop in a highly unusual way (that did not involve using it as an actual weapon). On a near closed board, where a bishop's long-range potency is often diminished, I inched the piece forward zig-zag style until finally it broke through Peter's defences to leave his position hopeless.

A few years later against Neil Clarke from Solihull, I played a better game still, even if the Leamington best game judges ultimately did not award it the trophy. We were playing their A team in a cup match and everything clicked perfectly. My pieces seemed to dance onto the perfect squares, my grip tightened, tactical possibilities abounded.

It is not unusual for teammates to half watch the other games that are going on during a cup match, but here, everybody seemed to be following intently. An audience of experts, but for once I got it right and a pawn thrust was followed by a piece sacrifice and rapid victory against a strong player. One of those few moments where I felt that

I had made something at the chess board that might stand up to scrutiny, a story that really did work. Sure enough the game was soon posted on websites and I received praise that I was very grateful for.

Praise always secretly mattered more to me than it would have done to my father, or at least that is what he would have wanted people to believe. Much later, I showed the games to my coach Andy Baruch, who pointed out that against both Peter and Neil, the moves I had played to force their resignations were only the second-best available. So what, you might say, if they were good enough to force immediate capitulation. However, Andy served to highlight that I had understood neither position as well as I had thought, and I could not look on either of the games in quite the same way after that.

Even in these very rare moments what might have been perfect was still flawed. Perhaps every story, like every chess game, is also such, that it is the price for its very being. It could be there are parts of *The Information* which work better than others. It might be noted that the so-called Game of the Century, in which a thirteen-year-old Bobby Fischer beat Donald Bryne, was later to be criticised by Gary Kasparov, who suggested a number of ways in which Bryne could have defended better.

My own family's stories were flawed too. There were things that might have turned out differently, relationships that could have been improved. My grandfather Martin in particular would have wanted the words he wrote to take him further, away from the shops, into something else. My own account is missing much, can only talk to

23

some of what happened, can only guess at other aspects of it. It will reveal more of my weaknesses than I might have wanted it to, that much is obvious to me without any need for computer analysis.

Chess and writing and family life might in the end all be part of the same thing. A desire to create and to challenge, to make something that lasts, that has a reason to be remembered, to work through the complications and the myriad of possibilities, to get it right. However hard it might seem, for all the inherent risks, we have no choice but to get on with it. Perhaps the best approach is to look on everything as a sheet that is waiting to be ripped.

2014
PART 1

Rigorously Pragmatic –
17 October 2014

I had been unsure whether I would do this again. "I hope so," he had said, holding my hand and lifting his head from the pillow to look directly at me. Frail, but his presence undimmed. On that Monday morning I didn't know what I hoped for. Not this. Probably not the alternatives either. Not really. I don't think.

"I'll see you on Friday," I nod, and head for the car, our history having left us poorly equipped to go deeper into the moment. It could have been anything. Taking on a future significance that it now will not, rather destined to join that collection of other moments stringing all of this together but not yet ending it.

Feeling ill and being told there was nothing wrong with him. Questions as to whether it might in fact be psychological. Then the private diagnosis that says, yes, you are ill. And actually, yes, it is terminal.

"I know what's wrong with you," the BUPA radiologist tells him; an exchange that, entirely in keeping, he does not mention for some time. "How many months have I got?" he asks at a later appointment in Cheltenham. "I think we are looking at weeks," says the consultant, evenly but firmly, with the practiced professional air of one who has given this news many times before. "I'm not as ill as the consultant thinks I am," he says later. There is more assertion than question in his tone.

So it is that I am back on the M5 in Friday night traffic. He is at his home now and this is where I am heading, in the greying light of an autumn evening, with both the air-conditioning and radio up, two noises competing with each other. The pins and needles in my left leg are more acute than normal and I am aware of my tiredness. Ahead soon, the roadworks that pre-date Dad's diagnosis, if not the illness itself, as, incredibly slowly, ageing metal motorway barrier gives way to new and stronger wall. Overhead signs will encourage the use of the hard shoulder; fifty mph beaded in white on overhead boards. Entering another limbo period framed by striped orange bollards and sentinel-like bright yellow average-speed cameras, where all I can do is drive. It makes me think back to Lego sets and Meccano. I once read that a motorway was like a skyscraper laid out horizontally. The road network is more complicated than you might think, yet still easier to fix than a human.

On several occasions recently I've driven past my exit. My sense of direction has never been good and it often fails me now, but even when I go wrong the monochrome concrete and metal of the motorway lend a more linear degree of certainty than I will be afforded on arrival. I think of the chess term zugzwang, which essentially means every move you lose, no matter which you choose. I feel a bit like that now but, as in the game, when it is your turn you really have no choice but to press on and hope that somehow all your fears will turn out to be unfounded. I have some apple turnovers in a bag on my seat, which Dad likes but is no longer able to eat. We both know why I still have to bring them.

After Mum, a counsellor said to me, "Life is now." But it is amazing what can be deferred if you put your mind to it. What you can choose not to think about, at least for a while. All of it ebbs and flows like the tide on the mud in Wootton Creek, continually open to revision and re-remembering. It is never the same, even around the hard stops, the silted-up points that nothing further can flow from. The weed on the rocks is a changing hue, depending on the strength of the wind and the light and the movement of the cloud. But I don't always choose what it is that I see, and it is impossible to ignore the rubbish that is increasingly washing up and sticking to the bank, the shades often darker now than they once were.

Another hard stop is approaching. It is all but an instant after all.

I drift back to the noise from the radio. A footballer has just been released from jail and the pundits on *Talk Sport* are discussing whether he should be allowed to play again. Darren Gough says, having done two and a half years of a five-year sentence, he shouldn't play for another two and a half years. I sense it's a line a producer has given him, but really, who cares? I press a button and there is music, which is better, and I wish there was another button that could be pressed which would make my father's problems disappear quite so easily. My own too.

Finally, motorway will turn into ever more minor roads and I will arrive at the house that was once home. It is not even that far really. Journeys never are, when you look back on them. It still surprises me that the house looks the same, solid and well-lit in the October darkness, even as time draws in. It has doubtless seen dramas like this with other casts play out in its history. A mismatch of Tudor, Victorian and 1970s build, with a small orchard off a private road, once pitted, now smooth. An extension to the dining room to accommodate a larger table, a conservatory, a second garage; those have been my parent's additions. The coal-fired heating, the damp and rotting floorboards, all but distant memories now. The new dining table was due to the growing number of grandchildren, but it had barely been used before it was just Dad left here to host.

The central core of the house is the oldest part. Kitchen, hallway, bathroom and the smallest bedroom are lined with beams which are painted black. There are tiny holes in places, treated wood-worm, ships' timbers originally, the story goes. This house has travelled. Within its ancient frame, the bathroom looks as if it has had a spaceship grafted on, the power shower a huge, gleaming tribute to modernity. Albeit, to use it for more than three minutes is to drain the tank, which will inevitably draw complaints and lead to recriminations.

The playroom and spare room are both high-ceilinged, Victorian. When we first moved in they were cold and unwelcoming. But now a large log fireplace centres the playroom, a significant upgrade on the old electric bar heater that never worked properly. Like all the other rooms it has been incrementally improved over the last thirty years. A huge television screen is screwed to one wall. Not in the best possible taste perhaps, but it keeps Dad happy, in sofar as anything does. A plaque declares that on this spot in 1897, nothing happened. I had assumed my mother would object to it, but as he screwed it into the wall at some point in her final years she seemed to find it amusing. There are expensive sofas, and a rich green carpet that still feels new even though it isn't, overhead cupboards, crammed with DVDs, video cassettes, Beatles records, old schoolbooks and reports, some theirs, some mine, some Matt's, with their grades and verdicts that no longer seem to matter quite so much. Some of the newer Christmas decorations are stored here too.

My father's parents once inadvertently trapped a bird in the sash windows of the spare room above. We found it fanned out in a smear. As was our custom, the incident was never mentioned once the debris had been cleared. Mum's red velvet wedding dress is folded away in one of the cupboards there. The rest of her clothes hang untouched in what was their bedroom.

Bookcases dominate the hall. Built by Martin soon after we moved in, they run floor to ceiling. There are other smaller ones throughout the house. Two-thirds Mum's – Shakespeare, Austin, Bronte, Hardy, A level study guides, a lot of poetry, more modern books that she used to teach her classes and like everything else of hers, Dad has not touched them in the years that have followed her death. *Enduring Love*, *A History of the World in 10½ Chapters*, things like that. He is more an Agatha Christie man. Asimov, books about astronomy, mathematics and Egypt, that sort of thing. They both read the Christies for a time, but beyond Shakespeare their literary tastes did not overlap much. He went to Egypt after her death, years on from first reading about the place, but the trip was not a complete success. It had been an organised tour, mainly of women, who didn't speak to the men much. But he saw the things he had wanted to see, and in the photographs he is smiling.

The dining room, sitting room, utility and two of the bedrooms, mine and my parents', were added in the 1970s. The kitchen looks out onto the Malvern Hills and there is a hatch between it and the sitting room that we used to climb through as children. My mother passed food and cups of tea through it with a relentless regularity that makes me feel guilty now. There are too many walls for modern living, though whether between sitting room and kitchen or kitchen and dining room, it's hard to tell. In recent weeks my mind has turned to what new owners might do. I almost look at the place afresh as they might, which never ceases to make me feel guilty and, at another level that I don't like very much, rigorously pragmatic.

My mother would have had a central role in all of this if she was still here. This thing that went from nothing to a crisis in the time it took for his private test results to come through, as well as everything which has happened since, has only served to heighten the sense of impending disaster. I feel her absence, just as I see it in his face and feel it in the rooms of a house that still speaks of both of them, six years on.

I have to do this for her as well as him, even if it is obvious to both of us that I am a poor substitute. I cannot cook, have a busy job an hour and a half away, a young family of my own. Yet these are all details. Really it is about reach. She understood him in a way that I do not. She could talk to him in a way that he and I cannot. Perhaps my pragmatism is really less about imagining new layouts for the downstairs and more about seeing all these limitations in both of us and pressing on anyway, on this drive to both the known and the unknown.

BOSBURY CHURCH:

FOUR

SEASONS

Introduction to Four Seasons

My mother was a creator too. I have a painting of a flower from her schooldays, which rests on our landing bookcase. The petals are perfectly formed, colours still clean and fresh after all these years, delicate and nuanced. The leg of the picture frame is broken and it is propped up a bit, but I do not want to attempt to fix it. Partly because of the risk of making things worse, but also out of a sense that this would disturb something, would be an intrusion. Mary Holmes is tidily written in one corner in blue ink. We all bustle past it day to day, but sometimes I stop to look or to point it out to the children yet again. They all nod politely and Maddie will talk about her grandmother's sponge cakes.

In some ways I am surprised that she did not write more and in other ways I am not. A handful of letters and poems (some of which were illustrated), a few fragments of diaries, some study notes. She was talented and capable but lacked confidence and energy. What energy she did have, she gave to everyone else. I sometimes think to how it might have been different. Whether she could have rested more and not tried to do so much, if we could have helped by asking for less. It is possible to imagine,

I suppose. But whilst a much easier person than Dad was in a lot of ways, I don't think she could have changed, or would have wanted to especially.

At Bristol I had a professor who said she loved teaching but hated writing. A rare thing for such a person to confess to in today's world of university league tables. I don't think it would be right to say that Mum hated writing. Rather, much like my professor, her most natural environment was the classroom, rather than the written page. I had seen it for myself, when with her in the college, which I often was as I would walk there from my sixth form college for a lift home. She was completely at one with her students, both mentor and, friend and it was with them that her knowledge and feel for literature was at its most intimate. She was a sharer, not a hoarder.

But there was a little writing too. I remember her writing the *Four Seasons* poems, and *Travellers Joy* which did not quite make the cut for her. Sitting at the dining room table with a rigour and seriousness of purpose, carefully thinking her way through the words she formed on the page. Channelling the history of the ageing village church, the enigma of the changing seasons, highlighting the ways in which people come to bear witness to this, if only for a time, much as she did. We are the live players on a stage that will outlast us. I cannot remember what the occasion was. A church festival or suggestion from the vicar, an idea of her own, I do not know. The poems were published in the local paper but I do not have the cutting. I think there is also a copy in the church archive.

I did wonder whether the four seasons might have

formed four groupings around which to structure this book, fusing everything that happened into the quadrants of the year. An artificial framework linked to her writing felt like quite a clever idea to me for a while. But it could not work like that. Too much of what I remember comes from summer and Christmas. Too many of the stories start in winter, whether literally or metaphorically. Every ending is also a beginning, and the stories and the sense of time do not work like that here, if they work at all.

Hence, these poems do not appear as huge anchor weights, adding ballast to shaky metaphorical chapter structures. Rather, they feature within this story entirely as what they were. Staging points in Mary Graff's mind, around the revolving year and the stone church that stood nearby unchanging throughout the seasons.

Another Spring

Spring was a long time coming this year
Snow clung to the hills, reluctant to depart,
'Waiting for more,' they said, 'to keep company.'
Only the cypress showed green in the churchyard
As frost scorched the daffodils on tombs
Mocking the frail birth of spring as though
Such a thing could never be after winter's dominion.
The flowerless lenten days creep slowly by
But churches have the habit of waiting,
Engendered by patient watching for soldiers gone
On vanished wars, carrying with them
Thoughts of an English spring. For it will come;
Hope of the spring gives men's minds direction:
From winter's desolation comes the resurrection.

M.G.

Anna's Letter –
Yarmouth Car Ferry – 1975

Below is a letter Anna wrote to my mother a few days after I was born. It had been a normal birth, then I went blue and spent a few days in an incubator, after which everything was fine. This is from my incubator period.

Anna was highly maternal, which meant as we grew older that we sometimes found her fussy. She was the first of her generation of the family to die, in 1994, at a time when I was just bridging into adulthood. I was pre-occupied on the day of the funeral by a phone call I needed to make to somebody who was about to dump me. This was a time when not everybody had a mobile and neither I nor my soon to be ex did. My thoughts were more on my life than on Anna's that day. It was only looking back at this letter and some other cards from this time that I appreciated how much it meant to her to see her daughter's children.

I remember her being ill when we were quite young and being nursed at a convent where we visited her. It was not until years later that I learnt of her battle with depression and indeed anti-depressants. I never saw any sign of any of this, but my observation skills were not especially acute. I tended to look inwards rather than outwards, so am not really in a position to say. Despite her challenges she always seemed to manage to function. Life can be hard sometimes, but Anna found her way through it just the same.

My dearest Mary,

It was a joy to get Colin's phone call just as we arrived indoors last pm and to learn that everything was fine. I felt sure by the look of him that all was well. He arrived a fortnight early and you had a speeded-up delivery which no doubt was a little shock to him. However, a few days in the incubator will put that right.

What you have to do is not worry about him. He is and will be 100%.

As I said to you before, we are thrilled for you both. It is like this is happening to us.

Another thing, rest on your bed in between his feeding etc. & sleep and read. It will help you to be more relaxed.

We thought he was a lovely little chap & Colin is simply wonderful. He knows far more than I do about the whole business and I feel sure he was a tower of strength to you.

Colin's mother rang at 10pm and wanted to know all about you & the baby. I reassured her that all was well. Of course, they are very much looking forward to seeing you both & Benjamin, but will leave it to you to give the OK. Will be in touch with Colin on the phone tonight.

Much love, sweetheart, and make the most of the rest. Put your legs up as much as possible and I hope the tights we found were OK.

Hope Charmian[1] will visit you again soon. She seems very nice. Please put your cards out and start to thoroughly enjoy yourself and your baby.

Much love
    Mum xxx

---

1   Charmian Knight taught with my mother and is my godmother. She and her husband Tim were lifelong friends of my parents and she wrote a letter after my father's death which appears later in this book.

Moving In – 1983

"I knew we would buy it straight away," he once said. "Your mum took about half an hour of convincing." I still remember that first afternoon, riding our bikes around the small orchard while Anna and Martin also looked on and my parents proudly surveyed the last house either of them would ever own. Anna and Martin's mission to get me and Matthew from the Isle of Wight, where we had been staying with them for a few days while my parents sorted the move from Aldershot, had been successfully completed. We travelled with them on the old passenger ferry *Brading* and then onward by train to Bristol, and Dad was there to meet us all at Temple Meads for the final stage of the journey to Bosbury.

"Is it this one? Is it this one?" we would ask as he increasingly seemed to be driving us into the middle of nowhere.

"Are there any sweets?"

"Can we stop in a minute? I need the toilet."

"Please don't punch your brother."

I do not know if we irritated him during the journey, if the way in which Dad had imagined driving his children to the new house for the first time was different from the reality. Much as Arthur's first meeting with Martin had also not quite gone to plan, was there a seed of frustration that was sown then that I never knew about?

Eventually we arrived and ran straight out into the orchard where our bikes were waiting.

"Watch out for nails," Dad says; "don't get a puncture," as we meander through the longish grass this way and that, marking our territory, observing the sap that oozes from the split trunk of one of the apple trees. Three-quarters of an acre. Quite something compared to the tiny town garden we have left behind. We have arrived, even if there is the inevitable paradox of something being both home and utterly unfamiliar.

That first night, listening to the quiet so removed from the continual hum of Aldershot traffic, it feels that we have come a long way, and not just in terms of miles. A new life ahead, things left behind, the occasional hoot from an owl breaking the peace. The night sky of the country is much darker than we are used to. We do not know that the rustling outside the window is the sound of bats, wings and that they have a nest inside the garage. There is a torch by my bed in case I need to go to the toilet in the night; the builders have already started fixing things, and finding my way around in the dark is not straightforward. There is little money left over and those floorboards on the landing that are rotten have been stripped out but not yet replaced. The possibility of injuring yourself if not careful is something we have been advised of a number of times. It adds to a sense of adventure and uncertainty.

A new school ahead, at which I will show from my toy

gold bullion truck a block of what I think is real gold, and another boy will bite it and declare that it isn't, gobbing and spitting all over it. The same boy later proposes a few of us should run away to sea, where we will survive by drinking sea water. I express my doubts, but these are as nothing compared to my delight at being included in the plan, that inevitably does not come to anything. But that was all future then and is past now, along with my participation in cricket teams, carol singing, village fetes, Christmas plays and school hall fundraisers. You cannot move into a place like Bosbury and be anything other than an outsider really. Belonging is being able to trace your lineage to the *Doomsday Book* and if you can't do that, then people will be aware of it, in a benign but still knowing sort of a way. I tell myself it is benign at any rate.

A field with two duck ponds stands across the way from the house and in winter we would slide across them. They looked like large, fogged mirrors, a misty moon you could stare at and see very little reflected back. The snow would fall in fluffy white buds, always sticking, framing the landscape and accentuating the quietness. It did not take much, a couple of hours perhaps, for us to be snowed in. School closed; everything else was far away, strangely remote. We sometimes used the toboggan in the pond field, occasionally using the wooden sledge Martin had made for us, always remembering too late how heavy it was.

It was colder in those days (it really was) and most

years the water would be thick with ice. We would tentatively put a foot onto the surface and see if it creaked. Very occasionally it might. Rarer still but more than once, when we were out toward the middle, it offered a warning groan, but there was never an incident beyond the usual bumping and bruising that came from falling over. We liked the sense of danger and adventure, albeit I am surprised now that our parents were both so relaxed about the whole thing. We would eventually return home for hot Ribena and dry clothes.

Living so far out brought a sense of remoteness that I spent years trying to escape from, until I realised that it was what centred me and increasingly called me back. Although if today I suggest to the children that we might move to the country, they will make clear that it is never going to happen.

"We are all going to live in our Warwick house forever," Gabriella will say.

Oh, how I wish.

When spring came Matt and I would hunt for tadpoles and caterpillars and sometimes snails to race. We would keep a variety of creatures in tins or jars or ice cream boxes in our bedrooms, though the snails would tend to wake up and escape, which could be awkward. With tadpoles it was always a question of timing in terms of when to put them back in the pond, which we sometimes got right and sometimes did not.

One springtime we saw Caspar swim across the pond to catch and kill the baby ducklings. Grey and black striped, with amber eyes and a smudge of black on his nose; a ferocity and intensity far removed from the creature who curled up on my lap purring loudly through his dribble. We watched frozen from the bank as he ripped into tiny bundles of feathers, the hopeless shrieks of the ducklings' parents making no difference in that season of renewal and new life that also spoke most to death.

It was the same spring that going into the old shed we discovered an orange tent on the concrete floor littered with bodies, all without their heads. Every sort of animal you would imagine a cat could catch, and some you would not. Mice, shrews, rats and garden birds for sure, but also moles, ferrets, weasels and a barn owl. Presumably he had found and transported the owl, rather than killed it himself. But who can tell? Perhaps it had been injured, or just especially unlucky. It might even be possible that Caspar had had nothing to do with the owl's death, that the bird had wandered in looking for food. There were no witnesses. The owl was one of the fresher carcases, slowly rotting in the increasingly putrid air of the tin shed. Caspar lived to twenty-three, spanning my life as a child and the coming of my own children. He now rests under the bush next to the bird table.

Our new home was a mile from the nearest village, in a hamlet of four houses, the middle of nowhere really. It was next to a thatched cottage that for most of our childhood was inhabited by a Mrs Sawmill, who loved her garden. She taught me that looking like a sweet old lady doesn't make it so.

"She was always unpleasant when she was younger, so what do you expect?" one of the villagers once said to my mother by way of consolation, who knew it but still let the old crone upset her.

When a fire tore through her roof, many years previously, the people who had lived in our house at the time said that they worked through the night to minimise the damage. In the morning, she said to them, "You are never there for me when I need you, are you?"

It was certainly the case that no ball that went over her hedge was ever returned, and it was apparently held on good authority in The Bell that she kept a huge box of them. At times Matt and I (mainly Matt) would embark on a daring raid across her garden to save a ball from this fate. Occasionally Mrs Sawmill would see him and throw tea in his direction. But for all of her cursing, she wasn't the fastest, and Dad was pretty immune to her subsequent complaints.

Sometimes we would light fires and fail to properly cook sausages and tins of beans. We went through a phase of trying to launch rockets made of old torch shells filled with wood and firelighters. Science wasn't our strong point and Dad never really showed much interest in our pyrotechnics.

There was a grapevine on the side of the old shed, but my attempts to make wine with its tiny beads of fruit proved unsuccessful. Above the garage was a loft, which we used as a den, playing games there which involved CB radios and stacks of food and were based on us and friends dividing into rival gangs of boys and acting out scenes from *The A-Team*, albeit without any actual welding gear. The loft was good for birthday parties but less interesting in later years when our age outgrew our imaginations, at least for a while.

"We'll Always Have Bognor"
– 8 August 1988

We take the train the one stop from Ryde Esplanade to Ryde Pier Head, listening to the clack of the wheels on the wooden structure, looking down on the mud and sea through the slats. We are on our way to get the newish catamaran, *Our Lady Patricia*, from Ryde to Portsmouth. Made in Tasmania, a silver plaque proudly pronounces. It smells of plastic and clean carpet, more like a toy boat than the huge hulking passenger ferries *Brading* and *Southsea*, with their rust-speckled hulls and warnings to keep off the propellers. They had now been withdrawn from service.

Martin said it would have cost more to fix *Brading*'s gear box than the ageing vessel was worth, so that was that. Besides, he told me that the catamarans save a lot of time, although I wonder if time really can be saved. I already suspect that it cannot be stored. I find myself thinking to things gone by and things no longer worth fixing, dreaming vaguely of one day buying the ferry company and wresting the vessels from their rusty, watery graveyard, making things again how once they were. In the summer sunshine when you are young all things seem both possible and unlikely in equal measure.

As ever, on the journey from Mum's parents to Dad's, the atmosphere starts out tense. Both are braced, neither necessarily looking forward to this. He is baked brown by the sun, wearing dark blue cords and a short-sleeved shirt. It never takes long, a morning on a beach and he will be a completely different colour, although he could never just do that; once he is there he is there, a real sun worshipper, no matter how bored and I Matt might become over the hours.

He has gold-framed spectacles with lenses that tint like sunglasses in the summer light. Somehow they add to his enigmatic aura. Jet black hair, a full head, his chest is still scar-less. Suede desert boots. A ruggedness and physicality about him that people notice. He smells faintly of aftershave and sweat. He doesn't say much. It is the near silence that draws people in, keeps them guessing. On his wrist a Rotary watch with leather strap and gold face that he rarely looks at.

Mum is in a flora-patterned summer dress and overlarge sunglasses. She carries a large bag with supplies and emergency provisions: water, biscuits, sweets, a bottle of suntan lotion, her paperback, *The Daily Telegraph* neatly folded on top for him. The crossword puzzle has already been half done. Her legs are scarred and it is only in the height of summer that she does not wear tights.

As a student she had been hit by a bus while crossing a road and a number of operations on her legs had followed. Along with the scarring, she has an allergy to penicillin that she has told me comes from having had to take so much of it after the accident. A general weakening perhaps, certainly a nervousness about driving where she doesn't know, even if this had all happened to her as a pedestrian.

She is worried that we might miss the catamaran, and it's true, we do end up running for it. I half remember him throwing a bag in her general direction on another occasion when we actually missed one, but I can't be sure. Today we will make it. "I knew we left too late," she says. He says nothing but looks irritated; to some extent his default expression.

He points to the board that shows the boat is only just docking, the queue of people waiting to get on. If this was in the science lab no experiment would be necessary, a conclusion can be drawn by using our eyes. We have missed nothing and the day is still on track.

Matt fidgets while we wait in the line, which doesn't improve either of their moods. Finally, passengers disembark and we run on, pushing our way through the queue to claim the aircraft-like seats by the bow windows, leaving Mum and Dad with the dilemma of claiming the neighbouring seats we have saved, which will entail admitting that they are travelling with us.

Then we are underway and there is a lifting of sorts, as *Our Lady Patricia* churns through the Solent, grey on silver today in the sunlight, a twist of salt in the air. Slowly out of the harbour, navigating the sailboats and other pleasure craft, and then faster in the deeper, less sheltered water. She bumps on her wash as the engine briefly reaches full throttle, spilling diesel fumes in the air.

We watch the view of car ferries and hovercraft, fishing and sailing boats, until all too soon she slows again as the battleship HMS *Warrior* comes into view and we are docked at Portsmouth Harbour, landing close to the green and white striped Gosport passenger ferries. '*It's shorter by water!*' they proclaim.

Then forty-five minutes or so on the south coast train, filled with holidaymakers and local youths in football shirts. There is no air conditioning and the floor feels sticky to the step. A group of teenagers are singing a rude song about one of their friends that our parents studiously ignore, while Matt and I snigger. Until he is told not to, Matt picks at the seat cover, which has been slit open by a knife and bleeds foam, by which point a whole new pool of debris has formed and is sticking to his legs. We stop at some but not all of the stations, and I watch the names go by Portsmouth Harbour, Portsmouth and Southsea, Fratton, Hilsea, Farlington Halt, Bedhampton, Havant, Warblington, Emsworth, Southbourne, Nutbourne, Bosham, Fishbourne, Chichester, Bognor Regis. At last we arrive.

Dave is waiting to pick us up at the station in his bright red Datsun, with the plastic covers over the seats and airfreshener hanging from the mirror. His white hair and chiselled features leave the potential for him to look distinguished, but his general demeanour, as much as anything, detracts from this possibility. He is in his usual attire: grey suit trousers slightly crumpled, white shirt, a tie that is not done up properly and hangs scruffily from his neck. A pen and pools coupon protrude from his shirt breast pocket. He seems to stand with the air of somebody who has learnt how to make himself appear invisible when need be.

"How are you, Col?" he asks. Dad nods warily. They half pat each other awkwardly. "Have you put on weight, Col?" Dave asks, but turns to us before he can even register my father's look. "Ben, Ben, Ben, Matt, Matt, Matt," Dave sings under his breath, embracing us both as we wriggle to escape. He smells of cheap aftershave and polo mint. "How's Ben? How's Matt? How are you, bubalahs? Have you got a girlfriend yet, Ben? Matt? The key thing is to marry an older woman for her pension. You've got to think about that. You should have made more progress by now."

Dad sighs. "You know they're ten and twelve?" He is sweating slightly in the heat and motions toward the car, but nobody moves for a moment.

"Please take no notice, boys," says Mum, "… he's only pulling your leg."

"Well…" says Dave but Dad interrupts to suggest we should all get into the car.

"Ben, Ben, Ben. Matt, Matt, Matt," Dave sings, half-breaking the spell. He slips us both a pound note, which we pocket, smiling. "Let's get you home and get some nosh in you." Mum winces slightly, which my grandfather takes as positive affirmation.

Finally, with all of us in the car and with seat belts on, he turns his head to the back seat where Mum is sitting with us. "Do you know, Mary? I've never read a book in my life."

"I'm sure that's not really the case, is it, Dave?" she says with a somewhat fixed smile. But she struggles to avoid taking the bait. "You must have read something at some point, surely?"

"Load of nonsense, all of it," he says grinning broadly, knowing he has won an early victory. "I get everything I need to know from *The Daily Mirror*. Do you read it, Mary? No? Well, you're missing out. Thatcher would ban it if she thought she could get away with it. It's all in there…

"Had a good win on my accumulator yesterday – seven pounds could have been a lot more if the last one hadn't fallen, but you know.

"Ben, Matt. I'm telling you, I'll win the pools before I'm done. Then it will be Rolls Royces all round. Anything you want.

"I'm telling you, Mary, we'll soon have Thatcher out and things will be different then, you'll see. When Arthur Scargill's prime minister. It'll all be different. The workers have had enough. It might take another strike but these Tories will all be in jail soon enough. They're all murderers. You mark my words. Let's get you all back and we'll have a good nosh."

It is not far to 8 Nyewood Gardens, where Theresa is preparing lunch in their first floor flat within a small retirement block. There are garages outside with pale blue doors, and often when we pull up a neighbour will be wiping a windscreen with an ageing shammy cloth, or peering under the bonnet of a vehicle that has seen better days. Dave will grunt knowingly at them and occasionally make a tentative introduction.

The whole exterior of the block of flats is tidy and well maintained. The flowerbeds are carefully kept. There is an order here, and somehow a mild form of retreat from the world.

Dave opens the front door at the bottom of a small hallway that leads to the stairs which take you up to the flat. We are greeted by the usual shrieking.

"Echo, Echo, Echo. My name is Echo, Echo, Echo. Who is a pretty bird, then? How do you do? Echo, Echo, Echo. My name is Echo, Echo, Echo. Whosa pretty bird, then? Whosa pretty bird, then?"

On and on it goes on, mixed with high-pitched whistles, screeching, clicking and flapping; there could well be a colony of topical parrots up there, judging by the noise.

Mum looks at Dad as we stand at the foot of the stairs. It's the same as last time, despite what was said then.

Dad looks at Dave. "We did talk about this, didn't we? You know Mary doesn't like birds?"

"Her brother chased her with a dead one when she was a child and she's never got over it," I interject, helpfully, puzzled that from the looks I get no one else seems to think that this is a useful intervention.

"Just stretching her wings, no harm in that; she always likes to see everyone. Especially Mary."

"Dad."

He hesitates.

"Bit of a shame to put her away on a day like this. I'm sure she'd like to see the boys.

"OK, OK." He finally sighs. "Wait there a second."

A lot more bird singing follows and there is the sound of flapping wings and muffled swearing (him, rather than the mynah bird I think), followed by breaking china as a vase falls from a shelf, more swearing, then silence.

"OK, you can come up now," says Dave nonchalantly, as if he had just popped up ahead of us to turn the heating on.

The gate at the top of the stairs has a piece of A4 paper attached to it which reads 'Burglars Beware ALARM ON'. Behind it, on a bookcase, a plastic yellow hand-shaped sign says 'Welcome To Our Home'. There is a dark wooden stairgate that Theresa opens as she makes her triumphant appearance to greet us.

"Hello my bubalas," she says, handing me and Matt the knitted giraffes she has made to mark the occasion, and planting wet kisses which we squirm to avoid.

"You look nice, Mary," she says doubtfully. "Are you hungry?"

The giraffes have sticks in their legs to enable them to stand up.

The table, pulled away from the wall specially, is stacked with breads, crisps, cherry tomatoes in a bowl, half a cucumber, processed meats, sausage rolls, quiches, jars of peanut butter, basic cheeses, pickles, bottles of fizzy drinks and a large biscuit barrel. A cheap bottle of wine that no one touches sits at the corner of the spread.

We load up plates of food and sit on the red plastic horseshoe sofa (red was my grandmother's favourite colour) looking out on the balcony and shared garden beyond. The residents don't like ball games being played down there, we know.

There are sideboards filled with photographs of me and my brother, and china figures locked in a never-ending card game, one with a secret card half-hidden under its bare foot. Copies of *The Daily Mirror* and unsuccessful betting slips fill other surfaces. A plastic tree with lights on it is propped up near the television, flashing different colours when switched on for special occasions such as these. There is an oil painting on the wall that they had got an artist to do of us from a photo. Everyone mocked it, but I always secretly thought it was quite sweet.

There's Dad's graduation photograph, in which he looks thin and serious, attired with gown and mortar board, against a London high-rise backdrop. It's not a thinness he will still have in 1988, and the 2014 variation will somehow be very different again. A bright blue 1960s Morris Minor is also in shot. It all speaks of future.

Theresa tells us again about the conversations she had had with the university welfare office, when Dad had taken a year out after his sister Helen's death.

"They were going to throw him out, but I told them that that simply was not going to happen." It was never something he seemed particularly grateful about.

Helen, at sixteen, stands in another photograph. She wears an orange dress and stands smiling in a park, by rows of flowers which are all in full bloom. The time left to them shorter than hers, but not by much. Here it is all spring or early summer and beginnings and newness, an accurate representation of the moment.

I've seen a lot of photographs and a few reels of film. Helen swimming, Helen sunbathing, a group photo of the four of them, a little formal and stiff, as was the photography style of the time.

A certificate from a secretarial course she had passed at Pitman College is framed and hangs in the spare bedroom, alongside a poster lamenting the trials of long-distance aeroplane travel. Her autograph book is on the desk below nestled next to my grandmother's typewriter. Other than family members, Bobby Davro is the only name I recognise.

Mum and Dad's wedding photo, Mum in a red velvet dress. They did not think a white dress would particularly work if it was not a church wedding, but I don't know why not. The eight of them in a row at the reception: Anna, Dave, Janet, Dad, Mum, Mike, Martin and Theresa. Mike with a 60's style beard that he shaved off when he saw the negatives. A registry service the best compromise that could be wrought, even if that did rest uneasily for many of the years that followed.

Theresa, trying to make amends, had brought a friend who was a priest to give a blessing. How this relationship was formed is unclear to me and is now lost in time. But it transpired he was an alcoholic and, whilst airbrushed out of the re-telling of the story in most accounts, Martin told me that he had been very drunk and his contribution had not necessarily been seen as being very helpful.

There had also been a subsequent secret church ceremony, which my father forgot was secret and brought up during his twenty-fifth wedding anniversary speech. I think there was an unspoken understanding that it wouldn't be mentioned again.

A lot of their story was in that retirement flat, which followed years in London. They had lived in a high-rise flat which we had been to, but it was on an entirely different scale to this, in a block that dominated the skyline menacingly. I barely remember the redness of the carpet and the lift that didn't work.

Theresa was a legal secretary who wouldn't take the necessary exams to become a solicitor, even though everyone said she would have passed them easily. My mother used to say that Theresa was very clever but was scared to step out of her comfort zone. Perhaps like Dave, career progression was never something that interested her; the pair of them focussed on travelling a different, less conventional path together. Dave had promised, when they moved to Bognor on retirement, that he would teach Theresa to drive, and she went on to fail her driving test many, many times, seeming to delight in the experience and the stories of near misses, clipped curbs and occasionally well executed three-point turns that were to follow. Her lack of any natural driving ability a genetic trait I was to inherit.

He worked as a museum guard, a security guard, didn't work. A picture of the Queen at the museum, with him in the background looking on, stood on their sideboard. He ran a laundry business for a time but it was not a success. If they had no money, he wouldn't charge, and that was that, my grandmother used to say, neutrally. Years later Dad said that Dave had once had a trainee management position but he'd only lasted in it for a few days. "He just couldn't be told what to do." Martin, Colin and I were all conformists in our career choices, we did what was expected and made the compromises that went with that, but Dave was truer to himself. It might have been less lucrative and caused others to despair on occasion, but there must be a certain respect due to someone who could never be told what to do.

During lunch we would sometimes go and stand out on the balcony, looking out on the manicured communal garden. The occasional black mynah bird feather could be found even out there. The residents in the flat below had a patio, with ageing blue and white deckchairs and brightly coloured pot plants. We were always advised not to chuck drinks away when leaning over the railings. There had been an incident once, but I think from memory Dave was the culprit.

Beyond the communal garden, a second house is being built in the grounds of one of the large properties that stands across the way. We look at the metal scaffolding and half-built brick walls. Dad rubs my back. "Nothing ever stands still," he says. It surprises me, but in that moment he had guessed what I was thinking.

After lunch, we would go to the seafront, a ten-minute walk, downhill on the way there, "Like sliding down a magic carpet," Dave says. One of the houses we always pass has a sign up offering tennis coaching.

Stone-covered beach and betting shops. Cheap cafes. Lots of old people. And yet, the sea on their doorstep and a sense of optimism and possibility Dave and Theresa both seemed to carry.

We would play mini-golf and argue about mini-golf.

Being the scorer always gave you an advantage, although there could be recriminations after the count. More than once I would have to explain why I'd misread my eight as a three. "If you don't get the ball in the hole, you can't score as if you have," Dad would say.

"Calm down, Col," would be Dave's retort, which usually irritated Dad further, as did his singing. We would eat ice cream and walk on the world's stoniest beach. Occasionally we would swim, which always made Dave nervous. He would wave us in, which compelled me to turn and swim further out. We would talk about the Bognor Birdman and the carnival, which we had been to once. It was certainly a spectacle to see people in an array of costumes, with wings of various degrees of plausibility, throw themselves from Bognor's pier in a forlorn attempt to fly. Whoever travelled the furthest through the air would win a prize. "Sometimes when I come to Bognor, I have a similar urge to throw myself over the edge," I once heard my mother mutter to my father.

All of our visits followed the same pattern. Some sort of incident with Echo, food, the beach, golf and then back to the flat for cups of tea and more biscuits, accompanied by final thoughts from Dave on Thatcherism while we watched the news. (Today is the eighth of the eighth of eighty-eight, Nicholas Witchell says, against a backdrop of multiple Japanese wedding ceremonies.) Then we re-trace our steps with a car journey to the station, by which time everything is generally quiet, Dave's assault on capitalism and culture over for another day.

He would be content mainly to hum under his breath,

occasionally fishing yet more biscuits out of a carrier bag in case we were hungry, perhaps sometimes giving us another pound, ignoring Mum's increasingly firm urgings that he should keep his eyes on the road and hands on the wheel. We would all be tired, but there would be a sense of both relief and accomplishment after he had said goodbye and we could continue on retracing our steps: Bognor Regis, Chichester, Fishbourne, Bosham, Nutbourne, Southbourne, Emsworth, Warblington, Havant, Bedhampton, Farlington Halt, Hilsea, Fratton, Portsmouth and Southsea, and finally Portsmouth Harbour. Re-crossing the Solent in fading summer light, air much cooler now, watching the lights from the boats fall across the water.

"How did it go?" Martin would ask when we met him at Ryde Esplanade in the glooming for a lift back to their house.

"Better than average," Mum said.

2014
PART 2

Arrivals –
17 October 2014

I step out of the car and push my poorly-fitting key into the front door, wrenching it open. My left eye feels a little heavy, as it sometimes does, and my legs are achy. I wonder about the forces at work in my own body right now, that I can still shrug off much more easily than he can, whatever is attacking him. Our respective battles to stay alive are not comparable, not today.

My father is the hamlet's longest residing resident, in this house that he chose with Mum and has gone on to nurture since. His house, his place in the world, though this October evening the sense that he is in peril, that rogue cells are wreaking more and more havoc, that time is running out, cannot be ignored.

This is still instinctively both home and a homecoming of sorts, albeit one that now happens every few days. He had recently installed a fountain outside, the final structural alteration he would ever make to this or any other house. In the summer we had sat at the table next to it, listening to the gush of water that poured through its metal filter, gleaming in the sunlight. To me it somehow seemed to mock the latest set of bad news or disappointing data through its very newness, the fact that everything about it worked perfectly. But we are well into autumn now and it has been switched off, though it still drips limply.

It does not feel like the sort of place that should interest the wider world much. It has its own quiet seasons and stories that belong to this and other times, just like anywhere else. For years, to come back here was to escape from something. To return to a place that was quieter and more sheltered than wherever I had travelled from, even if I was far from blind to its imperfections. The protective barriers and preconceptions were not absolute.

Just a few weeks ago, it was difficult to make it down Dad's drive, as the nation's press was camped out to cover a murder–suicide. Not the thatched cottage where Mrs Sawmill had once lived, but the house with white windows and a pretty gate across the pond from us. Those windows were always a bright green when we were young.

It is a curious juxtaposition. Neighbour on the front page one day, Cliff Richard the next. The media speculated as to what might have caused John to despair and end everything for both himself and his wife, Anne. Was it the travellers buying a neighbouring field and making camp, when he had passed up the opportunity to buy the land himself? He was known to think that this had wiped a considerable sum of money from the value of his property. Had managing Anne's Alzheimer's simply become too much for him? Was it a combination of factors? Did it make any difference? It was all done now.

Dad said that John had mentioned nearly killing

himself years ago. It was Katharine who had found out about John's secret love child. He had told her really, the way people always seemed to tell her things that they wouldn't share with others. I notice Dad did the same with her too.

Of course, by this point Dad had fallen out with his neighbours, having once been close. He didn't fully appreciate what would happen when he suggested playing a new variation of bridge with someone who had Alzheimer's. The consequences were disastrous. There was also something in it all about botched work their son had done on Dad's car. The son said no one had ever spoken to him in his life the way my father did.

I had phoned John a few days before he killed himself, to see if things could be patched up, being the parent I suppose. Before I'd said a word he said, "We are not available" and put the phone down. Not available now.

The press had filled the garden. Did we have any comment on the 'poor man'? Long lens cameras pointed through their windows. Cars and vans parked up on verges and in the field. Reporters phoning asking for my mother; aerial photos of the house appearing in all the newspapers.

My father held my hand when I told him and did not say anything for a long time. We watched villagers, many of whom didn't seem to know the deceased, give interviews to Sky and the BBC. Everything happens to someone.

A drama on a larger scale that fleetingly captured the national imagination and enveloped our own quieter, more everyday disaster, a comparable form of which would be playing out in other next doors, unknown to us.

Much as others will have looked at pregnancy tests that yielded a single blue line on 9/11, somewhere everything is happening. There is a saying that there is 'nothing new in chess', so to, in life. Most chess players would assume the origins of the quote came from the Russian player Viktor Korchnoi, but it is based on the more poetic Ecclesiastes 1:9.

'What has been will again,

What has been done will be done again;

There is nothing new under the sun.'

I still do not know whether the thought is a comfort or not, hardly in the context of this drama, perhaps more so in others.

Now the press have moved on and the lanes and fields are quiet once more. The house across the pond in darkness, no one there tonight, already on the market and priced for a quick sale. Mrs Sawmill is but a memory too; a young couple live in her thatched cottage now.

I am support and witness, even if I am poorly equipped for either task. Somebody I work with said to me, "You can only do your best." Whatever that is, I have to try and find it from somewhere, in amongst my fatigue and general sense of inadequacy and the mutual irritation my father and I sometimes feel toward each other.

The hall is still, the television off. I know where he will be. I head up the stairs with the paper bag containing the apple turnovers held awkwardly in one hand, phone in the other. Jane, who was once the cleaner but has now become one of his carers, is sitting with him. In recent weeks she has taken to asking him how much the paintings are worth. "And what about the cars?" she says.

As usual, I'm not entirely clear how to initiate a conversation, but this is what he is waiting for. He always makes me feel self-conscious without actually doing anything. Is it because it can't be said or doesn't need to be said? It is all understood, or is none of it? I'll never be able to answers these questions, not really. He does not make it easy to build a bridge to them and at one level I have stopped trying to force a connection. Yet he is the one who breaks the silence, who takes the lead, and I am grateful for it. In that moment he takes charge, is the parent once again, something else that is happening for the final time.

"What can you tell me?" he says, holding my hand. He props himself up on the bed, looking tired but focussed. The skin around his face has a yellowish tinge, is tighter now than it once was, but he is not ruined. If you were looking at his face for the first time you would still think that he was handsome, or at least be able to notice through the shadows that once he was.

The quilt hides the thinness of his body; the bedding literally just changed by Jane smells fresh. Radio 5 whispers away, a sense of comfort and normality even though these are not normal times. By the side of his bed are empty discarded packets of Rennies and an untouched glass of water. Everything smells of mint and the chalk of the indigestion tablets.

He has read the newspaper, which lies discarded on what was Mum's side of the bed. His question is part rhetorical, which does not make me any less grateful for it; somehow he knows how to make things easier.

I squeeze his hand and offer him an apple turnover. He smiles and says he will have one later.

Dad's Work

In his letters to Mum he had acknowledged some of the differences between them, that her leaning was artistic and his was scientific, and what surprised me first when I looked through his old work folders was the poetry, if it could quite be called that. There were a number of limericks that had been written by his colleagues at a work Christmas party, about him, even if, on the surface, they did not necessarily give me much insight into his character. That came more through the fact that anyone had thought to write them in the first place.

A Divisional 'Super' called Graff,
Was keen to retain all his staff.
A bit sad for him,
The Chief Scientist's whim
Reduced all his budgets by half!

A Divisional 'Super' called Graff,
Got on quite well with his staff;
Until one fine day,
He was heard clear to say,
The whole crowd were not worth a laugh!

There were several pages of these, as well as puzzles and word games, and they surprised me too. Unless it was Shakespeare, he was always quite dismissive of poetry, but he and his colleagues seemed to write more of it, more than I might have expected, which is to say any at all.

Were all scientists frustrated wordsmiths? Was he? Growing up I thought he had a disdain for all things arty, those things which had given me a dubious sense of intellectual superiority. Was I reading too much into a handful of limericks and other such playfulness now? I couldn't know, but he had chosen to keep them. Perhaps he and his colleagues were not the one-dimensional number bods I had vaguely imagined them to be as a teenager, if I even thought to them at all.

My own children, particularly Francesca, will often ask me what I do at work. "I write emails, I go to meetings, that sort of thing," I will say.

"Sounds really boring; what do you actually do?" she will ask.

I once heard it said that explaining what you do at work without feeling the need to kill yourself is meant to be one of the tests as to whether you are in the right job. It is not that I hate it, but if I hedge a little it is because there are other things I would rather talk to her about, things that interest me more, and it is only when I think to this that I wonder if I was too hard on Dad. It always used to frustrate me that he had no inclination to tell us much about what he was doing at work, and now I am doing the same. There's more of him in me than I immediately recognised.

The difference though was that what he did was secret.

Growing up it seemed obvious what Mum did. She was an English teacher at the Royal National College for the Blind in Hereford. It was entirely in keeping with Dad that what he actually did was something of a mystery to us. He never talked about it. Aldershot and Malvern. Defence. He kept his security pass with its metal chain by his bed. They wouldn't let him in without it. He had signed the Official Secrets Act. We used to joke that he had probably begged to sign it, while also wondering why any of his superiors would have thought it necessary, given how tight-lipped he was. Did he actually speak to any of them when he was there?

We could never walk on the bit of the Malvern Hills that overlooked his office as he did not want to catch sight of the place when he wasn't there. Yet by all accounts (well, Mum's really) he quite liked what he did, until the final few years at any rate. I have no way of knowing whether or not this is true, or whether it is even a question that he could have answered. He worked in Malvern from 1983 to 2007 and there must have been all sorts of moments, good, bad and indifferent, during that time. Perhaps sometimes in my quest to understand I am too quick to reach conclusions.

His misfortune perhaps was that he worked in the defence industry in that brief period when history seemed to be over. The Cold War had finished. There was no hint then as to what was to follow it, even if all of us were to live long enough to see that answered in the skyline over Manhattan.

Later he had been more involved in air traffic control, we knew that much. He was running larger teams by the end, and was significantly better off than when we were younger. The money only really came after we had started work ourselves. Prior to that there were a succession of ageing Volvos, and once a mini-van that never lived up to our parents' initial optimism for it. He made money in a share deal when QinetiQ was formed, but could have made more if he had applied for his full allocation. He seemed to have an unspoken fear of anything other than cash, and had not wanted to take the risk. Perhaps his financial caution was a product of growing up in a family where money was tight and cash was king. Ready money to hand was a safety net of sorts if the laundry customers had not paid, and it was the only way to trade in London's poorer markets. In later years, particularly after the Northern Rock Building Society was bailed out in the banking crisis, transferring cash from one bank account to another became a hobby, which added unforeseen complexity to the eventual untangling of his estate and made me reflect again that he had needed better things to do with his time. For all his caution, the QuinetiQ shares he did invest in were still enough for more work on the house and a number of nearly new German cars.

There was an 'open day' once, but I only remember corridors and files and a sense of surprise that I could see the similarities with my own school building. I had not realised that all institutions shared some of the same physical and metaphorical bearings.

Some of the detail that I did not know when he was

alive was filled in when I went through the boxes in the spare room, afterwards. In addition to the limericks, I found a CV and a number of development assessments undertaken by external professionals. There were newspaper cuttings, one with him on the front page of *The Malvern Gazette*. I remembered also that he had once been on Radio 5, whilst I was at Bristol. Quite late at night, but talking about something related to his job. I hadn't listened to it.

I wonder if my children would listen to me if I was on the radio, talking about work, or even if I would want them to? I wonder if it disappointed him that I had not listened when he was on, for what was his one and only national media appearance, there in the deep of night when even his own son was doing something else.

Some of the technical details may not seem scintillating of themselves but they are things I did not know and now, thanks to his papers, I do. They are a part of the process of discovery. It all started with a BSc in physics from the University of London, then an MSc in cryogenics from Southampton in 1969, where he met Mum. Then came a nomadic three years. The British Oxygen Company (who years later rejected me for their graduate scheme), Marconi, Ferranti. He seemed to be employed in systems engineering and mathematical modelling positions, whatever they were.

By the time I was born in 1975 he was working in the mathematics department at The Royal Aircraft Establishment in Aldershot. He was a section leader working on databases and supercomputers, building his career. In 1983 he moved to the Royal Signals and Radar Establishment, focussing on integrated air defence systems. By 1990 he was promoted to superintendent, and then again to director of Missile & Defence Solutions Focal Business in 2004.

About all of which I understood nothing, but I knew he was good at maths. He had done all my numbers-related homework for years. When in the fifth year at secondary school my teacher noted that my work was declining, it was actually the opposite. Dad and I had agreed that I needed to start doing more of my homework myself if I was to have any chance of scraping through my GCSE. Which is what happened. Just. Without his earlier help I assume the school would have thrown me out years before.

He had one over me in relation to my children in this regard. Their maths soon outstripped mine and we had to find others to help them with it. I thought he was distant in many ways but I had outsourced the particular challenge of doing sums, while he had not. He spent more time just doing homework with me than I do with my children more generally. He seemed more interested in it than I am with my own children, more patient. Is it the case that my children do not want or need the same level of help that I did? Or was he just more engaged than I sometimes give him credit for, and me more remote? How will that one play out when the children tell others what they thought I was like?

In a magazine called *Focus* from 1991 there is a full-page article on work being done to ease air traffic congestion.

Dad is quoted. 'This expansion will not, however, be allowed to have an adverse effect on the CAA programme,' said ADS's Superintendent Colin Graff. 'We very much see the equipment we're researching as supportive aids for the controller. If the air traffic levels were to remain the same as today's, many aspects of our work would simply result in making the controller's job easier. In fact, the air traffic load is going to increase – so we're endeavouring to provide the controller with the means to keep up.'

There is a *Malvern Gazette* from Friday, 3 December 1993, a long time in a box file and a little faded, with Dad on the front cover. 'DRA "holds key" to safer air travel' is the main headline. He has scribbled just above it 'I can't stand the publicity. Colin.' The article is about one hundred European scientists who are going to visit the Defence Research Agency to look at ways of making flying safer, work commissioned by the Civil Aviation Authority which was concerned about over-crowded flight paths. Dad is quoted, 'Mr Colin Graff, head of the division concerned, which includes about 45 people, said: "It is an honour for us. It is a European project, and it covers a dozen European nations. Malvern has done most of the work on the subject in this country and this conference which will demonstrate the research shows that we are one of the principal centres."'

It was the leadership assessments I learnt most from. It wasn't easy to imagine anyone talking to him about what he thought or felt, how he might develop, but the evidence is there that this did happen, that he did talk about these things, if not to us.

A *Harvard Business Review* article 'Leadership that Gets Results' by Daniel Goleman also surprised me. It is a seminal piece that many management teams over the years have worked through. There is a picture of a leader selecting the right club from a golf bag, to represent the different management styles that might be appropriate for different situations. I had done the assessment too, not that long ago. Another faint echo across our two careers, a sense of something shared.

In another assessment from 2004, he described his key strengths as 'Total commitment, drive and energy.' Feedback from his team read as follows: 'Highly business focussed, with immense experience, Colin gives exceptional leadership to a well-motivated top team. He is a compassionate leader and always takes time to talk to staff. He has earned strong loyalty...'

He and his reviewers agreed that the democratic style was the dominant part of his repertoire. He thought he was authoritative, but his direct reports come to this conclusion. I would have gone with him on that one, but not when you looked into the definition. The feedback said that whilst he thought he was good at describing the big picture, others would see the situation as more him doing his own thing. Other notes suggested that he could be better at looking for external reference points beyond his department and the company.

His peers said he was an 'experienced and straightforward senior manager who is very customer focussed, forceful and clear... commands great staff loyalty and respect... generates good cohesion in his business.' Another noted, 'Colin is an extremely good leader...'

The things people thought he should improve on were also noteworthy. For him it was '...broader scanning together with greater delegation of day to day details. I also need to do more coaching.' While a direct report said, 'He does not suffer fools gladly but when politics are involved, he maybe does not identify the fool correctly!' I could see that, perhaps.

I never really knew how well Dad read people, although I assumed he read others better than he did me. Albeit I remember the conversation I had with one of his fellow school governors at his graveside, along the lines that he was a really good guy but might occasionally have varied his influencing style a little more. I knew exactly what he meant.

Perhaps the most ominous feedback came from 'Other': "I do not believe that Colin's approach to creating, sustaining and finding business necessarily sits well with the inflated aspirations that the company has more recently espoused. This may put him at odds with the overall leadership and he may, therefore, be regarded as something of a dinosaur both in approach and style. However, a more conciliatory approach to those that he might regard as out of touch in the upper hierarchy would not hurt in his overall approach to company politics... if anything, he probably needs to be able to let go a bit more and be more supportive of changes that arise – or at least, not give the impression that they will be for the worst."

'Other' had read the signs… Dad moved to a different job. His performance objectives from this final role were also in the file, the only ones to survive. They spoke of his need to manage this new team of six people with the same level of enthusiasm and energy as he had his previous much larger team. But this proved to be impossible; he had been marginalised and everybody knew it. Finally there were emails between him and the HR director discussing the terms of his early retirement. *We want there to be something in it for us as well as for you* the faceless official had written, and following further back and forth my father retired a year early at fifty-nine.

Many of his work colleagues were at his funeral. He had been outlived by most, but they were there to remember him. One spoke to me about Dad first working for him, and then, much later, him working for Dad. When they first met, he wasn't sure that they would get on. But they did. Somehow, despite the quietness and the reserve, he could make things work. According to the feedback, he was democratic and compassionate. Perhaps he was not really one for opening up outside of career coaching sessions, but he was very good at maths homework. Better than I proved to be at any rate.

Martin's Journal – Schooldays

I remember when he was very young I told Ben some of my school stories and he was astonished to hear that I had once been young, let along young enough to ever have had need of a school. But I was and did, however it might appear to look at me now. The old chap who often sits next to me in the lounge was telling me about his time at school yesterday, but I got the sense that he was slightly confused as to whether he was still there now or not. Whatever afflictions I have, I am grateful that I still know where I am, insofar as anybody does. Although, of course, this place does have its similarities with a school, and these sorts of institutions are somewhat disorientating, so perhaps he was not as out of it as all that.

So here goes – these are my recollections of school.

At the age of five I started at St George's School. My mother duly delivered me to the door that first morning, telling me to be a good boy and to come straight home when school was over. It never occurred to her that it would be necessary to come and collect me!

St George's, a private school, was owned by two

sisters called Holmes (no relation); the head was young, cool, self-assured and well able to cope with small boys. Her sister, considerably older, looked and sounded like the witch we were all convinced she was. Reading, writing and simple arithmetic were quickly mastered in those days; it was certainly easier that way.

When I was seven, the school was sold to a Mr Davies, who had a French wife and a bilingual son called Jim. St George's then became a school for boys of all ages, and was moved to a large house in Cleveland Road (now demolished). A few years later the school moved to a house in Drum Street which has also now been demolished. Soon after this move, Mr Davies returned to his beloved France and the school was sold to a Mr Gill.

Assistant schoolmasters in those days tended to be slightly odd, always underqualified and generally underwhelming people. I do not think many would be allowed through the gate of a modern-day school. At least I would hope not. My form master at the time was a Mr Gronis, tall, gaunt and pale. From time to time during lessons he would throw the window wide open, shout "Excuse me, boys," and spit into the garden! He did not last very long.

His place was taken by a Mr Vine, who was tall, well dressed, athletic and a first-rate boxer. This man seemed from another world, talking easily of music and the London theatre. He seemed to have been everywhere and done everything. He did not have the

T-shirt. In the 1920s no one would have been seen dead in such a thing.

Mr Vine was also a scout master and during the Easter and summer holidays he would go camping in France, accompanied by two or perhaps three boy scouts. Foreign travel was unheard of in those days unless you were rich, so I longed to take part in the expeditions, but my father refused even to consider it. It was just the way he was. Perhaps it was fear as to what might happen to me. Perhaps it was the money. Perhaps it was about control; who can say? It was another note of discord between us.

Two days before the start of the summer term of 1930 my mother told me over breakfast that I would not be returning to St George's. Instead I would be going as a boarder to the old grammar school at Shaftesbury (founded 1702). All arrangements had been made, but this was the first I had heard of it! In retrospect I believe that having been so lavish in my praise of Mr Vine my parents had invited him to a dinner party, and realised that he was gay and therefore in their eyes a bad influence. It was not unusual for parents to make decisions about their children's futures in this way at that time. Children did not have a voice in things in the way that they do today. It was always the case that your parents knew best; that was just how things were.

In the first week of the war, many years later, Mr Vine paid a flying visit to the Island, and we had a drink together. We sat in a Ryde pub, not exactly as equals, for I still looked up to him, but at least on some sort of level. He was still fascinating, and for all that things did work out alright for me at boarding school, I do not think any of the teachers I met there came close to him and I wish I had been able to have had him as a teacher for longer.

It was whilst we were drinking that he revealed that for some years he had been working for British Military Intelligence and that his trips to the Continent were a cover for his activities, which entailed mapping airfields and identifying the sites of munitions factories. It was very much the case that he had lived and would continue to live a fulfilling life of adventure. In the 1970s one of the Ryde Rotary members encountered Mr Vine at a family dinner party in Derbyshire. He had recently retired and been awarded the OBE for services to NATO Intelligence.

However, that was all in the future and did not change my current predicament of being fourteen years of age and about to start a new life at a boarding school. My mother assured me that her brother had been very happy there. Well, yes, but this was a cricketing school and he had been good at that. He had also been a day boy, whereas I was going to be a boarder.

I was certainly apprehensive; leaving my parents for the first time, despite the strains in my relationship with my father, was always going to do that. Whatever you are leaving, there is nothing more frightening than the unknown. They say that in prison camps it is the pessimists rather than the optimists who are more likely to survive. If you think something is likely to be terrible, you have no expectations that can be dashed, no emotional needs that you are seeking to have fulfilled. If you have higher expectations, it is their dashing that will do for you. All of which is to make this somewhat too dramatic. Whilst I was pessimistic to begin with, the truth is, in the end, things did not work out too badly.

The old Shaftesbury Grammar School at which I was about to be admitted as its newest pupil no longer exists, thanks to the disastrous Shirley Williams, one-time minister for education. Rather, it was destroyed to make room for a massive comprehensive school, whose hideous buildings now cover the once famous playing fields.

It was the case that normally one would not have been admitted without passing the common entrance exam, but I was accepted because of my mother's brother, Bill. He was an old boy of the school and a mainstay of the Old Shaftonians cricket team which toured the south coast during the school holidays in August.

So it was that the day before term started we drove to Bill's farm about three miles out of town and had a brief interview with Dr Tovey, the principal. He was a larger than life character who managed to inspire affection, even though most people, young or old, were terrified of him. I never quite worked out whether it was all an act, or whether that was just the way he was. I suspect the latter; public school life bred and fostered a range of characters you just wouldn't see today.

During the interview he asked how I felt about coming all this way to school, a question my parents had never thought it necessary to ask, which I thought to again when he did ask me.

I was apprehensive, to put it politely. School stories were popular in those days, and I had read many *Tom Brown's School Days*. It was obvious from those books that schools were exceptionally violent places! One was likely to be caned by the headmaster, and even more likely to be beaten by prefects. Bullying was of course an ever-present hazard. You had to think to survival first. Anything more that might follow was a bonus.

If you liked sport, the school was the perfect place to be, and in particular it was a paradise for cricket players. Our 1st x11 played against much larger public schools such as Sherborne, and we sent our 2nd x11 to play the 1st x11 at minor public schools like Claymore. In the summer term, cricket was played every day, except Sunday, from lunchtime to suppertime. Prep was from supper to bedtime, then we were up at 6am to do more prep before breakfast. The school had one of the most beautiful playing fields in England with a view over seven counties, Shaftesbury being a hilltop town.

Whilst cricket was not my game, luckily I had inherited from my father a measure of skill in the gymnasium. They were very keen on gym at St George's. Boxing was compulsory, although I have to admit that I was not all that keen on it. I have an aversion to punching people on the nose and an even stronger aversion to being punched myself. However, I had had a measure of skill instilled in me by the mysterious Mr Vine and was able to hold my own, the key to survival at boarding school.

On arrival I was introduced to a boy called Bobby Baker. He had white blond hair and the air of having seen everything that could be seen. In those days Christian names were only used by close friends. Everybody at school was known only by their surname and initial. Young Bobby was in dormitory three, as I was, and duly showed me around the place, finishing up in the music room. He asked me what I thought of a song which he was sure would be a BIG hit. Popular music was played by bands at the time and most of us listened to the BBC Orchestra. I did not know the song, so Bobby sat at the piano, and played and sang 'Love is the sweetest thing'. I have to admit that I had not expected to be serenaded with love songs! In that moment I really could have been anywhere, but I somehow thought as I listened to him sing that perhaps things might work out alright here.

When he had finished singing, Bobby said, "I am fed up about Jimmy Kennedy leaving us, as you can imagine." Seeing a blank look on my face, he added, "You don't seem to know much, do you? It must be coming from the Isle of Wight, I suppose. Jimmy Kennedy is only the man who wrote this. The man was junior science master here, unlike the end of last term. He is now making so much money he no longer needs to work as a teacher."

Eventually Bobby reluctantly closed the piano lid. "We can't loll about in here, we had better go out into the playing field and chuck a cricket ball about," he said, so we joined a group of fellows doing just that. Amongst them was a chap called Sheyale (a name I had never heard before nor since.) He was cheery, self-effacing, and obviously very tough. It was to be a stroke of luck for me.

From that evening we were always together in our spare time. He was in the form below me. In those days your form was dependent on your ability to pass end of year exams, and you did not move up automatically. People were scared of Sheyale, so I was spared the kind of ragging that new boys usually had to contend with.

A protector is a powerful thing to have. My first morning in class, I found that by chance there was a prefect in the form, at least one year behind with his studies as he was considered academically to not be very bright. Daniel Young went on to build up a big business in agricultural machinery and is today a very wealthy man. I had known Daniel for years: his father owned the farm adjoining my Uncle Bill's, where I spent many of my holidays. My cheery "Hello David", was treated with a curt nod, and "Holmes". He was a prefect, a man apart and not to be engaged with familiarity by an ordinary boy!

Sheyale had warned me that there were two bullies

to contend with. One, Stevens, was a day boy in my form, and known to be a local street fighter. "Fight him if you have to," said Sheyale airily. "You probably won't win, but that won't matter if you put on a good show!" The other, a boarder called Roger, Sheyale dismissed with contempt, "You can take him out any time." To my somewhat doubtful "Can I?" he said, "Oh, he is a very big chap and enormously strong, and people are afraid of him, but he has no idea how to fight."

That first morning we had one period in the gym and arrived before the PT master, so started to mess about on the equipment. I climbed up the rope on the far left, without using my feet, did a Tarzan act from one rope to the other, before sliding down the one on the far right. Stevens was watching thoughtfully and must have been sufficiently impressed as he never gave me any bother. He was subsequently expelled when arrested by the police for stealing a car and joyriding. Yes, even in those days.

So it was that I established myself, made some friends and showed some athletic skills to a point, albeit not really when it came to cricket. I do pause to consider how I might fare should I try to scale some ropes today, but of course I know the answer. It had turned out not to be like *Tom Brown's School Days* after all, but it was very much the case that you needed to keep your wits about you. Danger lurked and it could take many forms – good preparation for life more generally perhaps. Well, perhaps.

When I was due to return to Shaftesbury for

my second term, there was a thick fog. In those days before radar this meant that no boats were running, so I arrived back at school one day late, just after lunch. My immediate concern was to discover if Sheyale had returned. He had told me there was a possibility that he might not. I hurried to find him, taking a shortcut behind the jail courts, a small yard at the back of the school separate from general view, which enabled you to head up to the dormitory without having to traipse through multiple corridors and up the main staircase.

Preoccupied, I failed to hear footsteps behind me, so was taken completely by surprise by a massive open-handed blow on my ear, which knocked me off my feet. I jumped up, feeling decidedly cross – and there was Roger, a broad grin on his face, accompanied by two Frenchmen who usually followed him about.

"You're out of luck, Holmes, your protector hasn't come back, and by the time I'm finished with you, you will wish you hadn't either!" With that he drew his enormous right fist well back for a good round arm swing, leaving his left arm loosely by his side. Sheyale was right: he had no idea how to fight; two short arm jabs to the unprotected solar plexus and he was on the ground, gasping for breath.

I smiled at his two distinguished gentlemen. "Just keep out of my way in future." Quite a pleasant moment. A somewhat exaggerated account of this fracas went rapidly round the school, and I lived in peace from then on.

About three or four times a term, one could ask

for a Sunday off. On those occasions I would leave after morning service at Holy Trinity Church, and head to my Uncle Bill's farm; it was like an escape into another world. I would take the main Westminster Road out of town, across the border into Wiltshire, turning right down a road, closed off in those days by a gate, as cattle were grazing on common land. Then halfway down a steep hill was the wonderful old stone farmhouse, facing the farmyard.

A warm welcome, a glass of sherry, a super Sunday lunch, possibly a ride on one of the horses in the afternoon, then a drive back to school in time for evensong at 6pm. The weekends I spent there in my last year at Shaftesbury in 1933 were a real pleasure. It saddens me now that they are all passed, that I cannot go back and see them one last time, one last glass of sherry and pony ride, but there we are. The memories are happy ones, which should not be tainted just because it pains me a little that they are from a world that does not exist anymore.

I have just eaten lunch. Somewhat chewy lamb and over-cooked roast potatoes, not so dissimilar from school fare back then, an experience, unlike the one described above, that I would have been happy to forgo repeating. At least the pudding was apple crumble and custard, not rhubarb. I will eat any food that is put in front of me, apart from rhubarb. Years and years of this pudding, seemingly every day, have left me with an aversion to the sight of a stick of the stuff that could not now be shaken.

So yes, onwards with this story, although perhaps it is a coincidence but my next memory is also about food. I was appointed a prefect, a position of power and privilege, toward the end of my time at the school. The head prefect, Peter Bathurst-Brough asked me for £2 at the start of the term, about £65 in today's money. With a similar amount from all six prefects he went off to a grocer's, who then made sure that the food served to us sitting together at the top table was vastly superior to that served to everybody else. The benefits that can come with age and rank!

As a prefect, one of my duties at bedtime was to take charge of dormitory three. I was now in charge, which was always make or break (and was very much a case of break for some who were destroyed by their charges.) Keeping order in dormitories was certainly a very important part of a prefect's job.

There were fourteen boys in dormitory three, aged thirtenn to fourteen beds down each end of the room, washbasins and jugs of water on a long stand down the middle. Shaftesbury, on its hilltop, is a very cold place in winter, and there were times when we had to break the ice before we could wash in the morning! It is unlikely that the conditions would be deemed legal in today's health and safety culture, but we managed.

On arriving at the dormitory you were required to kneel at your bedside and say your prayers. No talking was allowed until everybody had prayed. The space on the left-hand side of your bed was yours and you were not allowed to trespass into the space belonging to anyone else. Anyone breaking this or any other school rule was likely to be beaten by one of the prefects armed with a slipper. In fact, hard house shoes!

The boy in the next bed to me on my first night in charge was a pleasant enough chap called Galihouse. He obviously knew that newly appointed prefects were supposed to be tested to the limit. "So, we get you this term," said Galihouse. "We had Cartledge last term; he is a very strong fellow, you know."

"Yes, I agree."

"He is a friend of mine and he is very, very strong." Galihouse looked up at the steel beam above his head. "He used to do his exercises on that, you know. One day he went halfway across the dorm. You have to be very strong to do that."

Those poor little innocents had chosen to challenge me in the one field of athletics at which, unknown to them, I was reasonably expert. Ordering Galihouse to stand away from his bed, I used it as a trampoline to reach the RSJ (rolled steel joist), then without any real effort I went hand over hand to the other side of the dorm.

Facing my crestfallen troops I said, "You all thought Cartledge was strong when he got halfway across. I am obviously twice as strong as he is, as you will find out when I tan your bottoms!" No rebellion was likely from then on: I omitted to point out that Cartledge had eleven and a half stone to support, while I had only nine.

The other prefects were all members of the 1st x11

cricket team, so I was appointed scorer (I had been 2nd x11 scorer the year before). I also scored for the masters x11, which contained two or three Dorset players.

So that summer we played several matches a week at places like the county ground in Southampton, to schools and village teams in Somerset or at home on our own beautiful playing field, with superb lunches and teas. This was surely a wonderful summer, and a fitting end to my schooldays.

A short holiday camping with the St George's scouts in Jersey, then to work. From being a VIP at Shaftesbury to becoming the most junior member of our family business was a somewhat rapid descent to earth!

It is hard to imagine myself now as the small boy I was then. I have seen and learnt so much since those days, how can it not change your perspective somewhat? I do not think a father would send a child to school like that today, but it was more normal in the 1920s. Equally I am unsurprised that my happiest memories from that time are of my Uncle Bill, rather than of going home, but all of this it was and it cannot be changed.

You can go from being young to old in the blink of an eye. At least this is how it seems to me now. As I sit here today and write this, I feel somewhat old and fragile. But when I think to my former self shimmying up ropes or climbing across the dormitory it does make me smile. Such ability does not survive in my body but it does in my memory.

I expect some day someone will be amazed to learn that Ben went to school once too.

Playing Games – 1989-2014

We left Aldershot when we were seven and I don't remember much about it. A poster in which bright pink pigs urged you to wash your hands pinned to the school cloakroom wall. Not being able to read the word 'turquoise' on the classroom colours mobile. Playing with sand and water and making things out of pieces of card and plastic. A goldfish that died and was either given a funeral or flushed down the toilet; I half remember it both ways. Looking for bits of broken china and glass in the school flower beds. A picture of the Queen that hung in a school canteen of wooden, metal-framed hexagonally-shaped tables and orange plastic chairs. The whole place smelt of cheese, egg, cellophane and damp, and like most of the children I struggled to eat in it.

Swinging a boy by his gloves and snapping the string, his mother complaining. A teacher moving to the Scilly Isles. Dave turning up at the school gate once and me being unsure who he was. Walking on the range with its gorse bushes, mud and tanks, where the soldiers used to practise. The smell of exhaust fumes on the busy road that led to and from the school. A swan painted on a stone given to me by a friend's mother; I liked the feel of the coolness of the rock on one side and the smoothness of the paint on the other. A children's party, where I wanted a bar of chocolate, but when I got it, it was plain and bitter.

There had been a certain tension with the immediate next-door neighbours and our parents were never keen to have much to do with them. I think I remember that. It was only years later that we were told they had been wife-swappers. There was some sort of plant in their garden which apparently was meant to be a sign of this, Mum and Dad thought, next to their large caravan, which now I come to think of it could have been used for who knows what.

"Did they ever ask you?" I once said to Dad.

"Let's not even go there," he replied with a shake of his head and perhaps the hint of a grin. At least I think that is the conversation I remember.

We were back again for a weekend to stay with other neighbours, in their chaotic house, although they had moved to a different part of Aldershot soon after we had left. A large house with a big garden, but not kept in a way that met with my parents' approval. Bash Street Kids stickers on many of the walls. Piles of laundry and dishes, wine from boxes rather than bottles, which Dad said was never a good sign. Cat litter trays and bowls in multiple places. Paperwork piled up in corners. Her university course work, his Inland Revenue files.

"Why can't they tidy up a bit?" my father would mutter, and Mum would seem to sigh quietly in agreement. But in the garden, in the heat of a summer game, none of that seemed to matter. Dad was at his most natural here, present and engaged, properly one of us, a real player, far removed from the world of polite adult social chit-chat going on at the margins of the lawn and on the patio.

Mum said that our dad's parents hadn't encouraged him to play when he was a child and it was like he was making up for it now. They took all forms, our games on that Aldershot summer lawn scorched yellow by the sun, with so many of the families we had once lived close to back together for an afternoon. We usually played football, sometimes a game that wasn't quite rugby, occasionally cricket or rounders. Barbeque smoke scented with burnt meat and charcoal in the air, plastic cutlery and discarded serviettes blowing across the lawn, as the little grass that had survived the heat turned to dust under our feet.

Lee, who lived further up Cranmore Gardens, who had been fired from the local paper for embezzlement and now owned an art gallery, was very much the other key adult in the mix of the games. Years later Lee wrote to my father after Mum's death, to say that he felt an affinity with him as he too was a Jew who had married a Catholic, even if they had since divorced. "Never propose in the middle of a blazing row," was one of the pieces of advice Lee shared with me, shaking his head. It wasn't yet a funny story. I don't know if Dad ever wrote back to him. He did not find it easy to reciprocate gestures of openness from others and I know what my guess would be.

The games would last for hours. 30–29 score lines were not uncommon, as often we would agree that the 'next goal wins,' and then find ourselves unsated and wanting to play more. Often times somebody would be injured or storm off in a huff. Occasionally there would be complaints made to the players by other adults that things were perhaps getting a bit out of hand. We barely noticed. I was no athlete, but I had a kind of determination that made me quite good, or at least carried me into the action. I had near unlimited energy and in those moments the game was everything and all else disappeared. In a rare flash of insight, I once thought that this is what it is like to be young, as I forced the football through the jumper goal posts, a moment that mattered to me then but now of course will be remembered by no one else. I do not know if it counts for less because of this, or not. Once, after a particularly bruising game, Lee said that he must say something to me about how he thought I had played. I could tell from his tone that it was going to be a compliment, but then Dad interrupted him and he never did finish his sentence.

It was around the time of the Aldershot visit that my father taught us to play chess, sliding the lid from the box and removing brown and white weighted wooden pieces with care, as if about to perform a magic trick, which in a way he was. The pieces were not quite Staunton, the design a little off standard, the kings with turbans and the bishops with mitres of the opposing colour, but these were minor details and everything else was close enough. The board itself was made of stiff card that folded in two. Large squares of black and white, an oriental-style brown and black patterned back. 'Chess and Draughts Board' was embossed in solemn lettering on a rectangular patch of orange and white.

We took our first steps with him into the labyrinth and he showed patience for explaining and coaching, at odds with my more general impression of him. Sometimes we would play each other, sometimes I would play Matt and Dad would advise. At ten it would never have occurred to me that I would ever beat him. By twelve it was trivial, though that was more about being at a school with teachers who played in weekend tournaments, far ahead of hobbyists like him, than anything else. I always saw beating Dad in this context; my realisation as to the limitations of a parent's knowledge was to come later, and for different reasons.

Dad had been a right-footed left back at school but didn't make the team; his father, Dave, had played cricket for the army at Lords but had been knocked out first ball. But the facility was there and it often surprised; he was better at sport than you might have thought. Or perhaps more likely, if you were not his son you would have been more open to the possibility that he might have been good at things from the outset. Perhaps children are always destined to be their parents most critical judges, to see them as either all-knowing or embarrassing without much in between, which can but lead to a disappointed awakening or confirmation of what we already know. Either way it is not good. I know all this must go for how my children see or will ultimately see me too.

I was horrified when he took part in the fathers' race at sports day. He was older than some of his rivals, chunkier too, and I had enough to live down as it was. But from the moment the starting gun fired, his strength was obvious. There was real power in the core of his body as he ploughed along his green, white-striped furrow, coming home second much to my amazement, only run down in the last few yards by one of the farmers. The way he brushed off my congratulations afterwards surprised me less.

Once at a clay pigeon shoot, he hit with both of his shots, spraying fragments of clay across the field. Impressing his hosts, he grinned broadly at us, briefly the hero of everyone in that muddy field, even the local farmers. We were at one with our country neighbours that day.

We played most things and his skill level varied. He was alright at snooker, on the ageing table we kept in the garage, and about the same at darts as the rest of us. His golf was appalling, not an issue on Bognor's putting green, more so at Appley pitch and putt on the Island. At least he got value for money, given the number of strokes he would take.

Cricket was more of a leveller and would sometimes bring in other family members who did not take part in other games. Both Mum and Martin were known to play. I remember Martin in his eighties still able to bowl with spin on the damp sand, hand–eye coordination with the bat strong. Some of the training from his boarding school days was ingrained in him and he looked to me to be a better player than he said he had been in his journal.

Dad was pretty good with bat and ball, Mum's effort more nominal but appreciated. Sometimes we would play on Brook Beach and then go to Hannover House for afternoon tea, hot buttered toast, scones and cake. Not open all year. A green caravan that doubled as a travelling library parked under the large oak tree in the grounds, overlooking the sea. All of it bored me at the time.

Once, travelling down to the Island years before, a car bumped us in near stationary motorway traffic and Dad's power surprised me. He got out, bare-chested, looking straight at the much younger guy in the vehicle behind, who held his hands up in acknowledgement or fear. Dad slowly satisfied himself that there was no damage, before turning and strolling back to the driver's seat. I was impressed, but also conscious of the fact that I wasn't the only one who could find him unnerving.

"You know he's quite shy really, don't you?" a friend once said to me. He was certainly quiet when we were younger. It was easier to play with him than it was to talk. In later years, as he became successful and started to drink more, he was to become at first more bullish then belligerent. Talking about sport, playing games, some things we could do more easily than approach certain other topics.

Why David Cameron was the worst prime minister in history and things of that ilk formed equally safe ground. We once watched Barack Obama give a press conference where his microphone didn't work. He had to ask if anybody had another one, which we both thought was quite funny.

My father was impressed by very few people, or at least so far as I knew. Long-dead scientists and pyramid builders perhaps, Shakespeare, Andrew Lloyd Webber and The Beatles, I suppose. All politicians were automatically idiots, but Obama was the exception. A man of substance, somebody to be admired. This was something we were agreed upon.

Our own children joined the ranks for football in later years. That final match with Dad in the line-up, although we did not know it at the time, was on the day he first told me he didn't feel well. It was a Good Friday, at Matt's house. My mother had always said that she could not imagine Good Friday as a normal day, and this one in hindsight turned out not to be. Reuben jumping about, pretending to be a horse, as he often did. Maddie chatting away with Evie, Annabelle playing with care and thought, shepherding Gabriella away when she wandered onto the pitch to see what was going on. Francesca demonstrating skills that none of the rest of us had, partly the product of coaching but not just that. Dad played mainly as a goalkeeper, alert and neat with the ball but rarely pushing up field.

Later I was to wonder as to what he might have been thinking about as we played. Not so much whether he knew how ill he was as I do not think he did, more what seeing his children play with their children and with him was like on that perfect spring day. The natural order of things, I would suppose. We were following in the same traditions, now a generation on from games with Martin and the other grandparents and my mum, with him as the bridge, the oldest survivor in that moment. In that sense, we were parenting much as he had. Things were always at their easiest during a game.

Perhaps this was what had drawn me to chess, had pushed me deeper into it, after that day when he had taken the wooden pieces out of their box and shown them to us for the first time. There was much about chess that was simpler than real life, with all of its rituals and processes to be followed. Shake hands when you first greet your opponent at the board, then again just before you start and finally when the game is over. Ask your opponent if they "want to have a look at it", if you win, but in no way be offended if they do not. In extremes, if you have lost and are distraught, no words have to accompany the final handshake. But not to shake at the end will always be viewed as a breach of etiquette akin to deliberately running the victor's grandmother over in the car park.

For all the possibilities, chess generally rewards time invested in thinking and studying openings, middle games often generate positions with recognisable tactical themes, identifiable pawn chains, squares that are clearly strong or weak – a sense of what might need to be done. Endgames are hardest, but how to use your king, where to place your rooks, when you need to gain or lose a tempo, are all things that can be learnt, perhaps not perfectly but well enough to do for most. Even in those positions that seem to transcend all this, there are rules and tests to fall back on. Questions such as, what is threatened, or, what is the position of my worst placed piece and how can it be improved, mean a chess player is rarely wholly without resource.

Life is never really like that, perhaps because it is not confined to sixty-four simple squares and two players.

It is harder to predict who might do what, still less why. Chess pieces are much easier to assess. Knights generally seek central squares (a knight on the rim is very dim, the old saying goes), rooks need open files, bishops long diagonals, the king shelter – at least while there are a lot of pieces on the board. It is altogether a more certain and predictable world, which is why it provides refuge to so many. Even though he had gifted it to me, my father never really entered properly into its realm.

I don't think he ever told me what he thought I was like as a parent, beyond the occasional observation that we should be stricter. Perhaps the football and the many other games were all the affirmation he thought was needed, his participation how we knew that we were doing alright.

We watched a lot of sport together in his last few months. We talked about the limitations in Alastair Cook's captaincy of the England cricket team, about which we felt we knew a lot, and the technique behind Phil Mickelson's golf swing, about which we recognised we knew less.

He had been unlucky in football, that much was clear. Growing up in London, the non-local team that stole his heart turned out to be absolutely terrible. Whatever moment had grabbed his attention, there had not been many others. For all the pain it had brought him, few could challenge his support for Wolves as lacking in authenticity. It was a cut above being an Aldershot-born Manchester United fan, as I was, which made me a glory seeker in the eyes of many.

A Wolves game we watched though was not a success, if not for the usual reasons. The cheers from the stadium, even filtered through a television, proved too much for him. It was not the noise itself, just the distance between him and those cheering, happy people. He faced things that they did not, much more imminently at any rate.

In that last bit of time, we watched a programme about 9/11 with Maddie that discussed the way in which the conspiracy theories surrounding the day were actually part of an elaborate plot to distract attention from the real questions that were not being addressed. Namely, the failure of American intelligence in the run-up to the attacks, the role of Saudi Arabia during them, and the complete collapse of America's chain of command immediately afterwards. I ask my father what he makes of it all and he just shrugs.

"It's not so much that I don't think there is something in that, it's just I am tired," he says. "You always think things will become clearer to you, but everything seems just as inconclusive now as it ever did."

I am intrigued, but I can see in his face that he does not want me to pursue it. He would rather rest and then play another game.

We generally stuck to watching sport, then *The Big Bang Theory*.

We played Scrabble regularly in the conservatory. We had long since agreed that Monopoly was just a game of luck. Bridge and chess provided an insufficiently level playing field, but Scrabble was where we could meet. It was often just the two of us. Sometimes Matt, who was the strongest Scrabble player, or Sheila, my father's partner, would join us. His game was not much weaker than it had been, but he did lose more than he won.

"All I want is your best game," he said, re-racking the letters with a look of determination and focus. A week before he dies we play for the last time. He is behind, but the point deduction for unused letters at the end does for me and he wins by two.

All Our Christmases

It starts with choosing the tree from a neighbouring farm, always the same place, with its barns and tractors and winter mud. They make more from the trees than a lot of other stuff, apart from the European subsidies, the owner mutters to Dad, who nods and continues to assess the Norway spruces as if conducting one of his scientific experiments. Fortunately this does not take quite as long as those other experiments involving multiple test drives of numerous potential second-hand vehicles we might buy, or the dozens of tester pots of slightly differing shades of magnolia that will have to be daubed onto any wall before a decision can be made. Even so, there is a moment where the time we are spending on choosing a tree feels comparable to either of those scenarios. He always thought he could completely solve a problem if he applied the right tests, gave the problem enough thought.

The trees all look the same to me and Matt, but apparently this is not the case and the fact that we do not recognise this annoys him. Finally though, he will choose, and we will load the thing into the car and head for home. Putting the lights on will be an extremely long, tense task that Dad will make clear requires no input from any of us. Tempers fray, his especially. The tree often leans at the wrong angle in the pot, and one year leaves a mark on the ceiling as it stubbornly refuses to be manoeuvred into place. But, eventually, it will stand straight, and much later still his light-stringing agonies will be over and it will be time to decorate.

Baubles of blue and silver and gold, with frosted white patterns on them, will be lifted from tissue paper-filled shoe boxes. Some find prominent places every year, for others it can depend. There is never tinsel, but there are fir cones and tiny pretend parcels to hang, a felt Christmas tree made by Matt, red plastic apples, and a gold star for the top; you can smell the sweetness of the tree sap as it is pushed into place.

Caspar comes to sniff the pot and half-heartedly swipe at low-hanging spheres, before the need for sleep overwhelms him and he curls up in his basket by the Rayburn. We pin Christmas cards to the kitchen's ceiling beam and place others on the sitting room mantelpiece. There are certain cards that must be visible because of who sent them, with others it depends on the picture. Mum and Dad prepare the spare bedroom with fresh sheets and pillowcases, strategically placing a mat over the stain on the thin blue carpet, stacking any stray books and papers into one of the cupboards.

The larder groans with food. There are places we are not allowed to look.

The build-up will have seen school pantomimes and shows, weeks of rehearsals on ever darkening winter nights, Mum and Dad sitting proudly in the audience while we parrot our words, all those drives to rehearsals through November rain and December sleet now worth it. When offstage, we loll in the music room, eating chocolate Rice Krispie cakes and drinking Coke from throwaway cups, listening to the music thumping through the wall from the school hall. There is a pattern and a rhythm to the season. School shows, a trip to the theatre to see *The Wind in the Willows*, or some such, carol singing on poorly-lit frosty village streets, and then at last the day itself draws close.

It is always the same. Theresa and Dave will arrive mid-morning on Christmas Eve, car filled to the brim with food and presents. Those she's done tidily wrapped in red paper, his contribution often in newspaper, held together with masking tape. They are late converts to Christmas.

There will be crisps and sweets and biscuits and Turkish Delight and Christmas crackers and other things that will be viewed by Mum as being of varying degrees of help. The turkey they bring one year 'just in case,' will not be well received. Dave will insist on wearing his slippers as he goes to and from the car to unload, dragging country mud onto newly hoovered carpet.

When they are finally all unpacked, we will go to the pub for Christmas Eve lunch. Not The Bell, but further out, not so far from the fields that would later reveal the secrets of notorious serial killer and self-styled King of Ledbury, Fred West.

It is usually before the snow and the real country cold at this time of year. Rarely white, more brown and damp, in the day at least, the gloom of the low-ceilinged pub only softened by its own Christmas decorations that glint in artificial indoor light somehow diminished by the weakness of the winter sun.

The air is scented with smoke from the neighbouring snug bar and bleach from the toilet, if we are unlucky enough to be seated by the door. I will drink tonic water and eat croquet potatoes, chips and beans. Mum asks if anyone else has ever requested it, but apparently even at the bargain price of £1.50 they have not; they have put it on the menu so the bar staff will know what to charge. Matt will fidget. Theresa will suggest that her pie is in fact recycled leftovers. Dave will share thoughts on Thatcherism and will sing under his breath. "Ben, Ben, Ben. Matt, Matt, Matt." Mum will drink a large glass of wine.

On Christmas Eve afternoon, we will sometimes go to the Christingle service at Bosbury Church. Never Dave or Dad, occasionally Theresa, always Mum of course. The biggest tree of them all stands here, in the knave next to the board that lists all the vicars back to 900AD. I always sniggered at the thought of Dad trying to put the lights on this tree, and then felt guilty yet again.

We know most of the villagers. It is half full, which makes it one of the busiest services of the year. We have wrapped red ribbons around oranges. Four cocktail sticks, with fruits and sweets, which we nibble on as the service progresses. White candle in the middle, pushed deep into the flesh of the orange.

One year a girl's hair catches fire and for a moment the smell of it burning is stronger than that of the pine and stone and all of the memories of the ancient building that can be inhaled with every breath. Then the vicar hits the side of her head with his vestments and the crisis passes.

I always knew that I didn't really believe any of this. Not really. Still too young to experience the full surprise of realising that other people actually did. I guess it was the one thing Mum would have changed in me if she could have done, not that she ever said.

But on Christmas Eve, in a village church, it is impossible not to feel a part of something more. In amongst the candles and the decorations, family tombs and stained glass, cross above, gas heating glowing but unequal to the task of warming this ancient place with its smooth stone floor. Sitting on a pew that so many have sat on before you and so many more will long after you are gone, considering your own mortality, you think to them all. Their hopes and fears. Either washed away by time or still yet to form, probably not that different from our own. But here in this moment it is me and those around me who are carrying on these traditions. Ancestors and descendants watching on silently; the owners of other moments, other times, but still partial sharers in the here and now.

In later years I will wonder if it might have been different if she had been low church Protestant instead of Catholic. Discussions about the state of the church roof over coffee, vague half-doubtful, half-formed hopes quietly mumbled, more my thing perhaps. I accept that this might not be everyone's definition of low church, but it is just possible I might have found a place within it.

Pascal's Wager, you lose nothing by believing in God, never worked for me because of the second wager inherent within it; who's to say that God doesn't prefer the honest doubter to the scheming chancer? Perhaps I thought to all these things as we stood in the church, with the oranges and the candles, Christmas excitement mounting as the service draws to a close. But I think mostly I was focussed on what my presents might be.

Although I liked the idea of a faith with different views about the afterlife, I never really considered being Jewish from a religious perspective. I was aware of this side of me too late to feel it spiritually; it was more like a memory of something I might have been, something I still was in part, a whole history somehow beyond reach. In some ways it was hard enough to work out who you were meant to be without all these extra layers of ambiguity.

In the evening they will lock themselves away to wrap. It's a big job. We'd listen to the rustle of the paper and the screech of the Sellotape outside their door, the muffle of their voices, which are occasionally raised, until discovered and shooed away. Dave will read the *Mirror*. He might play the mouth organ or even his guitar, or ask to record us playing the piano, all of which we will find annoying. He will assume responsibility tomorrow for clearing away the rubbish, forcing discarded wrapping paper into black bin liners. At some point on Christmas Day he will offer to wash Dad's car. Theresa will knit, ball of wool at her feet; jumpers, scarves and cuddly toys emerging from the tangle, melding incrementally with every click of her needles. I'll watch television with Matt, Caspar nestled up on the sofa.

After what seems like many hours, Mum and Dad will emerge and bright blue pillowcases will be placed by the tree, empty at this stage. They will drink mulled wine, Theresa and Dave will pretend to, and they will all eat mince pies. We are in for Christmas.

A memory from much earlier still, watching a *Willo the Wisp* cartoon about Halloween one Christmas Eve. An interesting piece of scheduling, but I was at that age where things become firmly imprinted, such that I often think back to witches on broomsticks at this time of year. It might have been the same Aldershot winter that it did snow and the three of us walked through the wood as the evening bled into night. Somebody threw snowballs at us and we couldn't see who it was. Looking back now, perhaps it was Dad, it's hard to know. Either way, we felt safe with him, there in that wood on a Christmas Eve night, when we were very little.

Four o' clock in the morning starts became six, eventually later still. Pillowcases in the morning, main presents after lunch. Things for my railway, another engine; I was top heavy with them, but whenever I looked at model railway catalogues they were what interested me most, even if strictly speaking I did not need nine. I had an unorthodox set-up, ranging from a Cornish tin mining tank engine through to the *Flying Scotsman*. A real mix of liveries and eras, to the point when I would eventually decide it was all a preserved railway.

I would have done it differently had I not started it as a seven-year-old. Carriages, trucks, a signal box, new track, points and miniature trees and moss all featured over the years. Martin constructed all my station buildings himself in our garage, doing all the cutting and joining, while I handed him the screws and kept my hands warm by clasping a cup of coffee.

One of the engines which we bought together from a second-hand shop on the Isle of Wight would breathe actual steam, if you put oil in its funnel. I could chart the history of Christmas presents, birthday presents and summer holiday savings through my growing rail network, and if I looked more closely I could see Martin's hand in its incremental development as it sprawled over more and more of my bedroom. Perhaps the seminal moment had been when my grandfather had sawn my fitted wardrobe in half so that we could build a new station and siding complex over what was now the much lower top of it. We had both beamed with pride when the work was done and were somewhat taken aback by my mother's reaction. Where I was now going to hang my clothes had not entered into our calculations.

There were other presents too. Tapes: Elton John, *Now 17, Now 18*. Aftershave as worn by Paul Gascoigne, no less. The best of all was a chess computer, a Kasparov Stratos with its wood and felt pieces and super strong playing strength. Perhaps we will meet across the board someday, Kasparov said in the foreword to the instructions.

I did not discover books until I was sixteen, not really; and I don't remember any as Christmas presents, until *The Bonfire of the Vanities*, much later. Dave and Theresa would give us money and knitted jumpers; comics, calendars and diaries, water pistols from the market; one year a dart board; electronic gadgets, radio-controlled cars.

We would pull Christmas crackers and wear paper hats until they started to itch, sharing the terrible jokes, discovering combs and plastic games, occasionally pocket screwdrivers. One year I got a dark brown china fox, heavy and expensive. How it had got into a cracker I don't know, but I kept it on my desk for a long time. I'd run my finger down its smooth, cool back in times of stress.

All that food. Turkey (which I didn't eat), sausages (which I did), roast potatoes, parsnips, Yorkshire puddings, carrots, peas, and gravy (again, not for me). Red jelly encrusted with raspberries, nuts in different shades of chocolate, marzipan fruits, *After Eight* mints. Only I liked the Turkish Delight. White slabs of Christmas cake, with silver balls on top and yellow marzipan beneath the cool layer of icing, often reserved for afternoon tea.

In the evening there would be indoor fireworks in the kitchen. Dad would be the ringmaster as black snakes unfurled. Other devices would smoke and crackle and sparkle, filling the air with the smell of gunpowder and possibility. Him having fun, fully with us in the moment, all of us laughing. Mum pretending to worry about the state of her baking trays. Looking back, perhaps she was actually worried, but it was all quite funny.

Finally the smoke and ash would clear. All the main food would have been eaten and all the presents unwrapped. It would be done. Then we would nibble at sandwiches and crisps and watch the *Only Fools and Horses* Christmas special. Holding the world away.

Martin's Journal –
The Island at War

In the 1930s Europe was preparing for war again, even though the carnage and destruction of the previous one scarcely seemed to have abated. It increasingly dominated the news and conversations in pubs and shops, as if somehow talking of it might make the whole thing go away.

First there was Mussolini, who provoked real fear in people to begin with, even if he was ultimately dismissed as something of a joke, but he was soon followed by Adolf Hitler, whose menace was all too apparent. I would look at pictures of him in newspapers. The intensity in his eyes, the neatness of his clipped moustache, his uniform – he always sent a chill through me.

Our sleepy and peaceful land, through its determination to avoid more conflict, was slow to awake to the danger in any practical sense, denial trumping logical thinking perhaps. Few wanted to contemplate more of what had been before, and that was almost our undoing. But ultimately, evil was loose in the world, was spreading and would not be tempered, things were out of kilter and it appeared that tragically they could only be righted through more bloodshed.

On that fateful Sunday I sat in the garden with my parents and we listened to Mr Chamberlain announce that we were now at war with Germany. His life's work in ruins, the situation disastrous, and yet still a tone of quiet resolution and determination in his voice. It was a perfect late summer's day, the carefree birdsong and soft insect buzz hard to reconcile with the gravity of his words. The sun still felt pleasant on me; the soothing sensation of its warmth on my skin and my feeling of dread at what might be to come were a strangely odd mix in the moment and I recognised the contradiction. Perhaps nothing, not even an instant like this, is ever wholly one thing or another. I tried to read my father's expression as he listened but I could not.

It might have been that he was thinking back to his time as a World War One dispatch rider. I suppose he could have been, as he now viewed the onset of another war as an older man. He had been through the horrors of one conflict, and as he sat in the garden, just listening to the radio, we were starting on another. Perhaps he was thinking to those he had known who had fallen, perhaps not. He was of course too old to fight this time around, but I know that for many of his generation, another world war underscored yet again the futility of the first one. We did not have the kind of relationship that might have lent itself to us having talked about any of this; I might be wrong, but when you do not know for sure you can but speculate.

I do want to say a little more about Neville Chamberlain. There are certain things that have now become obscured that are worth repeating. Of all the prime ministers in my lifetime, none has matched the popularity and enthusiasm he generated when he returned from Munich with his famous (perhaps that should now be infamous) piece of paper. Peace in our time had resonated; how could it not? We did not know then what we know now about the full depths of Nazism and all its horrors. The desire to avoid more conflict, at least to explore this in the 1930s, only seems doomed and wholly misguided with the benefit of hindsight; despite my own sense of foreboding, when I looked at Hitler's face it somehow had the power to draw you to it when you looked at a newspaper.

We rally against appeasers today and I was never one, but I could always understand why people wanted to close their eyes. We were willing for Chamberlain's magic trick to work, even if ultimately it did not. Those who criticise the way he played his hand, with some justification, should also acknowledge that once it had all appeared to be a master stroke.

I smile and lift my head as I write this to stare at the television which is playing without sound on the other side of the room. Tony Blair has just been on and, as I write this, it makes me reflect that he is the only other prime minister that I have seen who ever got close to the popularity of Chamberlain around the time of Munich. Albeit he is in many ways easier to see through, a less complex character, I feel, and these are altogether less substantial times.

But there we were. All had failed and it was now to be war again. I had been facing my own personal struggles as the war approached. I was suffering from heart trouble that had been caused by a severe bout of pneumonia I had contracted seven years before. I already knew this was deemed to be serious and was likely to mean that I would not pass a war medical. I did worry about my health then and what this might mean for me, but I was also worried about the stigma that might come from not joining up, from not attempting to do something. I think at one level I both worried about and simultaneously did not accept the advice I had been given, if such a thing is possible.

On making enquiries in 1938 I had been advised that no medical was necessary to join the Auxiliary Fire Service, indeed it was more a case of 'just sign here,' which I did, and I had been training ever since. We were to be a final line of defence and protection for the Island, should the anticipated widespread bombing break out. I was ready to do my bit, albeit I was mindful of the risks, fire is its own master – yet one that we were determined to do all we could to hold at bay should the need arise.

My war started within minutes of Mr Chamberlain's declaration, when the air raid siren duly wailed. A new, uncertain era had begun. Hastily donning my uniform I cycled on to Ryde to report for duty. I wondered as I cycled how many others might be responding to the first call of sirens, the first chain reaction following the declaration of war – something had been put into motion now that would not be easily stopped. We were all tiny cogs subsumed by something bigger, and yet still all a living part of it, at least for now.

When I reported for duty, all was quiet. The station officer said it was a false alarm and I was to return home, which I did, surprised at the adrenalin that was pumping through me. Had I been needed then I was ready, but in the event it was a metaphor, perhaps, for the wider, 'phony war' that was now upon us. For all the pace of the German blitzkrieg through Europe, which started with Poland being attacked and conquered with contemptuous ease, it was to be months before anything happened here.

The main fire engines for our area were stationed in Ryde, but there were small units dispersed around the outskirts, just in case. My outfit was located at Binstead in the station of Brook House, now called Brook Edge. I can still see men in uniform and think to where our equipment used to be stored, how our rotas used to work, and all the other associated paraphernalia, when I pass the place today. It is possible for people to see very different things when looking at the same object or building, I think.

Most of my fellow firemen were from the building trade and were used to climbing ladders and walking nonchalantly along narrow parapets. Although in training I often carried people, and practised doing fireman's lifts out of upstairs windows and down ladders, I was never nonchalant, and fortunately was never called upon to do so in real emergencies. I did not feel like an imposter amongst them, but there were few I had known before joining up and it did feel far removed from the world of Holmes & Son. Like so many others, the war of course lifted us out of our normal lives and there was little that could be deemed normal about everything that was to happen.

Whilst the Auxiliary Fire Service was certainly something, I wanted to do more and hoped in spite of my previous medical troubles to be able to join the air-sea rescue. Perhaps it was always a forlorn hope, I don't know. It certainly seemed to be worth a shot. You can convince yourself of anything if you truly put your mind to it.

In the autumn of 1939 a small party of us from Ryde went over to Portsmouth to try out together. We all knew one another slightly then, but over the years that followed I got to know many of them better. The success stories and the failures, the early deaths and the alcoholism, the self-made fortunes and the jail sentences; there would have been no way of guessing which of these destinies would have befallen which of this group just to look at them that day, but it all came to pass. Yet for all that was to come, we were united in purpose that day, with the same hope of being accepted, of proving our worth.

There was a man called John who I knew well from the Round Table, who was large, powerful and an amateur heavyweight boxer. You would certainly want him with you in a fight as his sheer bulk was enough to stop any argument even before it had broken out. We found the building in Portsmouth, entered and there was an arrow pointing to the stairs. John and I, deep in conversation, failed to notice the words Medical Board on the first landing, so started up the second flight of stairs. A door behind us flew open and a little man bounded out.

"Where do you men think you are going? Come down at once! Can't you read?" Pointing at the notice, John turned and walked slowly toward the man, then picking him up by the front of his jacket, held him with his feet well clear of the ground. I could see the sweat dripping down the poor unfortunate's face as he wriggled in the air, legs flaying this way and that to no avail. Military commander to pinned and squealing runt in a moment.

"Right, Martin, still got him. You hit him!"

"John," I ventured. "Do you really think this would be a sound way to start our military careers?"

He looked over at me. "Perhaps you are right."

He put the chap back on his feet, patted his cheeks not too gently, saying, "Just mind your manners in future." The man scuttled off and we did not see him again that day.

I felt somehow both proud and embarrassed. I did wonder whether I perhaps lacked the necessary aggression for all of this. It was hard to say. I could not have imagined being driven to the same sort of reaction, but we are all different and who knows what we might do until the moment arrives.

We went on to join the rest of our group. One of them called Rodney was a well-known figure in Ryde. An insurance man, he cycled around calling on his customers to collect their premiums, which was how business was done back then. He ran other business ventures on the side, which was also not uncommon in those days. There was a black market during the war, as you might well imagine, and his day job gave him the perfect opportunity to make his real money. He had permed hair, a pencil-thin moustache, and went in for suits that were slightly too tight and seemed to accentuate his weediness.

I am sure most of us were wondering how this effeminate and unimposing young sap would manage in the armed services. We need not have worried. When he removed his clothes the real Rodney emerged, a muscleman with rippling biceps and a perfect physique. It really did look as if he was as strong as two ordinary men.

One of the attendants gave him a push. "Hey there, you!" He found his hand seized in a grip of iron, and a hyped-up Rodney staring menacingly into his eyes.

"Tell me where to go," said Rodney, "and I'll go there. Push me again and I'll break your arm!" We somehow felt that the boys from the Isle of Wight had made their mark that day.

However, whilst many were accepted, I was not. As a result of the medical I was deemed unfit for the armed services, and indeed the verdict was rather more severe than anticipated. In fact the doctors were relieved to hear that I was not going home alone. The chances of my living long enough to return to the Island seemed to them remote. At the time of writing, that was sixty-two years ago!

Having this prognosis did affect me though. How could it not? I had to somehow assimilate the advice I had been given that I would not live long and should make the most of each day. That everything could (and most probably would) come to an end at any moment.

In some ways I never really shook this, as subconsciously I feared that if I stopped worrying about it, that would be the thing that made it happen. Of course, it hardly matters now, and perhaps it mattered less then than it did to me later, as those were exceedingly uncertain times for everyone. No one really thought much about the long term in those years.

Given I was not fit to fight I was told that I would be directed into industry as a wartime occupation, whilst also continuing in the Auxiliary Fire Service. I was offered a job as a security man at Founders Roe, the aircraft factory at Cowes. Friends advised me not to go near that one as it made you very unpopular with your workmates. Nobody likes a grass and for all that the history books paint a picture of the time as one of great national unity, in many ways you had to be particularly careful to choose who you stood with.

There were two jobs going with the Electricity Board: a clerk in the general office, or a meter reader. I smile now that all these years later Ben works in the electricity industry, although I know he does different things. I chose meter reading, a strangely independent occupation.

At 5 pm you left the office armed with your rota for the following day. No one expected or wanted to see you until 4.30pm the following day. There were days when the work did not last until 4.30pm, and days when it was all over by 10.30am. I felt a curious sense both of connectivity and freedom, much as an artist or a writer might, even if I did not create something that lasted in the way that they did.

Saturday morning was for revisiting those houses where no one had been at home during the week. Estimated accounts were unknown, and you were only allowed a small quantity of non-reads.

Generally speaking the public were friendly. There were hazards of course. Dogs could be an absolute menace; so too could cups of tea, freely offered despite their being severely rationed. You can only drink so many, and loos were not always to hand! Even worse was to be handed a cup in a house that was utterly filthy!

Women could also be a problem. The very first day back at work after my honeymoon I called at a large house in Pelham Fields. A pretty girl answered the door saying, "I am sure you know where the meter is. When you've read it come and find me in the drawing room; I've just made a cup of tea."

I took a seat beside her on the sofa and was handed a cup. After a couple of sips, the girl took it away from me, saying, "Oh, for God's sake!" The next moment I was flat on my back being smothered with kisses, until I managed to sit up and draw breath. I noticed on the table beside me the photos of a very large, tough-looking captain in the commandos. "Is this your husband?"

"Yes" she said. "Isn't he gorgeous? Trouble is, he is overseas." I was convinced that he had returned unexpectedly and would come charging through the door at any moment, so I fled hurriedly before the dear girl could do any more! It wasn't like this was common, but it was certainly embarrassing for a newly married young man hopelessly in love with his wife. It would be hard to imagine me having such an effect on a woman now!

Six months after the war started all remained quiet. Then one lunchtime the air raid sirens wailed and we saw our first action. I reported to Binstead fire station, from where we watched as a wall of bombers flew overhead to drop their load on Portsmouth. The German war machine up close gleamed in the sun as if from another realm, the noise from the planes' engines a roar completely obliterating any sound from the waves. Fighter cover at that time was non-existent and our only defence was anti-aircraft fire.

Daylight raids continued for a time, as the war drew closer, whilst the Germans swept through France, followed by the miraculous escape of a large part of the British expeditionary fleet from Dunkirk. It felt like such a triumph at the time; it was only much later that it occurred to any of us that it was actually a defeat. Sometimes the framing counts for more than the reality.

None of us ever really thought that we might actually lose the war, which surprises me now when I look back at how grim things were in those early years. I think that that was Churchill's true gift. He was never as popular as people now think, either before or after, but in those moments his belief carried many of us with him.

After the first raids on Portsmouth, German planes would regularly fly across the Solent, always little more than a few feet above the waves, to avoid the flack from anti-aircraft guns. Even today, so many years on from this, when I look at Wootton Creek I can still see those planes and sometimes think to those times. This quiet corner of land and sea where I have essentially lived my whole life, during most of which it has been quiet, was in those moments at the vortex of a struggle that spanned whole continents.

On a number of occasions when the planes came over, I was at home. My father, being an officer in the Home Guard, had rifles stored in the house, and armed with one of those I used to fire at the planes from my bedroom window. I am a good shot, so it

127

is highly unlikely that my bullets failed to find their mark.

I did not imagine that my bullet would bring down an aircraft, but I hoped that with luck I could kill or disable the pilot and the plane would crash. If it had done, it would probably have wiped out half the population of Wootton, but I had not thought of that. Did any of my bullets strike home, or were they all completely harmless? We still don't know. I suspect not, but I am in that very small group of people who cannot be entirely sure whether or not they have killed somebody. Most will know one way or the other. The thought does not really trouble me, I don't think.

In 1942, Cowes, the industrial centre of the Island, with shipyards and aircraft manufacturing on either bank of the river, was itself the target of a German assault, and this was the height of my war. We arrived to find the whole town ablaze, explosives and incendiary bombs coming down like rain. The phrase is a cliché, but I cannot think of a better one to do justice to what the experience was like.

Our squad were directed to the main shipyard which was burning fiercely. You don't feel anything in moments like this: the adrenalin takes you forward, drives you on. It is only much later that you think to the danger, to what has happened to people and to what could have happened to you.

Not then, though. With one of my comrades I worked my way into the centre of the yard. It takes two men to hold a branch (the nozzle on the end of the hose), and we were completely surrounded by flames. The roof had gone completely and everything else was blazing; a scene of awesome beauty. I had the sense of seeing something that was not meant to have been seen, not meant to have been like this, and somehow drew strength from this sense of standing outside the normal run of things.

We felt relatively safe from the fire so long as water was coming through the hose. Finally, I felt a tap on my shoulder. It was an officer ordering us to withdraw. I protested that we should stay, as we were beginning to have an effect on the fire, and maybe we could have saved a boat or two. For answer, the officer pointed upwards. There in the sky were parachute flares lighting up the second wall of bombs that were about to arrive. A matter of minutes after we had left, another bomb landed on the very spot where we had been standing. Another of those turning points, which could have been my ending but instead was just another near miss.

We regrouped to a street where the first three of the terraced houses were on fire. Our pump was connected to an overland main; cast iron pipes that had been laid in the gutters. Ready for an emergency like this, pumps down by the river kept us supplied with water. This was how it worked. The first thing we had been taught was that when houses in a street are on fire, the heat is enough to cause the house next door to burst into flames without any need for direct contagion. By concentrating the flow of water on the fourth house we were able to contain the fire, until further bombs shattered the mains and our water supply failed.

We could only watch helplessly as the fire spread remorselessly along the street, consuming another ten houses before water was restored and we could get to work again. The power and the force of it, and the speed; it seemed impossible to think that it could be tamed, and of course it could not without water. So much ruined in that period that might otherwise have been saved. When we got the water to work again we re-grouped and tried to save what we could, picking a new house as a firebreak, but I am afraid that whilst we saved it the owners were to return to witness the damage that thousands of gallons of water pumped over it and into it could do, against a backdrop of a street half burnt away, almost like a mouth with black and rotting teeth.

When, that morning, we had finished damping down, we went back to the shipyard, now almost completely gone, and sat down by the river for tea and cornbread sandwiches. All was now peaceful and secure, we thought, being unaware that we were sitting within a few feet of a large unexploded bomb! It seems strange now, but it was almost funny at the time. Perhaps it was hysteria, a way of coping with what we were facing, to laugh at everything. I have read that this is often what the emergency services will do, often the only way of coping with everything that has to be faced. I think it was that way for us.

Finally the war turned and it was clear that we were in the ascendancy. I started to think to life afterwards, but what was there to think? I would be going back to the business and things would ultimately go back to the way they were meant to be, I supposed. Although of course I had Anna now, and this changed everything.

The preparation for the invasion of Normandy went on with increasing vigour, and I was able to watch it day by day. In the course of time a flotilla was assembled in the Solent, close inshore just to the west of Wootton Rocks. More and more ships and equipment arrived, until the Solent was so filled with ships of all sizes and floating islands that it seemed possible to walk from Wootton to Portsmouth. It was an extraordinary sight I can still visualise after all these years of peace. I pray that nobody will ever see the Solent looking like that again. But it was also a testament to what we could do, what we would do, to free the world from Hitler.

At a more mundane level we thought a lot about food in those days. It was very scarce (even on the black market as the war years rolled on) but, notwithstanding that, we made it an aim at Binstead fire station to try and cook something really good on Sundays.

One of our number, a month or so before D-Day, had brought along some partridges. A real treat and one he did not encourage us to ask too many questions about. These were perfectly roasted and ready to eat, when we received an emergency call out to Newport!

It was extremely hard to drag ourselves away from the smell of them, which took me back to meals before the war; better times that we hoped were going to come again soon. Still, we had a job to do, albeit there was very little sign of danger, we thought, as we drove along, adrenalin pumping as it always did, ready for a repeat of the Cowes attack.

We were far from pleased when we arrived at Newport market and discovered we were engaged in a training exercise, running hoses all over the place to fight non-existent fires. We were then required to stand around while top brass from London evaluated our efforts. Our thoughts were on the beautiful dinner now in ruins at Binstead, and we were feeling cold, so I put on my coat. Presently I was accosted by some high-ranking officer, who told me that this was a breach of the rules. Frustrated, I replied that I had been fighting fires for six years and would not attempt to do so whilst wearing a coat. I said that if he could show me where the fire was I would take it off. Otherwise, it was a cold night and I was keeping it on.

In the opinion of my comrades I would be court martialled and shot. I felt that the consequences were likely to be less severe. I could not be reduced to the ranks as I was already in the ranks. I could not suffer loss of pay, because I was underpaid. Indeed, nothing happened. Sometimes it is right to stand your ground.

At the Electricity Board where I worked we had a drama group. We were due to stage a production of *Tonight at 8.30*, a Noel Coward play. One evening as we arrived for a rehearsal the news came through that Germany had surrendered. This was VE day (Victory in Europe).

The rehearsal was abandoned. Our leading man, John Huesly[2], and I went off to celebrate. John became a professional actor soon after the war, appearing occasionally on television in supporting roles. Later he went to Hollywood, where he had a successful career in films and television as a supporting actor. Most of those films have faded in my memory over time, although he did appear with Roger Moore once I think.

After everything, finally the war was over. John and I went to a pub called the Black Horse at the bottom of George Street. It was packed to the doors, many people in uniform. John was a slightly built man, but with considerable strength he elbowed his way to the bar. We drank to victory, songs were sung, strangers embraced. People you knew well, people you didn't know at all, all mixed together in an atmosphere that invited more revelry with every drink. Whatever had gone before and whatever was coming next, there, in that moment, we had stood firm. We had prevailed.

I look back on this now, as all of my generation will, as the most dramatic and eventful few years of

2   My grandfather's handwriting never did give up all its secrets. All I can say for sure is that I have this name wrong. I would be intrigued to learn if anyone knows who my grandfather might have been writing about.

my life. I had not been able to fight, but I hope that I played my part by helping quell the Island's fires at night, and through the strangely peaceful and entirely contrasting meter reading in the day.

I feel that I was part of a time that will obviously last in history and be remembered long after I and all of the others who lived through it have gone. Of course, many of us have already passed on, and in the scheme of things I will go soon. Life is lived at lots of levels and those years were never just about the war for me, just as they weren't for anyone else either.

I had married Anna and a different future lay ahead, albeit one that would entail going back to Holmes & Son.

Chess Stories – Bobby Fischer
Broke My Heart

My father taught me to move the pieces, but he did not teach me how to play. I might have explained it this way once, before I discovered that teaching children the basics of chess is not easy.

Annabelle and Maddie had no particular interest, and from a time when she was quite little I knew of Annabelle's dislike both for the game and the amount of time I spent playing it. But the pull was too strong and I did not play less, simply choosing to accept that my choices did not reflect well on me.

My father had had no such equivalent activity which saw him leave the family to drive the roads on winter nights to Banbury, Solihull, Rugby, Olton, Nuneaton and other such places to play a game, pursue an interest outside of the family. Perhaps he was more generous with his time, and myself less so, than I had thought.

Francesca was promising, but football, karate and acting interested her more. I saw her sing in a school play once and it was beautiful, and not just in the way parents normally say, but in a way that hushed the hall. I had missed a chess match to be there and had resented it, until she opened her mouth to sing and then I felt ashamed.

Gabriella was the most natural player and I started teaching her earlier than I had the others. I saw in her my last chance to have a chess-playing child, but in the end I wanted it too much and she was reluctant to listen to anything I might say on the subject, any advice I might give.

I was baffled as to how to proceed. We would stare at the plastic pieces with a shared sense of frustration and we knew that this simply was not going to work. As a personal coach I had failed with her almost before I had started, and ended up asking a friend who was a much weaker player to try and teach her instead. So my father was a better chess coach than me too.

It was true that I wanted them to do their own things, to find their own way. But it saddened me that I could not bring any of them to chess. Chess had its history, its stories; it is not just a series of moves on a board where black follows white until eventually the matter is resolved. I learnt this but never managed to convey it to the kids.

What it really showed was that I had ideas about what might be best for them which sometimes differed from their own, just as my parents had had when they had wanted me to read law instead of English. It was a small thing, but it made me think that good intentions and more life experience were not sufficient to call the shots on behalf of others. You had to let your children figure out what they wanted to do for themselves. Reading law had been a mistake for me that I would undo if I could; my parents had been wrong to push me in that direction, no matter how good the intentions.

At secondary school, my teacher Mr Keohane gave me my first chess book, and as well as teaching me more about openings and endgames, I discovered the array of characters that had shaped the game. These were not always happy stories and there were some I would not have wanted my own children to know.

The 'pride and sorrow' of chess, Paul Morphy, came to Europe from America in the late 1850s and played beautifully, beating all serious opponents and creating masterpieces in his wake. He had played a game against the Duke of Brunswick and Count Isoaurd during an interval in an opera that still stands today as one of chess's finest. The sort of game I would have shown to my own children, had they been more interested.

Somewhat ironically, given my own circumstances, Paul Morphy did not want to be a chess player. He returned to America determined to be a lawyer and did not play again. All his clients were interested in was talking to him about chess, and Morphy was to spend the last fifteen years of his life grappling with serious mental illness, before dying in his bath of a stroke at the age of forty-seven.

It was hard for me to understand as a child how somebody could play like he could, could create as he did, and then not want to do it anymore and not be made happy by it. Perhaps the things we think might make others happy, might make ourselves happy even, are sometimes just destined not to be quite how we would imagine them. The same with writing and writers as with chess perhaps;

what we create, however beautiful or terrible others think it to be, is still separate from us and we are still alone.

Many years later the second American chess genius, Bobby Fischer, would follow a path with similar echoes, and this would be something I would talk to my father about as he had witnessed it first-hand. I idolised Fischer. I thought once that he was everything I wanted to be, and I would have swapped places with him in a moment.

I read about how for a while in the early 1970s, he had made chess the centre of the world. Against the backdrop of the Cold War, at a time when the game was seen as a powerful ideological tool by both America and the Soviet Union, Fischer played Boris Spassky for the world title in Reykjavik in 1972, three years before I was born. Insiders knew that Fischer and Spassky were both hopeless representatives of the systems they were meant to be role models for, but no matter. Fischer, the loner who asked for hotel rooms that did not have a view, the better for him to study, was far removed from being a poster child for the American way of life, however hard others tried to spin it. He was a product of nothing other than his incredible gift and relentless focus on the game.

Spassky, who could send the party faithful in any Soviet chess club running for the exits with his less than sound conversation (he was good enough at chess to get away with it), was later to defect to France. He was more interested in women, tennis, drink and Greek myths than he was in communism.

Fischer was only interested in chess, or at least that was how it had seemed to the public back then. He had

138

beaten three world class players in order to qualify to play Spassky, the defending champion. He destroyed the Russian Taimanov 6-0, perhaps the equivalent of a top tennis player losing a match without winning a game. There were no parallels in chess history.

Taimanov was subsequently severely censured by the Soviet authorities for his poor showing. It is said that he was rebuked by Soviet customs officials for having a book by the banned Solzhenitsyn in his luggage. The official told him that had he played better, he would have carried the volume for him himself.

Then Fischer beat Larsen 6-0 as well. He had been expected to win comfortably but not like that. Finally, former world champion Petrosian put up slightly stiffer resistance, but it was not enough and the Fisher-Spassky 'Match of the Century' was on. Perhaps.

Until the last minute it was not clear if Fischer's demands concerning money and cameras (his desire for an absence of cameras), and a multitude of other requests, were going to be met, or appropriate compromises struck.

Henry Kissinger called him.

A British financier doubled the purse.

Still, nobody could be sure if Fischer would play. Eventually he became the first player in history to lose a game in a world chess championship final by virtue of not turning up. Then he made a beginner's mistake in the second game, an extraordinary blunder which put him 2-0 down.

There were real fears that he would not turn up for the next game and that would have been that, the match would have been ended. But turn up he did, and everything changed. Fischer won comfortably, but the Russians thought Spassky had made too many concessions; even at one point agreeing to play in a back room behind the main stage. A harder-nosed individual who did not yield to any of Fischer's requests to vary the playing conditions might well have won by default. When asked about this many years later, Spassky had shrugged and said that he had known Fischer was the stronger player, but he had wanted to play him just the same. All chess players find it hard to walk away.

Yet after the match this was precisely what Fischer did, as he fell apart and his mental health collapsed. He became convinced that the Soviets were out to get him. He had the fillings removed from his teeth. He turned down millions of dollars to play in events or promote various products. He declined to endorse a brand of car because he did not drive it and thought it would be inauthentic to lend his name to it. Perhaps Holden Caulfield might have done the same.

Eventually, his demands in relation to the 1975 world title match with new challenger Anatoly Karpov were rejected and he was stripped of his title. Fischer would spend the next twenty years drifting from cheap hotel to cheap hotel, now more interested in obscure religious texts and anti-Semitic literature (even though he was Jewish) than he was in chess.

Fred Waitzkin wrote a book called *Searching for Bobby Fischer* in which he talked about his son Josh Waitzkin learning the game, and his own dream of somehow bringing Fischer back to the board. Convincing Fischer that the noise in the room or the position of the cameras did not really matter, urging him to compete once again. I loved the book. I would have liked Fred Waitzkin to be my father; he spoke to my imagination in a way that my own father, who had the more prosaic job of actually bringing me up, did not.

The book changed nothing. Fischer returning was something that the chess world had accepted was never going to happen. The greatest regret of my life was that I had not witnessed Fischer play, until I did, and then that turned into the greatest regret instead.

Astonishingly, in the early 1990s, a combination of huge amounts of Yugoslavian money, the encouragement of a much younger woman and a slight-of-hand by the chess authorities that allowed Fischer to claim he was still the world champion (even if everybody knew he was not) brought him back.

I was ecstatic. My hero was going to play again. Sure, there were whispers about his views, but I told myself they would turn out to be wrong, when he re-emerged blinking into the daylight, took his seat at the board, started to make the moves we had all been anticipating for so long. Chess was again going to be as big as it had been in the 1970s. A legend was being re-born.

He might have been completely crazy by this point, but he was not stupid. He had no interest in playing Gary Kasparov, the real current world champion, who Fischer hated and knew at this stage in his life would have humiliated him. Instead, he played Spassky again, and the legend was destroyed.

By 1992 he was now a fat, dishevelled bigot who spewed hatred and bile with every utterance. I watched in increasing horror and embarrassment as the man I had idolised since first reading about him proved completely unable to stop ranting about Jews.

At the opening press conference prior to the match he spat on the letter from the US Government asking him not to break sanctions by playing in Yugoslavia. He talked a lot about Zionists. He insisted he was not anti-Semitic, because Arabs were Semites and they were fine by him. He came over as creepy and unhinged. Then finally, he obliterated what was left of his aura with his actual play.

Spassky was by this point in semi-retirement and was ranked around number 100 in the world. Fischer took the first game quite well, and though the vagaries of time and his nomadic life simply caught up with him, Fisher eventually 'won' the match, despite suspicion in some quarters that Spassky was carrying him. He was still better than most, but routinely got into difficulties that the Fischer of old would have won through with ease. By most standards he was still very good, but compared to his heyday he was nothing, like an ageing boxer who could still punch but was no longer able to move. Which even then might not have mattered had he been capable of keeping his mouth shut.

Despite the fact that sanctions forbade it, the US Government took no action over him playing in Yugoslavia. For all the talk of other matches, it looked like he was going to disappear back into obscurity. He was not strong enough to realistically take on Kasparov or another of the game's real elite, and the man who once had every major organisation in the world vying for his signature was now an untouchable to any self-respecting blue-chip entity.

Then finally, on 9/11, around the time Katharine and I were looking at a single blue line on a pregnancy kit, Fischer took to the radio to continue his descent into madness. He said that the attacks were a time for rejoicing and that, for the US, what goes around comes around. He made still more observations about Jews and their role in running the world.

Suddenly the US authorities were interested in Fischer again and warrants were issued for his arrest. He spent jail time in Japan awaiting extradition, but finally was offered sanctuary in Iceland, the scene of his world championship triumph all those years ago. He hated the place but knew if he ever left he would be arrested. He spent the final few years there, increasingly paranoid and delusional, dying at sixty-four, the same number of years as there are squares on a chess board.

Bobby Fischer was the only chess player my father really knew about. He had watched the 1972 world championship on the television and he told me everyone had been rooting for Fischer back then. It was a match that had really taken the imagination, somehow all sorts of things had seemed possible and Fischer's very different sort of craziness had then been a part of his attraction.

Yet in the course of twenty years he had deteriorated mentally from a man whose fears centred on the noise of the crowd and the positioning of cameras into something altogether appalling. Apparently that darkness had always been there, if more quietly stated. Spassky's own possible anti-Semitism was also by now whispered about, and I could but shudder as to where this really left the so-called 'Match of the Century', to say nothing of the rematch. Neither man was who we wanted to pretend he was.

For Fischer, it seems to have stemmed from a hatred of his stepfather. Many in the chess world are Jewish. So was my father, which made me half Jewish, as was Gary Kasparov. It was clear from Kasparov's writings on Fischer that he had no liking for him. The two were never to meet. The opportunity never arose, I once heard Kasparov say in an interview.

At one level they were to have competing legacies, although even purely in terms of chess there are few who would place Fischer ahead of Kasparov now. Had he played on, who can say? Kasparov's view was that you had to enjoy Fischer's games, that it was Fischer the chess player who should be remembered.

My dad, who never played through or studied any chess games, so could not share in the things that Kasparov saw, was similarly sanguine. Fischer clearly had issues and needed help that he did not get, he said to me. "It's obvious to watch him that he's really very ill. What he is saying speaks only to that, really. You have to feel sorry for him; what is the point of feeling anything else? Maybe the whole situation was too much for him?"

When you win at anything 6-0 it is hard to know where you go from there. Those whom the gods wish to damn, first they grant them their wishes, and all that. My father had surprised me again; I would have put money on him being more judgemental, more critical. But he wasn't, even if deep down he knew that I was.

It wasn't that he remotely condoned any of it; of course he did not. "The things he says now disgust me," my father said, "but it is like looking at a shadow, a ghost. There is a different Bobby Fischer for you to remember."

He had tried to save my hero for me and I was grateful to him for that, even if it was a futile attempt. This was the only Fischer I had actually got to see live on screen. Unlike my father I did not live in the time of the earlier Fischer, and could only read about him.

There is a debate in chess as to whether the game drives sane people mad, or whether it keeps those who are at risk of going mad comparatively sane. Fischer certainly descended into madness rapidly when he stopped playing, however odd he was before. Perhaps it might have happened anyway, age and time presenting challenges that a game like chess (or any other game, for that matter) would not be able to overcome. Come to think of it, returning to the game did not exactly seem to help him either.

For me, Fischer was an idol, no more, but I could still read books about his early matches and play through his games and enjoy them. I was grateful that my father had been thoughtful on the subject and had tried to find a way for me still to reach the former champion, even if in truth I no longer could. Not like before.

I decided it might be no bad thing if my girls did not turn out to be chess players after all. Morphy and Fischer were far from isolated examples of chess players descending into madness.

I vowed also, should one of my girls' heroes come crashing back to earth in the future, to remember my father's approach with me. If they were to ask me what I thought about their former idol I would try and save for them what once that person had been. It is something a parent should do.

Other Visits –
Mountains and Rocking Horses

Attempting to go the Brecon Beacons and not being able to find them. Hours in the car, Dad increasingly frustrated; our questions as to whether we are nearly there yet not well received. Finally, we park at the foot of a hill that may or may not have been what we were looking for. We eat our picnic in near silence. Soggy sandwiches, flask of tea cold, chocolate biscuits melted into their wrappers. We walk through wiry mountain grass, past streams and rabbit droppings and the occasional sheep skull, the arguments of the journey still with us, conversation stilted. One of us needs the loo.

We are already late on a day that has not panned out as planned and cannot be rescued. A trip to Cheddar Gorge on the way home, sausages and chips in the restaurant, passably good but not enough to change anything. Our request to use the fruit machine rejected.

We are survivors of something, as we eat warm food and wistfully watch bells and fruit flash and spin against a backdrop of canned music and the occasional rattle of falling coins. Later I write an English essay about the trip, which my mother said worried her in terms of whether they were giving us a good childhood. It grew funnier in the re-telling. "Do you remember that time we went to a mountain range and couldn't find it?" But we didn't go again, if we had ever been in the first place.

The mountain venture was unusual for other reasons as Mum and Dad weren't really walkers. We would occasionally venture onto the bits of the Malvern Hills that you couldn't see Dad's work from, or more frequently do the loop around the back of Bosbury.

Coddington meant bikes. Dad hadn't learnt to ride as a child and was always a bit wobbly, but did good joke impressions of nearly falling off. Occasionally he did actually fall off, which was somehow less funny.

There was a vineyard that had been mentioned in the *Doomsday Book* we would whizz past, and a steep hill to negotiate around the halfway point. I'd make it all the way up on occasion; other times I would have to stop and push. Briefly, while at university, I was fit enough to run the thing and occasionally would, in the heat of a summer day, while listening to Chris Evans on Radio 1, inhaling the yeasty smell of the chicken farm near the main road.

Fields spanned all the way back to our house without needing to touch the road, if you knew what you were doing and were so inclined, which Matt and I sometimes were, and I would sometimes run through them by myself, invincible, impossible to imagine getting older and not being able to do this.

At the top of the hill in Coddington was an old schoolhouse opposite the church that a Mr Close, a retired teacher, lived in. We would sometimes go in for tea and cake. I don't know when the school closed or whether he had actually once taught there.

He would tell us amiably that he did not believe in the cane, but a cricket bat was alright. In the churchyard rested the tiny daughter of a friend. She had been born with a heart condition which nobody knew about until it was too late. A child I barely knew but still remember.

The fear that anything might happen to one of my own children is perhaps drawn in part from my knowledge that things can go terribly wrong, and being young is no safeguard against the randomness of nature and all that that entails.

I hated it when my own children went near the edge of bridges or buildings. Maddie and Francesca in particular would play to this, as if trying to induce a heart attack in me, setting a trap that I would always walk into. My father never had much of a head for heights either, but I lacked Maddie and Francesca's capacity to exploit that.

I worried when they were driven by others. I worried when I drove them myself. Maddie developed a peanut allergy that meant a nut could kill her. Gabriella, diabetes, which we were told would not. But we all knew the horror stories about what might happen if she chose not to look after herself properly when she was older and responsible for managing her own care.

Sometimes she would tell us that she didn't have diabetes anymore, that she had been cured. We had to tell her that if we could change things we would, but we could not and that the important thing was that we all worked together to look after her.

People would sometimes say that because she had been diagnosed so young, at three, she would never know anything different. That was not true either. It more seemed that she would have to react to the situation emotionally firstly as a three-year-old, then as a four-year-old, and so on.

We have to deal with today, Katharine and I would say to each other. Worrying about what hasn't happened is too much.

Matt had a bit of asthma but my MS (if that was what it was) did not develop in childhood, so perhaps our parents did not have quite such acute fears about our mortality as I do about my own children's. Except as I think to it now, they must have done. I do not worry any less about Annabelle simply because she can eat a peanut, or Francesca because she does not have diabetes. Perhaps the worries through the generations are the same. It is just the specific manifestations that differ.

The fear that we might die of boredom on a visit to a stately home was not one of those that resonated for my parents. We went to lots, and when we were younger it was always excruciating. Looking at old furniture, rooms long since hushed and roped.

There were probably fewer things to do in those days. But as we got older, I became more interested by the stories, if not the architecture. Those told explicitly in guidebooks, and others only half to be guessed at or imagined.

I remember a large doll's house in a nursery, that stood untended. A plaque spoke of the family that had played with it. I thought to those children, now long gone, their time playing with the house finished forever, and all the things it might have been to them: a meeting point, a negotiating arena, a stage for worlds created in their imagination and played out with china figures, watched on by maids. A backdrop to all sorts of discussions and arguments and normal afternoons and extraordinary happenings, dramatic then, now faded away. I thought to the stages through which they would have grown away from the house. Playing with it less as they became older, laying untouched for a while, enveloped in cobwebs perhaps – until their own children arrived and it was dusted down and pressed back into service. Though perhaps it was used less from one generation to the next, grandchildren being told to play gently – it's fragile now. Then, finally, they were gone too and it became what it is today, a grand but empty museum piece to which I stand witness in a time beyond which they could reach. But it is still theirs, not mine, abandoned or not.

Once, after our marriage, we had dinner with an older, very successful couple. He mentioned his meetings with Tony Blair and Gordon Brown while we drank champagne in their palatial house. "Tony is much easier to work with," I remember him saying. Then the conversation moved on and he said that while he did not believe in any of it, something strange had happened to them recently.

They had bought an old wooden rocking horse to place on the corner of their large stairwell. As soon as it was carried in, the dog went berserk and refused to go anywhere near it. Both their children burst into tears, one running away, the other standing transfixed. The older refused to speak when quizzed. The younger said there had been a child standing by the horse, just looking at him. "The boy could see me," he said. "He was waiting for something."

"So we had somebody take it away again," the father said. "I don't know what it was." He shrugged insouciantly and took another swig of his drink, but it was a subject he had raised. Who knows when we might be being watched unseen, from the corners of other times, by forgotten children who have reached across the void? Perhaps it happens more often than we think.

We are born, we play, we work, we are first child, then parent, perhaps even grand or great grandparent, and finally it is done. In all families, some objects survive us, even if they are less valuable than those to be found in stately homes and the houses of the rich.

My father's chess set is in my study now, all set up and waiting, though no longer for him. His old Totopoly set, a horse racing game with the cardboard cut-out figures, is sometimes used by Annabelle, Maddie and Francesca. His Scrabble box is on the bookcase in the dining room, and Gabriella has created her own word-making game that involves piling the tiles on top of each other in a way that no one else quite understands.

Over time all of these things will be used less, and one day, after I have gone, they will find their way into more obscure cupboards, and ultimately into a skip, although I will do all in my power to delay the inevitable for his chess set.

I do not think that he peers out from behind the

things that once he owned. There has been no event like that of the child and the rocking horse, but I can see him in his things and remember moments when we played and bonded over them.

It was always the games that papered over the cracks in our relationship. If one day, which will come, there is nobody left with these memories, and his old games are simply a collection of ageing plastic, wood and cardboard, with no meaning for those who look on them, then that too is part of the cycle. It will not diminish the power they once had, or what they once meant. Even objects are ultimately destined to die.

Still the cycle goes on and family life repeats itself, or at least comes close. The thing we call a family. Even now, the fact that my own children too are mortal has become obvious, has explicitly manifested itself for Maddie and Gabriella much earlier than it ever did for me.

As with chess, the precise pattern of each generation is different from the one before, but they are all recognisable and we are all constrained in some way by the power of the pieces ranged against us, the confines of the board. The difference is that chess is a game that can end in a draw, both kings can survive, whereas none of us are getting out of this one alive. Yet with luck there are many moves for us to make before all that. I will my children to make as many as possible.

The Mouth of Hell,
and Some Writers

Blackgang Chine, with its plastic dinosaurs and other 1950s-style attractions, was one of our summer playgrounds. Near Ventnor and vulnerable to landslides, as bits fell into the sea and were reconfigured, it never seemed to be the same from year to year. We were told that all the profits made went into rebuilding it.

The Mouth of Hell, which had to be passed through in order to reach salvation, was a dark fibreglass cave at the end of a red tunnel tight enough to make you consider whether you should ignore the warnings of eternal damnation and just walk back out the way you had come in instead.

Dinosaurland was home to large plastic creatures that were not meant to be climbed, but everybody did. Buffalo Creek had a pretend graveyard, a Wild West-style home to cowboys and outlaws. One of the inhabitants had been hanged by mistake according to the inscription on his wooden cross, which always made Dad laugh. Adventure Land, Rumpus Mansion, Nursery Land. Cowboy Town, Smuggerland, the model village. Blackgang Chine was ever being re-invented and re-imagined as stone succumbed to wind and wave.

There were other dinosaurs too. One of my first memories is of going to the Natural History Museum with Dad, the large skeleton in the entrance hall, the scale of the place beyond anything I had seen before. Dad buying me a woolly mammoth, which I got out of its box and placed on a London Underground escalator, losing one of the tusks in the process. Him annoyed but quickly concealing his irritation when I explained that I still liked it just as much. Later him taking me to Camden for a course, and Earls Court for a graduate placement, back to his roots. "Not these parts of London," he would say.

Taking the Underground together to get food in Trafalgar Square, his cockney a little richer, "It's a big city to find your way around alone," he said. Everywhere seems big when you are alone, I might have thought.

*

My parents both liked Hay-on-Wye with its many bookshops, and we went to the festival together several times. When I was in my twenties, but before the children had arrived, we saw Ian McEwan read a passage from *Atonement*. He said that in reading it aloud he could hear the things that needed fine tuning.

It occurred to me that writing was not just a case of pure inspiration. It needed nurturing and revision, a desire to test and re-try. You start with something, but whatever you first wrote was only that, a beginning and nothing more. Even the best writers were not like Mozart, insofar as one could generalise.

If McEwan was anything to go by, they did not wake

up with fully formed symphonies in their heads; the final melody needed to be developed, evolving slowly, incrementally, in its own time.

I read that Julian Barnes said he only wrote with a pen and paper to start with. Using a computer made the work look finished much too soon.

Novelists were less fun (if generally saner) than poets, perhaps because they had to put in office hours to get enough done. Having had this revelation about the need to work at your writing, that seemed to be enough for the next fifteen years or so, in which I did not follow through by actually writing anything.

At another literary festival I got Mum to ask Alain de Botton if he liked the characters in his books, and he said that he did. The question was triggered, as much as anything, by my own low self-esteem.

I remembered one of de Botton's protagonists having failed to get into Oxford, just as I had done, and I thought the author had rendered a kind of verdict on her, which he had not. The only judgements being made were by me on myself, another lesson I was slow to absorb.

Yet now, writing this, I do think again to the broader question of whether we necessarily like the people we choose to write about, beyond the obvious examples of when a serial killer or some such is being described.

I did not always like my father. He could be irritating, insensitive and annoying. His father Dave often used to embarrass me with his singing and observations on marriage. Anna could fuss. Theresa with her desire to shock, often did. Even my mother's multiple worries could be a bit much on occasion.

There is like and there is love. Like only takes you so far, only has meaning in a shallow sense. It works with acquaintances, less well with family. All of which is not to say that I did not like my family, rather that I could see both their strengths and limitations, as they could mine. I hope this book is a richer picture for all that, and a more complete one.

When in Hay, we browsed in the bookshops and drank tea in the marquees, coming home with paper and plastic bags filled with books. The sorts of things that had to be found and couldn't just be bought anywhere, at least before we fully understood what Amazon could do.

These trips fulfilled us at one level. Together, doing something that interested us, exploring and learning as a family. A collective purpose and sense of who we thought we were. Even if it also showed what I was not, listening to Ian McEwan read was no different to talking to Rachel Cusk or David Flusfeder. It moved me no closer to becoming a writer myself. In chess terms, when it came to writing, I was what would be termed a kibitzer, which is the name given to somebody who watches others play and perhaps passes comment on their moves but does not take to the board themselves.

The only way to avoid ever making a bad move, or drafting a poor sentence, perhaps a whole story that nobody liked, was simply to avoid playing, or writing. There is a certain comfort in being a kibitzer. Yet I knew that I wanted to do more, to write rather than simply to read, even if the desire still did not burn as much as did that to play chess. Perhaps it is more accurate to say that the demand to write pulled at me more slowly, even if I did my best for a long time to ignore it.

Mary and Colin Graff – Letters

The 1970s were still young as my parents made the transition from studying to working, from being separate to being together. This was an era before the internet and mobile phones, when the times for telephone conversations had to be agreed by letter, when money was tight for both of them and everything was just beginning.

The black ink of their letters made me think to a spider's web. But rather than silk, here it was old stories from previous generations being woven together, new ones being created. More durable than any cobweb could be, able to take on different forms through the years, to be more complex at the end than at the beginning; and still the stories they began would continue evolving after they had gone.

Perhaps we are not fully programmed to imagine our parents as young, or to recognise the fragility in the thing we later come to see as family in its formative stages, when nothing is certain, like a chess game, perhaps a few moves in but still lacking much by way of definition, and where it is unknown if the players have any intention of seeing it through.

For us, if we are lucky, our stories have a sense of

inevitability about them. We arrive, often followed or following other siblings, and if things unfold as hoped we grow up and grow on and almost take for granted how it all started, never fully realising that there was no certainty to any of this and that it could have all played out differently, in ways that would not have allowed our own story to even begin.

At the time of the first of these letters some challenges and questions remained, which were perhaps to form a quiet undercurrent to the years that followed. My father's recognition of their differences in interests, scientific (his), artistic (hers), and of religion, Jewish atheist (him), religious Catholic (her), are written about in a way that I never heard them discuss.

His quietness, her need for more conversation; her more of the worrier, though in amongst it all the letters showed that he worried too. I was surprised for instance that he thought he might get the sack if one of his projects did not produce results. The comment is perhaps a touch flippant but it did not seem to me that it was entirely so.

Thinking to this now, perhaps my relationship with my mother was easier because she did not have the same level of internal conflict that he did. She worried about things: the girl who did not want to share a house, her students, money. She was sometimes homesick when away from her parents, sometimes unsure what to do next, and he would comfort her. Still, there was no sense in her letters that she was ever other than who she really was, that people saw her differently to how she saw herself. She knew what mattered to her, what she wanted to do, and by and large throughout her life that was what she did.

In contrast, my father often talked about the difference between the way he seemed and the reality of it. A former girlfriend would think they had had meaningful conversations, when in his view this was not the case. (We only have his word for what the girlfriend really thought.) People would see him as one thing when he knew he was something else and he wrote at one point that this amused him. I cannot say whether or not it also troubled him a little.

He had no real lead on a long-lost friend he met in the pub one day and wrote about. It was all as echoed in the much later appraisal from a work colleague, who said that he did not assess others particularly well. Could it have been that his sense that others did not read him in some way formed a mirror image, a mutual fog within his relationships, that did not always make things easy for him? I wonder now if the same is also true for me, if again it transpires that we are actually more similar than I once thought.

Yet I think I was luckier, that over time I found a larger number of people where genuine mutual understanding and sympathy was achieved. I never had his inner anger. In some ways I also had better social skills, responding politely in circumstances where he might be scathing. I would look to steer conversations back to safer ground in ways that he did not.

It could be argued that all of this makes me more of a phony and serves only to demonstrate that, of the two of us, he was the one who was always truer to himself. Sometimes in my own appraisals at work it might be put to me that I could come across as too eager to please, and while I might inwardly think *fuck you*, outwardly I would only nod and say that I could see that there might be something in this. I thought his letters were more honest than anything I had ever written.

There were only a dozen or so of these letters between them that survived. I am sure there must have been many more once, but there is no way of knowing now. I first became aware of them in the period after her death and before his. They were in a bedside drawer in my old room, which was crammed full of other, less interesting, items: the extension plans for the dining room, a small tax bill, some of his Egyptian photographs, a handful of plastic farm animals, the guarantee for the conservatory, a railway truck that I had unsuccessfully tried to make look rusted with brown poster paint, a model of the space shuttle Columbia Dad had brought back from America, a broken rosary and its damaged green leather case, a communion present from the time before my mother had given up hope for us on the religious front. Some of our children's things were also wedged in, almost as an afterthought: a painting of a cow, or perhaps it was a pig, that Annabelle had done, aged four, a handful of green marbles that Maddie and Francesca were given one Christmas, a pair of baby shoes that looked like they might once have been Gabriella's. Like the drawers in many houses, this one had accumulated treasures across the generations.

He did nothing particularly to hide their letters and nothing to draw attention to them. I would read them illicitly in those last few months when I lay across the hall from him on what would inadvertently and unexpectedly become his deathbed, not that either of us could have known that then. I felt both guilty and not; I wanted to know more about Mum and more about them and this seemed to be one of the few ways through which this might be possible.

Perhaps I should have asked him about the letters, but that felt like it might be a violation. (Accepting that just reading them was also such.) In truth, I was more scared that if I did ask, he might destroy them, and while he might not have done, the prospect that mentioning them would cause him to open up seemed unlikely.

I thought they might become another thing we would argue over, something else I would have to regret for longer than he would. While more implausible, I thought it also possible that he did not know they were there at all. Though I felt with more certainty that if that was the case he would not want to be reminded of them. He never willingly travelled back to the past, or at least, if he did, they were not journeys that he shared with me.

I only remember him being able to speak of Mum a handful of times after she died, and those occasions were never easy or particularly revelatory. I remember towards the end, I would sometimes try and talk of Mum a little more to him, as a way of showing that we would still continue to speak of him, which was easier than making the point explicitly might have been. I was my father's son after all.

I do not know if they would have wanted me to share their letters. I would have to guess that he would not, and

I find it harder still to know what she would have thought. Nearly ten years on from her death, writing this book has given me a sense that she has slipped a little further away from me, is in some ways more remote than once she was. She seems more distant than he does, which is not how it was when they were both alive. Is it simply the passage of time? The order in which they went? The fact that there was not much that was unresolved between me and Mum? Has the intensity and duration of Dad's final illness crowded other things out? Were things not quite the way I always imagined them to be?

I have no answers, and in some ways the echo of the questions is all that can be left to any of us. I know that Mum can only ever drift to a certain point in my consciousness, and yet that is not the whole truth either. It is impossible to look back without also looking forward.

The one thing, the only thing, I want from my own children is that they should outlive me. Still, what would it feel like to know that, after my death, I became increasingly remote to them? I suppose it would not feel like anything; the point of death is that you no longer can feel, at least not in a way that anyone who is still on this planet might be capable of imagining.

Perhaps it is not so much a drifting but more the gentle bobbing of a boat on the water, moored on a buoy someway from the shore. Harder to reach than once it was but still held by a rope, even if it is not always easy to see through the early morning mist. I might like my children to see it this way.

However honourable my intentions, I do recognise

that in publishing these letters I surrender any pretence of moral authority over what those who follow me might choose to do with what I have written, either here or elsewhere. I am also convinced that one day there will be a stronger and more successful writer than myself. It might be Annabelle, Maddie, Francesca, Gabriella, Reuben, Evie, or perhaps someone from a future generation whom I cannot yet, and might never, know. Will they reference some of what I have written in their own books? Will they perhaps rip these words apart as I did Martin's journal, repackage and re-present them in a way that may or may not have met with my approval?

I would prefer that fate to being ignored altogether, vain as I am. In some ways it does not matter much. Families are their stories, and just as Martin wrote his journal, my parents wrote their letters and I wrote this book. Those who write next will find their own ways of doing so. After all, family stories are linked, like the threads of the spider's web.

Disastrous English Lesson

May 19th, 1970
Bristol,

Darling,

I missed you terribly today & haven't been able to get you out of my mind. I had hoped you would phone at lunch time – the fact that I can't get in touch with you at all is upsetting. I worry about you. I hope you got my last letter about phoning on Thursday at 7.30 – if you have suggested a different time & have written to me, I'll be there at the time you suggested.

I wrote off for one job today + intend to write for 2 more tomorrow.

I was in class today, thinking about what it would be like to see you at the end of the day, every day. The kids had some funny cracks about how I spent my evenings – & I wished I could. This is the latest of my disastrous English lessons:

Kevin: I like your dress, Miss.
Me: If you think you are going to get round me like that, Kevin, you're mistaken.
Robert: That's not what he really likes Miss (with awful laugh).
I collapse.
Then I was asked for an account of sex.
"When are you going to tell us, Miss?"
"I'm not."
"She don't know anything about it."

Small boy: "I knows all about it Miss, I just ask me dad &
he tells me."

Stephen: "I asked my mum & she said come back later, &
when I came back later she said ask your father, & I asked
him & he said someone at school will tell you – so will you
Miss?"

Honestly darling, I feel sure you could do a little profitable
instruction – I could invite you along as guest speaker –
"My experiences etc." How about it love?

By the way, we've got an invitation to a 21st. It's a
formal one, on a Saturday at Blandford – Dorset – it's
about an hour's train from Bristol, so you could come for
the weekend. I think it's July 4th.

Anyway, it should be very posh – at the farmhouse
where I went to stay that weekend. This time the
invitation was for both of us – how about that! So you'd
better come!

I do hope you've written as I keep worrying about you.

All my love darling. Take care. I miss you so much. Life
is really empty here.

Mary xxx

'A letter about things'

22 Kingsgate Est
London N.1
Wednesday evening

Dear Mary,

I think I'll write you a letter about things. You know that they pile up when you least expect them. Well, I was walking along the other day when two things ran up behind me and started yelling at me in a strange tongue. I could tell that they were things before I turned by the sound of their tiny webbed feet − all eight of them − on the pavement. I could see at once that they were related (brothers, you know) but under the circumstances I think I reacted very well. No panic at all. Though I say it myself, darling, I've always prided myself on my ability to cope with things.

"Good morning things," said I, jovially. I thought it best not to antagonise them − you know what it's like when they get out of hand.

"Splize," said one of them earnestly, shaking his head up and down and laying a quivering tentacle on my left shoulder. "Yith, Splize. Splize. Splize!" said the other.

"Come again, thing?" I said.

"Splize, splize, splize…" they jabbered in unison.

By this time they were jumping up and down and I must admit that I was beginning to feel a bit of an idiot. It was at that stage in the proceedings that I noticed a crowd had started to form on the other side of the street;

luckily I had sufficient presence of mind to hail a passing taxi. I bundled the things in, gave the driver the address of my flat and sat back feeling that at last I was beginning to get things under control.

It took a couple of hours and a lot of dry martinis (god knows where they put them) before I learnt their problem. Apparently it was the British weather. Every night when these things went to bed it didn't matter how well they tucked themselves in, they just got too cold to sleep. They'd tried hot-water bottles, electric blankets, toasters, hot-cross buns – the lot. All to no avail. Now darling, if you get cold in bed or I get cold in bed there are plenty of things we can do about it. But we all know what happens to a thing when it gets too cold. That's right, it shrinks. Thermal contraction you understand.

Of course, as soon as I'd understood their problem I could only admire their intelligence and tenacity in approaching me for a solution – after all, hadn't my fame as a cryogenic engineer spread throughout Southampton? Hadn't my knowledge and expertise in the field of low temperatures been wondrously acknowledged by all at the Albany? You know, darling, I couldn't help but feel a twinge of pride deep inside me. They had come to me for help – and that couldn't have been easy for them, being basically shy and timid creatures – and goddammit, I was going to help them.

Pills. That was it. In the trade we laughingly refer to them by their technical name, "anti-shrink pills!" I know that's a bit of a mouthful darling so in future I'll refer to them as "pills". There was one problem though; it's often difficult to tell how a particular patient will react to a given pill, and so it's advised that after the first dose has been administered the patient be kept under surveillance over a period of suitable coldness. I told them about the pills and explained that they'd have to spend a few hours in my flat after taking them so that I could check for possible side-effects.

"Thankth yoth, thankth yoth," they chorused. Their little heads were nodding up and down, tentacles flying around, beaks grinding together. Honestly darling they looked radiant.

I gave them a pill each and tucked them safely into bed. They wouldn't shrink that night I vowed! They fell asleep pretty quickly and so I thought "why waste an evening sitting here watching two things. I'd much rather be with Mary." So I phoned you up and you came round and you sat on my lap and we watched those two dear little sweet things snoring away, blissfully ignorant of the consequence of other pills. But so were we for that matter.

You noticed it first darling. Remember? One of the things started to grow. He started to swell out, like a balloon being pumped up, and before we'd had time to do anything about it he'd pushed his brother out of bed. Of course, you and I immediately helped him to his feet (all four of them) and the three of us tried to stop the expanding thing from getting any bigger. But it was no good.

It's obvious now what happened of course. I'd given our fat friend too large a dose, and so now the cold, instead of shrinking him, made him swell up. By this time he was floating two feet above the bed and the three of us were desperately trying to pull him down from above our heads. As I remember it that's when we all fell on the floor, fat friend and all, and I realised that things were getting on top of us.

But there was nothing I could do about it darling, I know you'll agree with me there. He just got bigger and bigger. One of his tentacles had pushed the window out from its frame and the rest of him was slowly disappearing through a gaping hole in the ceiling. It was then that I knew that this thing was getting bigger than both of us.

So we went out and had a good meal!

All my love

Colin

xxx

Diametrically Unopposed

22, Kingsgate Est,
Tottenham Road
London N.1
Friday afternoon

Darling,
At the moment I'm sitting downstairs feeling bored stiff and
listening to a story on the radio about a hedgehog house.
Very stimulating. So I thought I'd write to you because
according to my calculations I owe you about nine letters.
As you've probably gathered now I'm feeling completely
better; after feeling ill on Wednesday. I think I've made an
incredibly [word partly crossed out and corrected] (I can't
spell!) brilliant recovery, which is due in part no doubt to
having heard about other poor souls who succumbed to
the same complaint. I know you may find this hard to
believe darling but I've had a three day bug which lasted
for three days. By the way, before I forget, let me draw you
a "tough old black boot."

(I won't colour it black because I don't want to spoil the overall aura of the sketch.)

I must admit I am looking forward to meeting the new you. Are you going to take me out if I'm good darling? Perhaps as a special treat you'd take me to the theatre one day? Would you like me to buy some nice freaked-out ties?!

Honestly you great big golumptious gook. It's time someone told you that you in no way resemble a boot of any kind; I think of you in terms of silks & white & pale blue things and frilly dresses, to boot. Please don't take what I've told you too harshly my little glushplush – after all, a man's got to do what...

Seriously though, it was very good receiving your letters & calls during the past week. Please don't make the mistake of labelling me a sort of invalid incapable of taking any responsibility or difficulty. Actually, labels don't worry me very much. I learnt a long time ago that there's no point in worrying about people pinning the wrong label on you – thinking you're thick when you're really clever, brazen when subtle, etc. What you really are always comes out eventually; I know how much I carry & make no apologies for always wanting to do just that bit more. My attitude has always been one of outward aggression. One of the reasons I love you is that you know what I really am beneath the façade. I can enjoy being with someone like Janet for a limited length of time, during which we talk (or at least we think we do) about great profundities & philosophies & people; but it's incomparably better to be with someone with whom one can talk not first to maintain some "image" but when one wants to say something. And then to be able to relax.

I really can't understand why we don't talk more darling. You mentioned that in one of your earlier letters. The obvious reason is that there just isn't time (that's what I call a good sense of values!). But when we were in Southampton we had time. I suppose that when I was down there I was so busy arguing (which my "discussions" often descend to) with everybody that I wanted us to be in love. This business about people who are so diametrically opposed getting on so well is alright I suppose, but I'd rather be diametrically unopposed. Actually, I think that bit came out slightly wrong, still the point is that I love you apart from which I reckon you're a smasher. There, the ultimate.

From what you were saying on the phone last night I get the impression that you now think I find your presence somehow upsetting or disturbing. Let's knock that one on the head right away (you as well if you're not careful!). I wasn't feeling particularly brilliant last weekend until about half an hour before I met you at the station; I should think it was obvious from the weekend we had that being with you was marvellous. Believe me love, when I tell you that you're incredibly sexy & very passionate & very loving & womanly. You don't talk about what a woman's got to do – you just do it! (No! No! No! I'm thinking spiritually. (I'm not dead either!) You're not preggers. (I have my doubts about me but you're definitely not!).

I'll be going driving tomorrow. I think I've discovered

the reason I haven't passed my test so far. No my love, it's not because I can't drive. It's because I always drive on test as though I'm not a learner – I tend to be overconfident, this doesn't make me drive badly but it tends to create the wrong attitude with respect to the examiner. I must try & be a bit more humble next time – how about me crawling to the car with a blank cheque hanging from my mouth?! Or perhaps you could don your se*y knickers & mini mini skirt & take the test for me. On second thoughts that's not such a good idea because you might burn out the clutch. Or something.

Darling, I love you. You must know that – don't be frightened of loving me. Take care,

Colin xx

PS – It's bad enough you have to spend so much on trains, let alone taxis. The enclosed is what I saved by not going to work.

Another Bash

22, Kingsgate Est,
Tottenham Road
London N.1
Thursday
11th December 1969

Darling,

I spoke to you over the phone a few hours ago. Since then I've been having another bash at my project & have actually managed to draw 2 graphs (I thought I'd manage at least 6 – this just about sums up my rate of progress on this damn report). It's now 12.20 & I'm in bed. This means that at most I'll get less than 7 hours kip tonight – what's the betting that tomorrow morning my boss decides to put me through it & expects me to have a fresh and lively mind!?

Darling, I've been thinking about you since we left Cannock & I think that you think I don't love you or care for you. I think that you think I only want you physically & that I don't really believe we have any future together. We have a lot of differences, darling – background, religion. Artistic as opposed to scientific interests etc. Don't you understand that the fact we're together now in spite of all these differences means that we are now in the process of overcoming them? I know that I can't envisage being without you. I tried to explain to you once before that I didn't think our weekend meetings were helping us to find and understand one another more; I'm definitely not suggesting that we stop meeting at weekends – what I'm saying is that it's wrong for you to judge me by what you see then. I am not a sex-starved maniac who always wants to stay in & have early nights & watch television & read about football. Similarly – & this is more to the point in view of your present upset condition – you are not always tired & going off in huffs & needing me to lean on & wanting me to be physical and making me spend lots of money.

What I'm trying to say is that we mustn't judge each other by what we see at the weekends and that I want there to be a future for us & that at the moment the thought of being without you is just ridiculous.

I am about to fall asleep, my eyes are watering and if I don't stop now I'll probably die. Darling – I may not write you bloody 9-side foolscap essays every day & I might not tell you every 35 seconds that I love you.

But I love you and I want you to love me and I really do care about you & whether you like it or not I'm going to look after you. Your problems are my problems darling.

Love Colin

Letter continues on a separate sheet of paper–

Darling,

I'm not at work having spent most of the morning talking to Geoff about my results. I thought I'd slip this in quickly before I posted your letter. It was hard luck you not getting the flat with that woman but I must say that she sounds a bit drippy and you're probably better off without her. Try & remember that you've only been in Bristol a few months now & it's bound to take some time for you to find your feet there (although from what I know about your feet it shouldn't be too difficult). I remember that after you first started work you were complaining about not knowing anyone down there & not having many friends. Well I know that things have improved a bit in that direction & that you do go out sometimes, even if it's only to metal-work classes! Well, it's a start darling. You'll soon find a flat darling & a bird to share it with (with whom to share it?).

Just stop trying to take too many problems on your shoulders & stop worrying & scheming & try & remember a few good things. Like that heatwave we had in Southampton, & that time we bumped into one of my lecturers at 8.30 in the morning!

We'll do a lot more things together love. Take care, stop crying, and start thinking about the things that are right instead of concentrating on what you think's wrong.

Love,
Colin xxx

Cars and Fred

22 Kingsgate Est
Tottenham Rd
London N.1
13/2/70

Darling,

I love you. I suppose one day I'll get the message across but until then I'll just have to batter away in the only way I know. It was very disheartening to listen to you on the phone last night informing me that I never thought about you, didn't miss you & was probably going out with someone else anyway. At the moment I feel a little bitter about the way things are; you know that things are a bloody nightmare at home and I've told you over & over that I need you. When you talk to me the way you did last night it's as though you're throwing everything back in my face. I seem to have acquired a skill for alienating everybody, even you. Stop attacking me darling – you're the one person I can't fight back. Also, please don't present me with ultimatums. Of course we'll go and see Fred. There's no need for you to emphasise that you're going whether I'm coming or not. Do I ever say things like that to you? Did I say come to Jamie's place or I'll take someone else? Of course not. No relationship can thrive on that sort of thing. I'm now convinced that you don't know how much I want you. This is probably because I don't say it over & over again. But can't you understand why? Little kids of 16 & 17, when they go out have a knack of really falling in "love" & saying so over and over again to each other. This is probably partly to convince themselves as well as each other. Well I don't want that. You've read all the books & poems about love & so you should realise that it's something essentially very deep. There should be no need to repeatedly state the case; no darling – don't twist what I've said and regard me as an opponent of affection and lovingness. You know me better than that. I love you so much that it hurts and the only thing that's going to make things work out between us is mutual respect based on our love for each other.

Stop telling me I don't love you. That's my first and last ultimatum to you!

And now to more mundane matters. The next week at work is going to be the most crucial week of my career so far – and I'm not kidding. The experiment I designed is undergoing its final tests & we should have the results in about 10 days. This is a very nail-biting time. Everybody knows that my reputation is staked on the results; my boss has promised me a bottle of whisky if it works. I'm not sure what I'll get if it doesn't. The boot, probably. So keep your fingers crossed for me – I can't cross mine at the moment because I am too busy touching wood!

I'm still looking round for a car. I'll be taking Dad's car into work one day next week just to see how long it takes me. I've also worked out routes to Bristol & Fishbourne by car. Things'll be much better when we have transport, you'll see.

Right now I feel incredibly frustrated and I want you

here very much. Just think of being snuggled up in a nice warm bed – just the three of us!

Returning to the Fred weekend, it'll have to be the 6th March because I'll have business to attend to in Southampton on the 21st – graduation day! (I hope!)

Don't worry, I won't put my foot in it... I'll read up a few arty & sociological books before I go so that we can all have a nice quiet weekend discussing the theatre & pictures & politics etc.

Don't underrate me Mary. I'm not like some of the twits you've been meeting lately. I suppose that it's partly my fault that you sometimes misjudge me because I don't always say what I'm feeling. I've tried to explain that.

I need you, I want you, I love you.

Plain enough?

Now go away & look forward to next weekend.

Love

Colin

   X

All We Can Keep

20 Stockmead
Langford
Bristol
April 27th, Monday

My Darling,

Once Jim said (and I didn't agree with him) that all we can keep in life is memories. I keep seeing you on Saturday night & there is some truth in what he said. The first time I stayed with you & so many other first times for me I will remember. You are so gorgeous.

You know what I mean, even though it is obscure. (I am afraid that this letter might go astray like the others did & then I would be forever wondering what had happened to it!)

Anyway darling I'm delighted to know that you are O.K. & that work is bearable & that it's mathematics forever. I'll show you just how much I know about maths ("O" level Standard – below rather!).

You + me = I or n or $\prod r$ 2.

So there. Juggle those figures, my mathematical tycoon. The answer should be something in the region of 15 (prs of knickers!?).

Now, having worried myself funny over the interview with the head, over you & your job & you and your flat, I'll find something else to dedicate my creative talents too. (English! Ugh!) I read somewhere that the greater proportion of things one worries about never happen. So having proved this right, I'll just keep on worrying in case they do!!

NO. I refuse.

Instead I'll tell you how much I want to be with you. I was glad to see you need me this weekend. Honestly darling I do want to help you. You do seem so confident sometimes. Yet not others. I know exactly how you felt because I feel much the same and have done for years – even though I was near home – when I had to go back to college & here.

As I told you, I've been homesick for my parents and the Isle of Wight just lately.

I'm ever so tired now love after a session of lesson planning & report writing & after a school meeting, so I'll stop, but I'll write again very soon.

All the very best darling at work – I believe you're a match for any of them.

All my love darling,

I think of you so often.

Mary

Down In The Dumps

20, Stockmead,
Langford,
Bristol.
Tues.

Darling,

I've just come back from the phone feeling down in the dumps again. Obviously I've no right to deprive you of your holiday & one way or another you ought to have one & I won't stop you.

I've just been thinking over my financial situation though, & it's not quite as bad as I thought. When I added up approximately what I should earn for June, July & August + what I already have I should have about £300. It may not be quite as much as that owing to unforeseen expenses, but it's certainly more hopeful. Tell me what you think on Thursday darling – I hope you get this before you phone. I could certainly afford something, don't you think? Even perhaps Greece?

I had to write to you about this. I expect you may be feeling a little resentful about the fact that I don't appear to trust you. You said a long time ago that love is founded on mutual trust & respect. I agree & I'm not really doubting you darling. Deep down I trust you implicitly with other women – but at the back of my mind there's always the feeling that they may have more to offer than me, at least in the obvious way. It's childish, I agree. But even though you might go into something lightly & not mean it, I would still feel slighted.

I'll stop talking this way. Even as I write I can see it's all nonsense. But I do expect a lot from you just as you do from me. And I do trust you, whatever you may think from what I say on the spur of the moment.

I must stop now darling as I'm very tired. School work is piling up as ever.

I do love you my darling, I'll speak to you soon – you must get through.

I really do think I'll be able to come with you now darling. Obviously something cheaper would be better, but I might manage Greece. But as I said I'd like your opinion.

All my love, darling.

I'm falling asleep.

Wish I could hold you tight.

Mary

Tahiti Blue

22, Kingsgate Est,
Tottenham Rd,
London N.1
Tuesday 21st April, 1970

Darling,

I'm really sorry that I couldn't write yesterday but before you start going mad let me explain what's happening. When we got back on Sunday evening I suddenly realised that I hadn't give you your pound back & that you probably needed it quite urgently. So I dashed upstairs, put it in an envelope & posted it straight away in the hope that I could get the 7.30 post & you'd get your pound on Monday morning. It wasn't till I got to the post box that I realised there wasn't a 7.30 post but I thought I'd post it anyway. That's why there wasn't any note with it – I didn't want to miss the post by writing a note.

Yesterday morning I bought the car we saw on Sunday. I'll be picking it up tomorrow night. It's a pretty basic sort of a car but I've had a heater fitted + one other luxury: yellow number plates! The colour is called Tahiti Blue but the salesman wouldn't let me have the version that came with the native women in grass skirts! I drove it around for about ^{2} hr and it's definitely a very nippy car – a bit like your father's. I think we'll get a lot of pleasure from it and although it was a bit of a strain this weekend looking for cars I think you'll agree we've ended up with the right one. After buying the car in the morning I went home for something to eat & spent about an hour writing off to various people cancelling interviews (I got another one yesterday – it was virtually an offer of a job. By a complete coincidence it came from Elliot Brothers, Rochester, who apparently got my name from an agency!) and then I went to Frinley to have another look for flats. The journey was completely unsuccessful, and I'm going to have to start looking further afield for something satisfactory. I'll go down again on Thursday – in the new vehicle of course – and see what I can find.

I hope you got back to Bristol all right & didn't have too much trouble on Monday morning at school. As far as your new job is concerned I think that it'll be easier for you to find somewhere & then for me to move near you rather than vice versa. Everything seems to be in a state of flux at the moment but things will be much better when we're together again. We'll be able to go to lots of places (the car's very cheap to run) and if we don't want to do that we can stay at home and do whatever we like. I think it'll even be nice to argue with you all the time because at least that will mean you're there! I can't say that I'm exactly looking forward to being by myself from next week so you'll have to promise to come & see me often – if not frequently. I'll be able to pick you up in Reading and take you straight back to my place where we can discuss all sorts of things – computer program if you like! That sounds familiar somehow.

Anyway, I have to go now darling. I'm going to the West-End to see if I can buy some books about systems engineering so that at least I'll be able to find the right department on Monday morning. Take care of yourself my love. I love you very much. Even if you can't cook!

See you soon.
Love
Colin xx

Life Apart

My darling,
Today I have missed you so much. I miss you coming up behind me & giving me a big kiss, & I miss the secure feeling of knowing that you are there, sitting on your knee in the evening – it's not a bit the same sitting on my own. I love you.

Today I worked all day till this evening when I felt sleepy & wanted to cuddle you. I hope you are not too much alone in your little room. I don't know if you are playing bridge. If not I can only presume that you are cooking eggs rather brilliantly & watching Panorama. You might of course be playing Patience if you remembered your cards but I don't mind about that as long as you haven't got any Margarets or Chrises to entertain you.

I can promise you that today I have met no strange men, no young or old liberals, have not got drunk, nor have I done anything of which you would disapprove except worry about you. (Not really.)

Dad was asked at the Rotary club today by one of his friends when I was getting engaged to that nice young man. All I can say is if they could hear you early in the morning… I still love you.

I don't think that there is much more news except that I have finished the exam papers and am now writing feverishly about "Wuthering Heights".

Kay & I talked for a couple of hours last night so I'm

a bit tired now. They must be having a horrid drive up to Lancaster today, what with the fog.

I won't write you a poem tonight, but I think about all the good things we did last week & feel happy.

How is your car?

Only drawing for today.
I look forward to seeing you again very soon, my love.
I miss you,

Mary

Xxxxxx

Missing You

My darling,

I felt stricken when I realised that you might be over tomorrow evening & I hadn't even written one line to tell you that I love you.

I felt terribly sad leaving you on Sunday evening. You were so sweet to me & kept saying that I should have a rest. Which was very loving of you. On the boat I felt strange, because you've been with me so much lately that I feel utterly lost on my own. To be without you now would be unthinkable.

I am so looking forward to you coming over & hope that the sun stays as hot as it is now – you'd love it.

In the sun you're just like a pussy – no! You're handsome, strong & sexy – & curl up like a pussy. I'm not mad, but I love you, I love you, I love you.

At the moment I'm supposed to be cooking lunch as Mum is working. It's super out, but I haven't been in the sun yet today as I decided to make a quick trip to Ryde. You haven't phoned since I've been in, so I hope I haven't missed you. I'm still not very brown so you'll have plenty of chance to catch up provided the weather lasts.

I love you so much, my darling.

From Mary xxxxx

Worry So Much

20 Stockmead,
Langford,
Bristol.
Thursday

Darling,

I miss you. I don't know what happened tonight. I waited from 6.55-7.25 and you didn't phone. During that time I had visions of you being ill, being with another girl & doing about 50 other things. I do hope you're OK & that you haven't been gadding about. I've suddenly realised that you may not like being alone & am trying to reconcile myself to what may happen. If I go on any longer I'll convince myself…

This evening I've been worried. I hate not seeing you at the weekend, two weeks goes by so slowly — one is bad enough.

I won't go on darling. You should get this on Saturday morning, by which time I really hope to have spoken to you. I got this letter when I got in this evening. I'm thrilled about your new place. I just hope you want me there still. Your job sounds ideal, money and all! I've just discovered that predictably enough, my pay rise has been swallowed up by Union fees. Big deal!

Do have a rest, my love, & do take care. I worry so much about you.

All my love Mary

You're Super

My darling,
I've just torn up one letter to you & I've no time to write
properly. This is just to say that you're super, my writing's
awful & I miss you.

Thank you for phoning just now.
I'm as nervous as anything.
Take care love
See you very soon
All love

Mary

Boats

Martin's boat was called *October*. It had sail and engine, a small cabin with a blue canopy and a white seaweed-flecked hull. It was not always easy to get her to start and we would wait on the pontoon while he fiddled with the starter motor, trying not to put him off. We would watch him swear softly under his breath, which somehow did not detract from his vaguely noble presence. After what seemed like forever, exasperation and tinkering would yield results and *October* would sputter into life. We would all climb on board, finally in business, knowing not to remark on the struggle that had just ensued. The noise from the engine, the smell of the motor and the breeze were all more acute when on deck, at the beginning of another summer day.

We would use the engine to get out of Wootton Creek, weaving past moored-up vessels of all shapes and sizes. Elite racing sailing boats, a catamaran that had circumvented the globe which was owned by an airline pilot, big rusted metal fishing boats, and an array of smaller motor and sailing craft all resting at their buoys. Their names spoke to poetry and possibility: *Black Knight of Wight, Avril, Red Admiral.*

At the mouth of the estuary, at the Fishbourne terminal,

we would pass the car ferries loading and unloading. The thump of wheels on metal, the service announcements carrying across the water, and we would wave to the passengers as they took up their vantage points on the outside decks.

The ferries had grown much as we had. When we were smaller, it was *Fishbourne, Camber Queen, Cuthered* and *Cadman*, all replaced over time by the much larger Saint class of boats. More space but less soul, and locals complained that they brought with them too much traffic for the Island's roads, and that they caused coastal erosion to the land around the terminal's fringes. Of the old ferries *Cuthered* had been my favourite; with its box-like frame, a certain stoutness, she was the first one I had actual memories of sailing on.

Once our engine stalled as we stood in *Cadman's* path, threatening to crush *October* like balsa wood under her metal frame, pulling what remained into her wake. Small as she was for a ferry, she was a lot bigger than us. We were like prey, just waiting to be eaten. Could they see us from the bridge, and if they could, then would they be able to do anything?

Martin, completely calm now faced with a real emergency, fiddled with the engine. I could see the look of urgency on his face and the focus. He knew what could be tried, what might work, and he meticulously executed the options, not speaking, all his energy focussed on the problem in hand, gently coaxing *October* back to life as if through some mix of magic and alchemy. He had no time for swearing now. A moment that turned out to be nothing and might have been nothing anyway, but I remembered it – for his calmness and skill, bringing about a resolution before *Cadman* was close enough to give a sense of what, if anything, she might have done had we not moved.

Often we would fish for mackerel with spinners. Martin would later gut the fish and everyone apart from me would eat them. They would tug violently on the line and he would help us reel them in, extracting hooks from their bloodied mouths, glassy eyes staring up at us. The mackerel would flash silver and green and sometimes keep breathing and flapping for a long time in the ice bucket. I didn't like the way they seemed to stare up at me, both accusing and unknowing. New smells mixing with the fumes from our engine. Secretly I was always relieved when I reeled in clumps of seaweed.

We would take a picnic sometimes, occasionally using the inflatable to go to shore and eat sandwiches and crisps, fruit and biscuits, flasks of tea, cartons of juice, all kept cool in the fridge box. We might put the cricket on the radio or explore the rock pools. Swim. We would have competitions as to who of me, Matt or Dad could start swimming first, the Solent always chilled, irrespective of the sun.

I rarely won these contests. Long summer days, when if we wanted to swim or picnic or sail in Martin's boat we could do so, together. I had no sense as a child that these things might be finite, but of course the adults must have known that there could only ever be so many fishing trips or near adventures with oncoming ferries. I think my older three children are already at an age when they know that nothing lasts forever, though I would guess that Gabriella is not. I envy her that and want to preserve that innocence for her for as long as possible, as perhaps they all once did for me.

Martin was always aware of when the tide was going to turn and of the latest moment we could scuttle back up the creek to home, always leaving time to get the sail out so that we could tack our way back.

I was hit hard by the beam more than once. We never really learnt to sail independently. I'm not sure why. They could not have afforded lessons, but Martin could well have taught us. He described me as an 'experienced boater'. I suppose I lacked the inclination to go beyond this. I don't remember ever asking or wanting to do more.

I have seen Annabelle and Maddie grow up with sea scouts and go on camps where they sail Lasers, Mirrors, Toppers and Topaz. Annabelle says that Lasers are her favourite, but I would not know which were which if you lined them up in front of me. It is only because landlocked Warwick happens to have a river and a Sea Scouts that they can now do what I could not.

Uncle Mike's boats were different. Hulking fishing vessels, *Wham* then *Janet Marie*. These were working boats that formed the basis of his livelihood once and were kept long after that. Long after, we noticed a thinning out of the number of similar vessels moored in the creek. They were more powerful than *October*, so we would go further afield, into the middle of the Solent to the real fishing grounds, near the wartime circular forts that still stood guard. Holiday homes with helicopters now. My ideal place to live I sometimes thought. Around there you could pull up twenty mackerel in a matter of minutes, or none. It depended and you could never be sure.

For years, Mike would take us to Cowes' fireworks. We'd head out in the dark, boat well lit, hundreds of other vessels doing the same, *Royal Yacht Britannia* often in attendance, ferries hired out as spectator vessels. He would play pop music and the sky would dazzle with a kaleidoscope of colour. Golds and silvers, purples and reds, boats honking in approval as bangs filled the air.

As I became a teenager it spoke of a togetherness that made me feel more separate, growing into and away from something at the same time, without really being able to make sense of or to explain any of it. Time can start to gnaw at you, even when still young. My father was never a confident boater and would often meet my eye with a mock grimace as we rolled in the wash from the mass of other vessels.

Sometimes it was possible to get back up the creek after the fireworks, other times we would have to moor at the yacht club. Occasionally we were not sure how far we might get. I remember a late-night walk home in the dark once, Matt excited, Mum and Anna more worried. A cat flashing past us on the unlit path, which made everybody jump.

By the time we were going with our own children, it was different again. Not just the people, but the boats. Mike with a Sunseeker now. "A gin palace," Martin would have said dismissively. But it spoke to his success and continuing sense of adventure – our family still on the sea.

The children had no memories of Anna or Martin, no overlap even, and few of Mary, just as I had no recollection of Martin and Anna's parents and grandparents, or most of the others he wrote about. Yet it is possible not to overlap, not to consciously remember, but still to be a part of something that predates you and might even go on after you, and for the whole thing to feel entirely natural. Perhaps we are all so destined to seek our place, to understand it, that we might miss noticing when we are actually there. Although sometimes I worry that I simply think too much. For all of us, it was to do with the boats and the creek and summer days as vivid as each other, spread over many years.

Martin's Journal – Holmes & Son

Of course, I know quite a bit about my fellow residents by now. What they did and what in some cases they still do – mainly what they did. At least how they put it themselves, which may or may not be true, although in my experience by the time people reach my age they go one of two ways. Either they are so convinced by the stories that they have told that they have come to believe them, or else they are more reflective about it all. What did and did not work and what might have been different. It is all the same in the end. On occasion I think outwardly I am more in the former camp, but I want to try and get beyond that now, to tell the story of what happened and to describe some of the characters along the way.

My grandfather, Arthur, started the business, my father expanded it and I managed the decline. That would be how I would summarise the history of the thing in a single line. Beginning, middle and end, so to speak.

It all started with my grandfather, Alfred Holmes, who was born in Sussex in 1853. He was the son of a cabinetmaker, and I sometimes wonder if I inherited some of my own skill and inclination to work with wood from this great grandfather. I am not sure what else I directly inherited from my lineage. Alfred must have left school at fourteen years of age. He spoke with impeccable grammar and was a first-rate accountant, and what he lacked in formal education he made up for through guile and ability to strike a good deal. He was driven and ambitious and had a way of making things happen.

Alfred worked in menswear retailing, rapidly rising to become the manager of the menswear department in a store known as Walter Bros. of Worthing. In 1880 he married Caroline Walter (daughter of one of the two Walter brothers). He then moved to Ryde, Isle of Wight, buying a small shop and two cottages in Ryde High Street.

Alfred had very little capital but received backing from Sir Maurice Leog, chairman of a clothing manufacturing company, a vital connection, cleverly cultivated. Sir Maurice used to travel the south coast and had known Alfred well in his capacity as a menswear buyer at Walter Bros. Through him and his firm, he was able to buy stock on a continued six-month credit agreement, an arrangement that lasted from 1880 to 1939, which served as the life blood or the backbone, if you will, for all his enterprises.

This was all a time of great promise. Railways were being built in the late nineteenth century, connections were being formed, places that were once inaccessible now were much less so, and this brought large numbers of tourists to the beach. Alfred had seen a gap in the market. Stocking up with the clothes these men required proved to be a booming trade. Perhaps not the garments one would necessarily envisage today, but back then it was all about corduroys, moleskin trousers, waistcoats, thick woollen vests and casual shirts. He sold them all and his store was the place to come. This Holmes shop prospered to the extent that Alfred was able to demolish his property and build a three-storey Victorian edifice with two shops and two flats. He was on the rise and business was booming.

At Holmes & Son, the staff, in addition to father Alfred and son Arthur, comprised two senior salesmen, two apprentices, a cashier and a porter. You would not run such a place with so many staff now. In fact there are not really shops like Holmes & Son anymore. The world has moved on and progress has had its way. The big department stores like Topshop and Woolworths, the huge out of town Tesco, this is what retail is now and doubtless always will be. It is hard to think to a time beyond it, that is for sure.

Alfred was always called the Old Governor, and Arthur the Young Governor. This title stayed with him until he retired in his mid-seventies. There was a formality to things then that you do not see so much today. We all had our clearly defined places, which had its limitations but also brought some certainty and structure, a sense of belonging perhaps.

The shop was cool and dark, an array of

merchandise meticulously set out, perfectly arranged and presented for the discerning customer. I remember the smell of linen and cotton and thread that seemed to hang in the air, oh so gently, much as you can sometimes smell paper when walking through a library. A world far removed from that of the street outside.

The shops had round windows and were lofty, long and narrow, lit by gas lamps – according to Stanley Coffen who worked for the firm for the first sixty-five years of the twentieth century. Not that these ever quite dispensed the gloom. The fire risks were considerable, but fortunately there was never actually a blaze on the premises.

Ryde's fire brigade in those days, and until the early 1930s, operated a horse-drawn fire engine with a steam pump. When Ryde's first motorised fire engine arrived, this writer was one of a crowd of small boys who followed its trail to discover if it was able to climb our steep hills! Little did I know then how acquainted I was to become with fire engines when war broke out.

But I digress, as I sometimes seem to a little more these days. The shop was open from 9am to 7pm Monday to Wednesday, and Thursday was 9am to 1pm. This early closing day started during Arthur's apprenticeship and the shop workers could not believe their luck. Friday closing was at 9pm. Saturday, midnight! I was told that my grandfather would be standing by the door at this time. Precisely at the stroke of twelve, the porter would make his way through the shop carrying the pole with which to pull down the shutters. My grandfather would take his gold watch from his waistcoat pocket saying, "Don't be in too much of a hurry to close, Hobbs. Give the clock a chance to cool down."

The senior staff member when I joined the firm was Mr Morris (Percy, but Christian names were never used in business). Mr Morris had joined as a boy apprentice. Some two years later a family event was taking place in Southampton. His parents told him to ask for a day off in order to attend and were convinced that 'nice Mr Holmes' would consent. The following dialogue ensued.

"Please, sir, can I speak to you?"

"Yes, what is it, boy, what is it?"

"I wanted a day off, sir, because—"

"Day off, boy! Whatever are you talking about? Suppose we all wanted a day off? Have to close the shop, wouldn't we? Go back to your work and let me hear no more about it." And that was that.

When I was a small boy we had living next door to us a Mr Joiner: tall, dignified, bearded. Formerly one of our senior salesmen, he had had to retire early because of ill health. Every Saturday morning my father would give me a small brown envelope to deliver to Mr Joiner, who always liked me to thank my grandfather very much. As this happened every week I wondered if these thanks were really necessary. The envelope contained a £1 note. My grandfather was paying a pension, which he was under no obligation to do, out of his own pocket.

There was a generosity in him that was not in keeping with his general air and demeanour; my father had that about him too, at least deep down.

The staff retirement pension at the time was ten shillings a week – half of one pound. Mr Joiner was really doing very well, evidently. This service to retired employees continued with Mr Morris and Stanley Coffen.

Percy Morris was typical of Isle of Wight characters of those days – a strange mixture of ability, intelligence and stubborn ignorance. Perhaps the insularity came from island living; we were a breed apart in a lot of ways. I do not think many of us could have contemplated being on the mainland for any length of time, although I always felt that I had a greater degree of curiosity about things than many of those around me, albeit I would not see this as a particularly unusual thought.

Percy Morris was nationally respected as a leading breeder of canaries. Many people kept joy birds in cages at the time. The money he made from his birds he invested in houses, and he owned quite a number of small cottages in Ryde. It would be difficult to imagine anybody managing to build up a property portfolio in this way today!

Stanley Coffen served an apprenticeship with my grandfather, then worked in Brighton for several years, before returning to Holmes' shops after service in the Isle of Wight Rifles during the 14-18 war. He was another complex character. I knew him first as a small dapper man who drove an Austin 7. Car owning by shop workers was almost unknown prior to 1939, and this was often commented on and yet never really explored. There was a tendency to leave well enough alone in relation to things that you had no business knowing the ins and outs of.

He was a competent, considerate painter, an exceptional photographer and a violin player. A bachelor, he courted his 'young lady' for the last forty years of his life. He had a wryly amusing attitude to life. I think to him now all these years later in part because it would be hard to imagine anyone quite like him today, certainly not with his experiences and history.

During his service with the Isle of Wight Rifles he showed a tremendous aptitude for rifle shooting. He served in the Middle East: and recalled an occasion when his unit had some Turkish troops pinned down in a trench. There he was, sheltered behind some rocks, rifle trained should any of the enemy show themselves above the parapet.

The Turks were short of water, and eventually one appeared carrying a bucket, trying to reach a nearby well. Private Coffen, for his own satisfaction and amusement, put a hole through the bucket, causing its owner to dive headfirst back into the trench. He was able to repeat this performance several hours later, with the same effect. To my query as to whether he should have shot the man rather than the bucket, he looked quite horrified. "But I might have killed the poor chap!"

His only experience of a full-on battle was to be a disappointment to him; although, as I think to the above, perhaps it was also something of a relief, even if he would never have said as much. His platoon commander led his men into action, pipe in mouth, walking stick in hand, in the nonchalant British way, so at last Private Coffen was about to use his rifle in earnest. However, before he could fire a shot in anger his right leg was shattered by an enemy bullet, and his fighting days were over. He could never forget that all his skill with a rifle had been for no purpose, other than to put holes in a couple of buckets! He was forced to draw a disability pension.

From time to time he would visit the Ryde shop to dress windows. On one such occasion, in my early days, he did a display with tweed overcoats amid bales of hay and tree branches. My father commented, "Nice window, Coffen; you've done a good job there."

Stanley displaying his peculiar sense of humour replied, "Thank you, sir; next week I thought we could have a plague of locusts!"

The few mourners at his funeral included the disconsolate 'young lady' he had courted for forty years to no avail. Sadly, she was still firmly tied to the apron strings of her elderly, domineering, widowed mother.

When Stan Coffen died, I felt it somehow ended our link with the nineteenth century. Certainly as the years moved on Holmes & Son became less profitable and our problems seemed to mount. Many businesses struggle to move with the times, to do things other than in the way that they have always done them, and this in part was our undoing. What people wanted from a menswear shop changed faster than we did. My father to some extent lost his touch, and for me it was always a case of trying to manage and defend against a myriad of near insurmountable problems. But these things do ultimately pass, and I can just think now to the shop at midnight, with the clock not yet cool and Stanley Coffen and all the others from that time who are now gone.

Helen

To what extent can you have a relationship with someone who dies before you are born? Whom two people speak of for the rest of their lives as if she was still present but your father never mentions, ever? The stomach ulcers that developed soon after her death made him violently sick on and off for many years, always at night, until a new drug fixed the problem instantly and completely, not long before he died. I would listen to him throwing up from my bedroom, which was next to the bathroom, a sound I have never heard anywhere else – raging, guttural, going on and on beyond what you might think would be possible. Mum often comforting him, rubbing his back, saying soothing words. Did he think to Helen in these moments? As with so many things, Helen was something in him that he could not share and I did not know.

Helen had been seventeen. A little more than two years older than Annabelle is now. A child just starting out on things; then the routine appendix operation that does not go quite right, although still is not a cause of immediate concern. The time in hospital in which she contracts MRSA, which to begin with is just something else that needs to be fixed, but she struggles over a week, two weeks, until suddenly the situation has become something else. No longer about antibiotics and science, luck is needed now and it simply is not there. In those last few days, hope is replaced with a grim realisation of what might be coming, and then it is over.

The funeral will be the next day, as Jewish funerals are. Dave and Colin will go, but Theresa will not. At that time Jewish women did not attend, and she did not witness her daughter being moved from bed to box and into the ground all within the space of a few hours.

Helen had been training to be a legal secretary. She had certificates and hopes and dreams of which I cannot know. Her photograph is on our mantelpiece, but I would guess few others. Too many years have passed, too many of those who might remember, would want to remember, have now gone. Even though I did not know her, our lives did not overlap, I want her to be remembered as part of this story. For herself as well as for those who knew and loved her – it always saddened me that my father could not talk about Helen.

I wondered if there might have come a point when he would, in those last few months, as time grew short. But what right did I have to ask? I regret not doing so now, but if I could go back I know it wouldn't be any different; asking was not the right thing to do.

Whether I could take my own advice in the end I do not know, might never know. But when you are dying, denial only takes you so far. Better to see what is coming as your final project. To have the conversations, to tell the stories, to put things in context; a last chance to frame everything for those around you. Unless of course you do think to all this, but what you are holding is so secret, so personal that it, belongs only to you. I think all of this was the case with Dad and that this was how he saw things. Also, more simply, that it made him sad. A life spent trying to outrun the deaths of Helen when he was young and Mum when he was middle-aged. When you know what death is and what it does, perhaps it is possible to see why you might choose not to dwell on your own. I cannot know; perhaps this is too simplistic: the opposite could also be true. The pain that he had known could have been the reason for his guardedness. A desire to protect others from what he had come to live with, also a wariness of getting too close to others who might then let him down by dying and inflicting still more pain on him. Instead of choosing not to dwell on his death, perhaps he thought to little else, just quietly and privately, much as he had lived.

I sometimes wondered if things might have been different with Theresa and Dave, had Helen still been alive when Dad married out of the faith. Would they have accepted us in the same way? I think yes, but who can know anything for sure? Having children of my own gave me new insight into their loss, but not his. Not really.

No one ever mentioned when we were younger that my father was Jewish. I found his skullcap in a bedside drawer once and he was irate. I had inadvertently uncovered yet another part of him that for whatever reason he did not want to talk about. I do not know if my parents agreed it should be a secret, if it was simply because she was religious and he was not.

As we got older it was acknowledged more, if still not explicitly mentioned as such. Impossible to avoid when we started going to Jewish funerals, and a pretence developed that we had always known about it, even though we had not. He regularly went to synagogue in the years before Helen died, but then he stopped. He did not attend any place of worship again outside of other funerals until after my mother's death, when he would go to services at St Wulston's and light candles and tend her grave and give the parish over-large donations.

Theresa and Dave would go to their daughter's grave every year, 'to visit Helen'. A day trip with flask and sandwiches, a car journey filled with 'do you remembers' and hopefully laughter. An adventure – the closest they could get to her physically now. The joy of her still in them, along with the sadness; both blissful and excruciating, I would guess.

Theresa would talk about what Helen would have liked or thought, lightly, with complete naturalness. I should have listened better. I have only an impression, nothing more. Toward the end of her own life, Theresa said it was a dilemma: to be with her or to be with all of us. "Helen has been calling me for a long time," she would say with a smile, serene in the thought that her daughter was waiting for her.

How Brave Helen Was

Dear Mr and Mrs Graff and Colin,

We have been to the hospital and learned the sad news of Helen. May we express our sympathy to you all at this time.

We know there is little that we can say that can be of consolation to you and hope that you will find a measure of comfort in each other.

We came to know how brave Helen was and we had a great admiration as well as liking for her. We prayed with you all that she might get well.

We have thought so often of you since we heard the news and hope that before very long you will be able to look back on the happier times and without the sadness that must be with you now.

Wishing you both long life.

Our kind regards to you all.

Yours sincerely

Chris and Francis

How Much More We Miss

4th April 1966

Dear Mr & Mrs Graff,

It is with deep regret that I have heard the news of your sad loss, and I wish to extend to you my deepest sympathy, along with Helen's other friends from the office.

You must have been wondering why I had not been to see Helen, but this was due to the fact that I have had disc pressure in my back, and have not found it easy moving, for which I have had to attend Hospital. It was very remiss of me not to have written, which I now very much regret and I can only apologise for this.

Whilst writing Mr Harris has requested me to ask if it would be possible for us to visit you as he has to settle up with you. He has suggested Sunday, 17th April sometime in the afternoon if this would be alright with you. Perhaps when you are feeling up to it you could let me know about this.

Once again, I extend my sympathy for I know how you must be feeling as we all realise how much more we miss Helen now.

Yours sincerely

(illegible).

Summer Wedding

The church waits for another bride to walk
Through the lych gate, past the square bell tower,
Into the greyness of its cold stone walls,
Never warm, though July blazes and shimmers
All around. Nine hundred years weigh down
On those who linger in search of quiet prayer
Distracted by the chill and scent of years.
Fields and lanes have long been decked with white,
Oblivious stood the stony church till now:
Inside the heavy walls sweet flowers teem
Obliterating dark and wintry thoughts,
Brief victors, conquerors of the musty air,
Your fragile piercing beauty blooms unbridled
For on this wedding day cold stone is kindled.

M.G.

215

Martin's Journal –
My Mother's Family

So this is the dusty bit of this work – stories about my mother's family, many of whom will be known to only a few, if any, of those who read this. I see now how it all happens. We live, we die. We are remembered and then we are forgotten.

I look at my fellow patients and cannot help but wonder how long it will be until both they, and indeed I, are no longer remembered. Writing things down prolongs things and this is why I want to tell these stories about that side of the family, as there is nobody else left to do so. I hope you will indulge me.

They were an eccentric and eclectic group of hard-working, hard drinkers who were originally from Dorset and Wiltshire. I am convinced that Thomas Hardy knew my ancestors and may well have based characters in his novels on them, although I am not saying which. Some of his books were all too close to home, the people too recognisable from the stories that were handed down to me. I am not surprised they provided plenty of material.

Perhaps we should start with the remarkable story

of Jack, my mother's brother. Jack was at college doing a course in engineering and usually returned home at weekends. On this particular weekend, sometime in 1911 I think, he had his dinner as usual and then said that he had better go upstairs to pack.

"Going away for the weekend?" queried his father.

"No," said Jack casually, "I am leaving for Australia tomorrow."

This was the first the family had heard of it! In those days, of course, Australia was several weeks' journey by ship. Jack already had several cousins in Australia. They had been given grants of land, providing they cleared it and developed it for farming. Today those Sydney-based farms are hugely successful and all the relatives involved have become very wealthy. Other worlds, other choices.

Jack left home promising faithfully to write frequently. His family never heard a word. I always find it strange that people can turn away from their family, but this was how it was with him. It transpired that he was actually working as an engine driver on the railways in the years before war broke out. Then in 1917 my mother received a telegram from the War Office stating that Jack was dying in a military hospital and was asking for her.

He had lost a leg, blown off by a shell while fighting in France with Australian forces. My mother, who was of course a registered nurse, left me with my grandparents and travelled to the hospital. Jack, who was very weak, took my mother's hand.

217

"Wonderful of you to come, sis; just hold my hand while I die."

My mother in her usual forthright fashion said, "You are not going to die, Jack, not now that I am here."

Whether she had any doubts, which she hid, I do not know. My guess is not, but who can tell? Few doubted her strength of purpose when she had made her mind up about something.

She marched off to the commander's office. The secretary who tried to intercept her was swept imperiously to one side. She showed the commanding officer the telegram, then announced that she would nurse her brother herself until he was out of danger.

She did not go to bed for the first two nights, remaining with him constantly. I sometimes think to this vigil now. It is of a kind that has played out all through history, the bedside attendance, outcome uncertain. Things capable of either turning for the better or the dramatically worse with the strengthening or weakening of a heartbeat, the rise or fall of a temperature, the depths of the night always the time of most danger.

But it came to pass that he lived and came to see my mother before he was repatriated to Australia. It was a very moving sight.

"Sis, you are the most wonderful woman in the world," he told her. "You saved my life, and I will never forget you as long as I live. We will never be out of touch with each other again, I promise you; I will write to you every month."

She never saw or heard a word from him again.

I cannot explain this. He was not a letter writer, that much is clear. Perhaps he just became preoccupied with his own affairs, lost track of the rolling years and then finally thought it was too late. Who can say?

I never heard my mother comment on his lack of communication; I do not know if she was hurt by it or not, albeit it would be easy to imagine that she must have been. Although, in the moment of their lives where he needed her most, she was there for him and able to make a difference, and I hope that counted for something with her.

Through others, we did hear some of his story from a distance. Apparently when Jack returned to Australia he got a job on a vast cattle station and before long he married the owner's daughter. He prospered well into his seventies and died a very wealthy man.

My mother's youngest sister, Dorothy, contracted TB when at college. That was in the 1920s when there was no known cure for TB other than fresh air. There was a big TB hospital at Ventnor, where the botanical gardens are now, but the best place was considered to be Switzerland, and Dorothy was sent there to be cured and ended up marrying Harry Warket, a German Swiss who owned a fabulous beauty salon in Geneva.

Sadly, Dorothy's health deteriorated, and her sister Lily, a London-trained children's nurse, went to look after her, but unfortunately Dorothy was not as lucky as Jack had been and she was destined to die young.

Afterwards, Lily married her brother-in-law and had two daughters, Sonia and Erica. When the children were seven and five, the marriage broke up, and Lily returned to her native Dorset to bring up the girls on her own while working as a housekeeper to a widower farmer.

My parents were seriously considering adopting Sonia, not just as a matter of family duty but also because they had always wanted a daughter. Before anything definite had been decided, Harry came to England to visit his family. By now he had gone bankrupt and was no longer living in Switzerland, having moved to Germany to work for his sister's husband. When he left to return to Germany, he took Sonia with him for a holiday. It was August 1939!

War broke out, and all contact with Sonia was lost. After the war, Lily wrote to her ex-husband's last known address, but there was no reply. Years went by, with Lily grieving for her lost daughter. Then Erica had the bright idea of calling at the Swiss Embassy in London to see if they could find her sister.

In a matter of days they came up with an address in Germany. Sonia had married a German, Yanz Wreade, and was the private secretary to the managing director of a large organisation.

Overjoyed, Erica flew to Germany, arriving unannounced on the front doorstep. The door opened. "Yes, what do you want?"

Erica said, "Sonia, it's me, your sister."

"I can see who you are," said Sonia. "All these years, you and Mum have not bothered about me, so why have you come now?"

Fortunately Erica was able to convince her that they had both been broken-hearted, and all between them was well. Separations and reunions, a misunderstanding rectified, another tiny crack created by the war ultimately smoothed over.

A year or two later I met Sonia for the first time. Erica is so typically a West Country farmer's daughter, and there was her sister, a beautiful, elegant, very continental lady, very much her father's girl. When the war broke out, Harry joined the German army, leaving Sonia at a convent to be cared for by nuns. After the war, he married again and went to live in Australia. Sonia told her he was always very kind, but there was no warmth in their relationship, a mistake made, as it is all too easy to do.

The family believed at first that Harry had suffered great hardship in the army, serving on the Russian front. It later transpired that he had been a staff officer based in Berlin. Staff officers are not famous for suffering hardship. He owed his position largely to the fact that he spoke most European languages fluently, and it was because of this ability that the Russians kept him on in his job after they occupied the city.

Erica married a man called Phillip Hodge, a boatbuilder in Eastmouth. When I first met Phillip he was such a quiet man, who said little and suffered from depression. When he had a bit of a breakdown a psychiatrist decided he was in the wrong occupation and that he should have been an accountant! The family regarded the advice with derision. The advice was seen as being typical from a profession where the doctors were obviously wealthier than their patients. That said, and I do not recall precisely how this came about, Phillip did in point of fact go on to train as an accountant. Today he is a happy man with a lovely wit, and is a most amusing companion. He and Erica live happily together but have no children.

When Sonia and Erica are together they speak French. Although Sonia grew up speaking English to her mother and was at school in England for two or three years, she had almost forgotten her mother language. It is funny how it is possible to become separated even from something as fundamental to you as your own language; truly nothing is really secure.

The youngest of my mother's family, Bill, was fifteen years of age when he joined the army in 1915. He'd said he was eighteen. He fought in the Middle East, and survived. Later he leased Hath Farm near Semley: a romantic stone house with a narrow flag-stoned garden facing the farmyard, and a large garden in the rear. It had no electricity or running water, and was set on a long hillside.

The house was haunted, a terrible murder having been committed on the main staircase. I always used the back stairs to go to the bedroom that was mine for a number of years; the main staircase was as if it had an invisible force field around it. Mainly invisible at any rate. Hugh and I had many holidays there, being wakened in the very early morning by the sound of cows being brought into the yard for milking just underneath our bedroom window, but I was never quite able to shake the thought of all that had occurred.

The house continued to be ill-fated. Bill married a pretty, bubbly lady called Phyllis and they had a baby daughter called Joy. In the '20s, before the discovery of antibiotics, Joy developed pneumonia and died. They never had another child.

Bill was a hard-working powerful man, difficult, as all the family are, but capable of considerable charm when it suited him. He was a keen fox-hunting man, out as often as possible with the South and West hunt, and a fearless point-to-point rider.

When Hugh and I arrived to stay at the farm, we travelled by train, disembarking at Semley station. We would walk across the footbridge and out onto the road, where Jack would be waiting with his milk cart; Jack was a real hero of ours and we always felt safe in his friendly hands. The farm was about fifteen miles from the station, the road winding through often common land, then up a steeply-wooded hillside to the farm. It was a daily thrill to take the milk to the station.

Once the afternoon milking was over, Jack and my uncle would load the churns onto the two-wheeled cart, then we would pile in. Jack would flap the reins and the horse would set off at a smart trot. A few yards from the farmhouse the hill became very steep indeed, and the horse would go faster than ever. We were always terrified that he would come down and there would an almighty wreck with us in the middle of it, then we would start to ease as the hill became a gentle slope. It may well have been a miracle, but the horse never did fall.

Sadly there was another horse that did. In 1934 Bill was out exercising one of his hunters when it tripped on a loose wire and came crashing down. Bill, wearing only a soft cap on his head, sustained a fractured skull and died a couple of hours later. We were all stunned by this terrible turn of events. Phyllis, totally shattered, came to Ryde to stay with us for several weeks, then when she returned to the farm to settle up the affairs I went with her and stayed for three weeks. Perhaps some houses are best avoided after all.

The farm was taken over by John Abbot: a little older than me, but a fellow old boy of F.G.S. His wife was the sister of one of my beloved friends. During my visits to Shaftesbury I used to call at Hath Farm from time to time.

Only about three years after my uncle's death, John Abbott died in a car accident. His widow stayed on and subsequently married again. Her second husband died soon afterwards of a brain tumour. The old house was living up to its reputation!

A few years ago I went down the narrow lane and parked in the wide space near the farm entrance.

There was a lady working in the courtyard garden, so I introduced myself and was invited in for a drink with her husband.

They had removed the Victorian-tiled surround, revealing a large open fireplace. They had also stripped out the cupboards in the hall that had enclosed a stone wall, and they had done a similar job on the staircase.

I thought to the horrors that I knew of and those that had been passed down from others. Despite the hospitality and the air of calm that seemed to prevail in the moment, I was glad to drink my tea and be gone again.

One Time Abroad

First time abroad, first aeroplane, our big trip has long been planned and now it is here. We fly from Birmingham, just the four of us, to Paris. I had been desperate to go, but as soon as we are on our way I want to turn back. It is all very different to the Isle of Wight and Bognor. Alien.

While we are still on the tarmac Matt and I have eaten the sweets that are meant to stop our ears popping on take-off, and as a result both feel sick. Mum is a slightly nervous flyer, but Dad has shut himself off from all of it and is walled into his seat with his newspaper. He has the air of the experienced, seasoned traveller, which of course he is, as well as that of a somewhat exasperated father, which he also is.

England pulls at me throughout. Ian Botham has been recalled to the England cricket team. Graeme Hick has been dropped. Botham takes an early wicket and hits the winning runs. I listen through my transistor radio's headpiece as we trudge around the city, with its heat and noise and sense of otherness, remembering earlier years on the Island when we marvelled as Botham hit sixes while we paddled at the Solent's edge. I am present and not present. It is partly my age I suppose. Wherever I am these days I instinctively want to be somewhere else.

The sense of indifference all cities radiate towards those who enter them is particularly strong. I think it was Henry Miller who described how impossible it was to make a friend in Paris, and while I didn't know those lines then, I somehow sensed them. But I'd only been to London a handful of times at that point, so perhaps I wasn't well placed to judge how big cities really work, if they do at all – their utter indifference is not personal.

I struggled to see beyond what I could literally see. The Paris of writers and artists was in my future reading, not the here and now, and I would not have been open to it if it was. I just see a tangle of language and traffic and people who walk with a sense of purpose that I envy, their way forward more obvious to them than mine is to me.

My mother asks a lady for directions in French and is disappointed when the reply comes in English.

"That wouldn't have happened once," she says softly.

The woman is a few years younger than she is and more glamorously dressed. She has a certain confidence and I can sense Mum thinking to something as she walks away, but I can't quite read what.

We take a riverboat down the Seine. The water smells, and the couple sat in front of us argue loudly in German. The headphones for the commentary don't work properly. We visit art galleries and then the Catacombs, walking past row after row of piled-up skeletons, glad to emerge blinking into the sunlight, different from them and relieved at the thought.

I can't eat the food. No meat to a French restaurant seems to translate as ham. But we find a place that can make a plain omelette and I insist we go there after that. We are always pleased when the waiter recognises us and is welcoming: a veneer of familiarity in a strange city.

Dad lets us sip his beer. Mum frets about where we are going to stock up on more bottled water. I'm not actually even sure that I like omelettes especially, but I have long since recognised that this is as good as it is going to get.

We ride the Metro and walk the streets. I like the feeling of safety that comes with being underground, the world somehow simplified into clean straight lines, a clearer story that is easier to follow.

In the hotel room I listen to Cathy Dennis and dream of being invited to parties by Kylie Minogue. I am acutely aware of how thin my legs look in shorts, the number of spots I have and, however much I wash it, the greasiness of my hair. Some things are only plausible in my imagination.

There are posters everywhere, on most of the billboards, featuring a photograph of a person's head. All sorts of different people, different races, ages and genders, but the caption is always the same – Yes, I have AIDS. Will you still speak to me?

I am scared someone will inject me with AIDS as we meander through the crowds. A fear of death grips me. It seems inevitable and soon. I am told I am being melodramatic. The actual likelihood of me contracting AIDS at this point is zero.

A tramp drinks whisky from a bottle outside the hotel. English newspapers at the kiosks are expensive and have to be rationed.

"You can't get one every day," my father says.

At night the Eiffel Tower is lit, and looking at it makes me feel lonely, separate somehow. We do not climb it. All the familiar sights are powerful and strident and appear to mock me. They have a place here, a permanence that I do not. It is possible that I am over-sensitive.

I am relieved when it is time to go home. On the way back we are told in pigeon English that 'the plane is broken.' We can only fly to London. Matt and I laugh, but Mum doesn't think it is funny. Dad is on the case and, annoyed but focussed by the challenge, looks into hiring a car to take us on to Birmingham. In the end we are put on a second flight.

"Paris! That's a bit grand, isn't it?" someone at school had asked when she knew this was where we had been.

As usual, I had no answer.

This was our first time abroad as a family of four, but it was only as I wrote this chapter that I realised it was also our only time. Just a single week of plain omelettes and broken planes in a period of my adolescence that I am glad has long since passed.

Our parents were to go abroad together many times in later years – Italy, France, Greece. Mum was not keen on the idea of America, or long-haul flights more generally, but in terms of the four of us, this was it.

For our children it has been very different. They have been on aeroplanes and boats, cable cars and trams, through the Channel Tunnel and on many ferries and cruise ships. We go on a cruise and they do not want to get off the boat. Their default expression in an airport is one of boredom; they have seen all that there is to see before. We have more money than my parents did; a lot of it was once theirs.

"Do we have to go to Barcelona?" they will lament.

An exploration of Rome will not go well either.

We think they are spoilt, that they take things for granted. They don't understand that they have opportunities which we did not when we were their age.

I expect they find me irritable.

I expect my father thought we were spoilt when we were younger too. He would have had no access to boats or expensive houses when he was young.

You can but live in the world you find yourself in. It is the cycle of things. I hope my children will look back on the good bits and forgive the bad.

If truth be told, I thought Rome was quite dusty too.

Mary's Journal – 1990

It was just on sheets of lined paper, in a box in a cupboard. A journal started, then abandoned, before being taken up again thirteen years later and abandoned again. This first part from 1990 does not cover personal events of the magnitude of 2003-2004, but for all the drama in families, in some ways it is the normal days where life is most lived. This account captures some of those, from a time when there were still many more days to come.

* * *

13 February – Ash Wednesday

I went to 10.00 am service in Bosbury, very cold, snow 6" deep & frozen. Main roads clear, but many of the farms and hamlets are completely cut off. Church chill, white breath on frosted air. Old service – again felt sense of past scenes of worship over hundreds of years. Many more people then, not like the solitary few today, whose numbers thin still further year on year.

Mrs Smith missing, Mr Smith there. Found afterwards she was in hospital. He was very frail, but

coping. She may have had a stroke. It was such sadness
+ I grieved for them: being separated after so many years
is a cruelty. Cannot get them out of my mind on this
coldest of days and feel frustrated as to what I can do.
Very little in truth.

The beginning of Easter can be the cruellest of times.

14 February

Valentine's day but hardly saw Colin as he had to go
away with work. He has a big project on, which means
that when he is here, he paces a lot and says little.
Just a case of letting him think his way through it,
things generally right themselves for him workwise in
the end.

Matt still at home but getting better from the throat,
cough etc. he's had since Sunday. Ben says he is skiving
but I think he is ill. Back to school tomorrow. Cleaned
out larder – very dull & depressing job – Lenten task
I suppose. All the usual delights at the back of the
cupboard, I have to accept that I am the only one in the
family who is ever going to read a label on a packet or
a jar and act accordingly if the information is not good.
Lost Caspar.

15 February

Caspar found locked in roof cupboard. Much rejoicing.
He seemed entirely un-phased by the experience. Rushed
boys off to bus & spent morning shopping in Ledbury
in time-wasting way impossible in term time. I thought
a bit to shopping in the days before the children, before

Colin even. Carefree trips into Ryde as a school girl. Things were simpler then, but I would not go back.

Snow clearing at last – it felt warmer & spirits lifted. The snowploughs have been at work on the more minor roads now and there are banks of snow stacked up by thin winter hedges. They drip thinly in the slightly warming air. Ben went to chess club – had to drive to Malvern to take him. Colin returned in very bad mood. Ben in a bad mood too. Neither of them offered any further comment.

16 February – Saturday
Stayed in bed late. Colin restored to humour. Called on Mr Smith in afternoon to deliver card & present for Enid. Found him very upset as she's been moved for possible op on a brain tumour – not a stroke after all. I pray she'll pull through in spite of her age as he's lost without her. Tried to encourage him but felt inadequate. Howl, howl, howl… It may be 10 days before he sees her again. May God help them both.

Is this what it comes to? The years go by and then suddenly things no longer work as they should, no longer make sense. You are no longer who you once were and do not know where it will end. People turn their backs on you in your decline and then… It doesn't bear thinking about. I dread the thought of being old, but what is the alternative? I have made Ben promise never to put us in an old people's home where they organise sing-a-longs. That is what I dread most, although of course objectively there are worse things.

I think mainly to Mr and Mrs Smith. Whatever my future fears, this is happening to them now.

17 February

There was a baptism at church which was followed by preparation for Matt's confirmation, went on till 12.40. We went out to lunch at Slip tavern. Very restful, the children have reached the age where eating with them in public can actually be a pleasant experience. Short walk on return. Still feels like the depths of winter, it is colder again now and the yielding of the snow has not brought with it any sense of Spring. It will come in its own time, we can only wait.

18 February

Felt v virtuous after making marmalade – a much needed holiday task but better than cleaning as there was something to show for it. I like the scent of the boiling fruit as it fills the kitchen with a tang of orange zest. I wonder how many years ago somebody first made marmalade in this room, too long to know, but a thought to imagine. Bombs in London railway stations – Colin delayed on way up & finally back at 10pm.

I've always hated London, with its noise and bustle at the best of times and I hate him having to go there even more in these turbulent times. The world feels increasingly less safe. If we could pull up a metaphorical draw bridge I would.

18 February

Boys had hair cut this morning, the hairdresser commented on how much easier Ben's hair is to cut these days. He is growing into himself and growing in confidence, that much is clear.

Matt and I went to Hereford this afternoon and had afternoon tea in Chad's. He was quite chatty.

Rushed back to get ready for Matt's confirmation service. Bishop very droll – hated singing while he was confirming people. Matt very sensitive, for once.

A proud day.

20 February

Matt had music practice at Church in Ledbury, something about the darkness of the place reminded me of a story Herbert once told me, about a solitary organ practice he undertook in Bosbury. Coffin laid out waiting for burial on the following morn. He said it was impossible to concentrate on his music and in the end he was compelled to flee, even though he wasn't like that, knew logically that there couldn't be any threat to him. Old churches, new bodies, a winter evening, I think it would have scared many.

Ben working hard & very gloomy. Says his life is nothing but work. I saw Mrs Jones this morning who said that they were well on with the lambing. The first this year had arrived on Christmas day! I do sometimes envy those who work on the land and imagine the benefits. That closer connection to nature, an ability to measure the seasons through the arrival of new born animals; to notice changes in the growth of a hedgerow that will pass by those of us with more sentinel roles. No more need to care about the latest crazy government education edicts. This is a somewhat romantic way of looking at life on the land of course. The work is backbreaking and repetitive and it is not my world. My students, my books and family of course, these are my life, but it always does me good to think out of myself from time to time, however silly the thought.

21 February
Back to college. Same old story. John very depressed about mess up re foundation training. Actually had good lecture with GCSE mob on interviews – assessing candidates & references etc. We are well into things now and I can see progress being made. Just occasionally we feel that we are making a difference.

22 February – Friday
More work. Boys at home alone but coping well. Took Matt's flute to be mended. War raging on in Gulf – ground war imminent. It dominates every news bulletin, every newspaper. Glorified and sensationalised. I pray for all of them.

23 February
Sunday – Church followed by Matt's music practice. Ben still gloomy as is bogged down in GCSE work. Planted tress (plum & magnolia) bought yesterday in

garden. All four of us were involved, which was fun. Felt a little like Spring – warmer + some sun. I wonder how long these trees will stand here, longer than any of us all being well.

24 February

All back to school etc. today. The rhythm of the year picking up pace, exam preparation looming into focus, it will be summer before we know it. Then another year will be gone. I know I must not think like this but the way time moves scares me sometimes. I look at the boys and think, where did you come from? I look at myself in the mirror and think… Well, I don't know quite what I think.

Did usual tasks – Colin away in London. Another bomb scare closed all mainline stations, again I worry for him. This is not an easy time. Ground war began in Gulf. God help them all. We never seem able to move beyond conflicts like this, however disastrous all know they are in terms of human cost.

25 February

Helped Ian G with his poetry reading. He is a very talented writer/ musician & a funny man. Programme went well, but was not well attended.

26 February

Dreadful images of war on TV screens – cannot bear to watch at all. Ben's parents evening – he is doing v. well & everyone was pleased with him. Wished Colin was there. Got back about 9.45. Very tired. Colin home at last, also tired and quiet. I can only guess at what he is thinking sometimes.

27 February
War seems to be petering out. Iraq will be defeated. I am very glad the nightmare will end. Visited Mrs Smith, hospital – she's OK – but so so frail. I held her hand and she stroked my hair. We did talk, but that was not what seemed important. You can only hold onto the moment.

28 February
Gulf war over! Glory, glory.

Felt v tired, but so relieved. Kept wondering whether Mrs Smith will cope when let out of hospital. She's longing to be home, with him, back where she belongs. I know things will be uncertain for them both now, but I will do what I can to support them and to pray for them.

We have to stand for as long as we can.

Golden Anniversary, and
Other Football Stories

After months of pleading we are going to Old Trafford to see Manchester United: Me, Matt and Dad. Nobody seems to mind that this is the day of Theresa and Dave's fiftieth. So long as they are together they are happy.

"Say it," Theresa says. And I feel resentful. It's an intrusion. There are more important things to be thinking about now. At sixteen I am not at my most gracious. We stand at the bottom of the stairs, facing each other for a moment. "Happy Anniversary, Grandma!" I say. She looks ecstatic and plants a wet kiss that I struggle out from under.

Fifty years.

Dave emerges beaming from the dining room and hugs her. He reminds me that if I find myself an older woman I can benefit from her pension. Fifty years. They have come a long way from that first meeting at a London Underground station during the Blitz.

"He couldn't survive without her," Mum says. She is taking them out for lunch. Dad has made his case as to why he is doing an equally important job. We are playing Arsenal. Dad has got the tickets through a friend from work and there will be a group of his colleagues at the match. We follow the motorway north and park up to eat sandwiches, but I cannot eat: my stomach tingles with excitement.

Outside the ground, Dad nips to the loo and a miracle happens. The whole Manchester United team starts to file past and I thrust my notebook at them as they do. Andrei Kanchelskis, the pacey Ukrainian winger, is one of the first to sign. Dennis Irwin. Mike Phelan drops my pen and scowls, but when I pick it up he signs. Neil Webb and his wife Shelly are arguing by an expensive-looking car and nobody intrudes.

Finally, the biggest miracle of all, Bobby Charlton is stood in front of me. He couldn't be more polite.

"I'll sign all your things, lads," and he does, managing the bustle around him with an experience that can only be gained through years of adulation. Dad returns and asks if he has missed anything.

The beat of the music, the sense of event, the smell of cheap fast food, cigarette smoke and lager; I love all of it. The Scorpions, *Wind of Change* rings out around the stadium. You have not really heard music until you have felt its beat in a packed arena, have lost yourself in the moment; few other places can provide such a refuge from life, even if that sense ebbs away as the clock runs down prior to the final whistle.

We draw 1-1. Arsenal in yellow and black, the better more successful team in recent years by far. Our agonising wait to win the League still has a little further to run, but we are equal to them today.

Yet change is coming, for me and for the team. For all of us really, and it will twist every which way imaginable. But here and now a sense of togetherness and shared purpose seems to trump all that.

UNITED!

Someone in the work group is drunk. He throws up and sits with his head in his hands, not watching any of it. Sick flecks the seat in front of him.

"He's meant to be out with his missus tonight and he's totally fucked," one of them says.

"No change there then, the stupid tosser," says another. Civil servants at play…

Someone shouts at Ryan Giggs, the kid who is only two years older than me, to 'get in the game' and I see him flinch. David Rocastle is playing for Arsenal, not many years left to him, but the imperious master of the moment.

"It's fast," says Dad, and I note he is impressed, if still a touch guarded. I don't know what else he thinks about the day, how much he enjoyed it. He would never really say, but there will be other visits and I will take that as my clue.

When finally we get home after that first trip I show Theresa and Dave the autographs, but the names don't mean anything to them. Dad asks how Dave expects to win the pools when he doesn't actually know anything about football.

"Don't worry, I know what I'm doing, son," he says.

We will do this a bit in years to come. Sometimes he will drive and sometimes we will get a coach. We will see Eric

Cantona make his home debut against Norwich. Watch him shake hands with Mark Robins, now a Norwich player, before the kick-off. The goal that had saved Alex Ferguson's career had not been enough to keep Robins at United. Despite the free plastic macs they hand out as we enter the stadium, we will get rained on during the rebuilding work, again against Norwich I think. Norwich must have been one of the easier games to get tickets for.

Clayton Blackmore was in our defence for that first game I went to with my father, and a decade later, at a fans forum I have gone to with Darren, I will ask Clayton about it. He says he doesn't remember and we talk about the subsequent match with Arsenal where a big fight between the players broke out. Then we will turn to other things, social chit-chat, visiting parents and so on, and it will occur to me that even being a Manchester United footballer only makes you different to a point.

I go a couple of times a year with Darren, in the period after we have started working together. We will take off an afternoon and morning and usually watch mid-week Champions League games. We play pool and take our chances in Sam Platt's, and tell each other how successful we are. It is not really the other we are trying to convince. We eat breakfast in the Red Café inside the stadium. One year we do a stadium tour. I take a picture of Darren standing at the dugout that will be used at his funeral. I will chat with other fans over lager, possible team selection, the obvious things, but Darren is usually quieter, more reflective; perhaps he subconsciously knows that his time is short, is using the moment to a better end, closing in on his own thoughts whilst he still can.

An alcoholic who hid it well; I didn't know but some did. A group of us piece the whole thing back together in the days before his cremation. His drinking that had somehow morphed from pints with his friends to vodka alone, by the bottle. The lost job; no one was sure if this was because of his drinking, or a trigger to more of it. Likewise, whether he drank because he was depressed, or whether the drinking itself caused the depression. As with all questions in such circumstances, they came too late to make any difference.

There was the car accident he had when three times over the limit, the suspended jail sentence nobody knew about, his black Mazda sports car folded around a lamp post, stricken and useless like a beached ferry. Him unhurt, or at least so far as could be seen. Installing an IT system at the local library that was part of his community service, which he completed because he wanted to even though he did not have to.

A new job offer that was withdrawn because he did not tell his prospective employers about his criminal record, which showed up in the background check. They might still have hired him if he had told them. He said the offer had been dropped because they had decided to restructure, that there would be other job offers, but there weren't.

A few weeks before he dies we eat together at his immaculate house.

"It's going to be OK, Steff," he tells me, and I have no

reason to doubt it. He always called me Steff, as in Steffi Graf, the tennis player, just as in the group we had at that time he was nicknamed Boss, even though he wasn't, that particular role being taken by the unusually named David David (or Dai Dai). While most of us were waiting for our lives to start, we spent a lot of time in the pubs and clubs and curry houses of Coventry, but this turned out to be Darren's life.

I write Darren an email just before Christmas telling him to hang in there, that things will improve. He writes back and his mood has changed. He tells me that they'd better improve. No money, no job, he says. I cannot think what to say and do not reply, and the next I hear, he is dead, discovered by a mutual friend. We are both among those who carry his coffin, in the Bedford crematorium that none of us should be in that day.

The undertakers organised something from the club for his parents. A nice letter from Alex Ferguson, saying he had just heard of Darren's death and that the thoughts of all associated with Manchester United are with them.

I don't go to Old Trafford again for a long time. When I do, it is with my own children, the shadows of my father and of Darren visible to me, if to no one else.

Francesca is the keenest fan, and we first go together to watch them play Swansea. She is eight and wears a huge white England scarf that looks really cute and makes everybody smile. Given David Moyes is our manager, there is not much else to smile about, although we do win that day. Ryan Giggs is playing. A kid when I first watched him, veteran now. She is a Manchester United fan because I am. It is in her now and I am glad of it.

Another time, the two of us go with Annabelle to watch the Europa League quarter final against Anderlecht. Maddie is not interested and tells us that if she comes she will just be a real pain. It is agreed that at four it is too soon for Gabriella. When you are a bit taller, we tell her.

Annabelle asks me what it will be like. I ask what the biggest sports event she has been to before was and she says it was her school sports day.

"It probably won't be anything like that," I say.

There is security now to get close to the ground, which there never used to be. Everything is changing, the world has become less trusting, this the only way to try and keep people safe against the rage that now seems to course right through it. Perhaps the anger is no different to that all those years ago on 9/11, when planes flew into buildings and people held hands and threw themselves from burning infernos raging a hundred floors or more into the sky. It is a further ripple from that day.

In the face of that which appals, there is nothing for it but to cling to the banalities, and some of these have not changed so much. The fish and chips we buy are pretty dubious and part of mine is still frozen in globs of ice, swathed in fat.

We sit against a wall on one of the terraced streets that fringes the ground. Francesca shouts hello as a policeman on horseback rides past us. He smiles; how could he not? Everybody smiles when they meet Francesca. She has a natural way with people that neither I nor my father ever had. Tests have shown that she has a photographic memory for faces, and with her warmth and tendency to hug people I worry about her the least of all my children, which is still a lot. The whole world will always hug her back.

"You look very comfortable down there," he grins as he rides on.

Finally we are in the stadium. Francesca is the old hand; all of this, new to Annabelle, who loves it.

"It's so intense!" she exclaims, and asks me how old Paul Pogba is. I am not entirely sure that it is his then status as the world's most expensive footballer that has piqued her attention.

"Very old," I say.

The stadium is loud, and the game is intense. Ibrahimović and Rojo suffer bad injuries, but eventually we win in extra time.

"That was amazing," says Annabelle as we make our way back to the hotel.

"Of course it was," says Francesca.

On the way back to the hotel Francesca inevitably wants more food, so we go into a petrol station. Annabelle sits on the wall outside and when we return I am relieved to find that she has not been stolen. The queue had been longer than I had expected, but she does not look impressed to hear that I was worried for her. She tells me that she is more than old enough to sit on a wall for a few minutes in a brightly lit, well populated part of Manchester. I wonder if she will be as relaxed when it is her kid sat on a wall. Either way, I hope to be there to see it.

I am glad that they have enjoyed it, that this is

something we have found that we have in common. But as ever, I am not wholly in the moment now that my minor panic has subsided, just as my father was not all those years before. I am thinking to the last game I watched with Darren. Of those who played that day only Rooney and Carrick are still at the club. He wouldn't have known many of the other players.

Things change fast. The moment of togetherness in the stadium is just that. One day, not many years after I am gone, Manchester United will field a team full of players I have never heard of. Yet the memories last longer. I remember the times with my father and with Darren, and I hope that Annabelle and Francesca, and hopefully Maddie and Gabriella on future trips, will remember these things, even when the players have changed again and I am no longer here to recall.

Martin's Journal – Joan

The story of Joan and her family I have turned into a novel that no one will ever publish, indeed no one will ever read, because it is handwritten in my illegible handwriting! Do I regret that it will never be read? It is hard to say. In some ways I would like the story to be remembered at a time when I am no longer capable of telling it, a time I fear is soon approaching. Yet there is also something in having written something that is known only to you and is not diluted through sharing.

But as I sit here now, so many years after both the events and even the secret novel, I have decided to give the outlines of a story that is dramatic in its way and very personal to me. It is not exactly the case that it feels as if all of this could have happened yesterday, but it would be fair to say that it is still very real to me.

My treatment has been ongoing for a while now and I am well set in the rhythm of this place, which makes few demands on me, if truth be told. I feel tireder than I did at the start of all this, but I was always told that that was to be expected. Besides, thinking to some of these things from so long ago takes me out of myself somehow.

Joan was an amazingly beautiful girl who went to Oxford and completely captivated me. I remember her coming down with an MA. You could in those days convert your BA to an MA on payment of £5, which Joan did, and I could only admire her worldliness and a sense somehow that the world would open up for her in a way that it did not always seem to do for me.

Joan and I saw each other often enough over the years, but one summer holiday just before the war we became very close. We seemed to be able to talk to each other in a way that I hadn't with anyone else. We had a connection, an understanding, or at least I thought we did. I could see the world that was before me and she was the only one in it. It is only when you look back at these things that you can spot warning signs, read things into interactions in hindsight that were invisible at the time, or at least not visible to you.

She always showed a lot of interest in the financial side of Holmes & Son and was very curious as to our income and how I saw our future business prospects. But in truth I was infatuated and would have been happy to talk to her about whatever she wanted. I saw it then as making plans; I only realised later that it was just part of the process through which she was determining whether or not she wanted to make plans. I never really thought then as to how the story of her father's failure and her family's poverty (however removed it actually was from the reality) might have affected her, might have had an impact on what she was looking for next.

I was oblivious to all of this, on the cusp, so I thought, of a momentous moment, the weekend when I fully expected that we would get engaged. We had arranged to meet in Shaftesbury, when I was there for the old school dinner and Joan was due to visit her mother at the hotel at the same time.

I cycled with an increasing sense of anticipation. This was our moment, our time, yet when I arrived at Sunridge there was a Rolls Royce in the car park and I started to feel uneasy without quite knowing why. I asked the receptionist for Miss Joan. "She is in the family's private sitting room, sir. I will tell her you are here," said the receptionist neutrally. When I think back to that moment I can still pick up on no hint of a warning in her tone.

Joan appeared, gave me a big kiss, then taking me by the hand, she led me into the sitting room. I will never forget the way she looked at me, even though that look is hard to describe. Affectionate but wary, as if she was somehow there but not entirely there, a plan going into effect that must have been thought through many times in her head but was now a reality being enacted.

When we entered, her father and mother were there, but also sitting on the sofa with them was a well-dressed elderly bloke (he was forty). He had an air about him, a sense of entitlement perhaps, but he did not look at me. Just the briefest of half nods and murmurs, they had clearly talked about me; he knew who I was even if I did not yet know who he was, except of course instinctively and in the only sense that mattered.

His face seemed to redden slightly and he studiously sipped at his tea, as if slightly unsure as to how exactly this would play out, but he knew the odds were very much in his favour.

After what seemed like forever, but probably wasn't, Joan announced, "This is John," and we finally shook hands, the least sincere handshake of my life. "My fiancé," she said whilst I was still grasping his warm and clammy paw.

It surprises me in hindsight how I reacted to this news. I was offered a cup of coffee, which somewhat dazed I sat down and drank, doubtless engaging in polite small talk. Not that I can remember any of that now.

Storming out would not have been the done thing and I never considered it then, although looking back now I wished I had. John, it appeared, was a Harley Street lawyer, and the Rolls Royce outside, of course, was his.

As soon as possible, I made my excuses and left. Joan came with me to the door. I went from being stunned to angry, as none of this made any sense to me. It did not fit with what had gone between us before, was not part of any scenario I had hitherto envisaged. Yet here we were.

"How," I demanded, "could you possibly marry that old man?"

"Don't say anything, Martin," Joan pleaded. "I

can't bear the thought of being poor, and John is a wealthy man. I love my poor father, but he is a hopeless failure; I am marrying a man who is a success!"

One last kiss and I was gone. Everything around me looked the same as I made my way back, but none of it was. I did not attend the wedding.

On their honeymoon Joan discovered the secret that John had carefully hidden from her: he was an alcoholic; and shortly after their wedding his glittering career crashed in ruins as he could no longer maintain the facade. He managed to get a job as an accountant in Bournemouth, but the police were on his trail and he was charged with drink driving! This was before the era of breathalysing, and evidence of erratic behaviour had to be given together with the conclusion of the police surgeon.

Given his fame as one of the country's most famous barristers in his former career, the trial was reported in the national press. Many years later, following further press intrusion, he sued for libel, putting Joan in the witness box.

"Ladies and gentlemen of the jury, look at this beautiful young woman. The police would have you believe that my client was a habitual drunkard. I ask you, would this lovely lady remain happily married to such a man?" They won the case.

In spite of this, things remained very difficult for them. Joan's life was far removed from the one she thought she was going to have, and I did feel for her from a distance. But that was all.

So Joan did break my heart, maybe, but not for long. For all of my anger and sense of disappointment at the time, I quickly realised that marriage between the two of us would have been a total disaster, and my lovely Anna was waiting just around the corner.

I saw Joan only once after that dramatic November day. Mary was about three years old, and we were staying nearby and dutifully called on her parents, Nell and Horan. It was Joan who answered the door. We had arrived in time for afternoon tea. At the table, Joan sat next to me, Anna and Mary were opposite. I noticed Joan, looking at Mary, her eyes filled with tears. Suddenly she put her hand over mine and squeezed it hard. "Oh, my darling Martin, isn't she beautiful." What thoughts were going through her mind, I can only guess. It was the last time we ever met.

I cannot say that I have thought about Joan much during the many happy years that followed with Anna, but as I sit here now convalescing I do find myself thinking back to days gone by and moments like this a little more. Not with a sense of regret, by no means, but with just a realisation of the role chance plays in all our lives. I was all set to embark on something that would not have ended well, was determined to that end, and it was only fate that saved me and brought me to Anna.

They have just been round with the tea trolley. There are a handful of us in the lounge, dozing, reading the paper, staring at the television. A young person would think us the most boring group on earth, no doubt, but I am sure my fellow patients could all tell their own stories about the loves of their youth and beyond. The roads we travel and those we don't. I hope for them too that things turned out alright, but I have no way of knowing.

Bristol – 1994

During term time, I would sometimes come home at weekends, taking the train from Bristol Meads to Newport and then a second, shorter one to Ledbury; I was studying in the city where my father had been carved open a few months before.

I think he grew darker and more withdrawn in the period leading up to his first major health problems. Perhaps it was his age, latish forties, or my own, latish teens, but we particularly did not hit it off at this time. I found him easily irritated, seeming to misunderstand everything I was trying to do, generally unsupportive. He would probably have said the same about me. It was all the usual: Where are you going, where were you, why weren't you here, are you planning on doing some work? – that's all none of your business.

Then chest pains, inconclusive hospital tests, a big mow of the lawn the day before, back to the GP, a test on a treadmill.

"Please just sit down, Mr Graff. That's right, try not to move too much. I'm just going to call an ambulance as your heart is barely working."

Ambulance to Bristol, heart by-pass the following day,

which was conducted by a surgeon later struck off in a scandal involving operations on children.

"Look after Mary if anything happens to me," he had said to Mike and Janet. That night I had a friend round. It had been pre-arranged, which seemed like a good enough reason then but does not now. A girl who was into amateur dramatics and not renowned for her sensitivity, but even with him in hospital and about to go under the knife, I was still a slave to my hormones.

"What is she doing here?" Mum said, somewhat distraught. But after the girl had gone, there wasn't much to say. We never usually struggled to talk to each other, but I couldn't find the right words for what was happening. She worried about everything, so how could she not worry about this? It was beyond my experience and I had no reference point.

I kept thinking of the mower, that this was better than it might have been, but I wasn't sure that the observation would help. I thought that if someone had told me my father was dead and then asked if I wanted a game of snooker in the garage, I would have said yes. I was disturbed by the thought, even if at another level I doubted it was true, not really.

What I did know was that whatever happened over the next few hours, one day she would lose him, a certainty I carried for fourteen years before it turned out to be wrong.

Dave and Theresa were coming up the next morning. Mum was going to the hospital around the time Dad was due to come out of surgery. It was going to be alright, I said.

We heard from the hospital sooner than expected. She hadn't even left for Bristol. I have no idea why we weren't going with her – visitor restrictions, I suppose – and I can't remember who took her as she wouldn't drive on motorways or in cities, or on many other sorts of roads.

"He's not dead, is he?" Mum asks, as Dave takes the phone.

"No, he's OK," says Dave. "He's coming round." He looks at Theresa. "The nurse is called Helen."

The recovery is slow and painful. When home in bed he yells out in pain. He tells Mum not to say anything to the doctor.

"How can I not when you cry out like this?" she says. The GP visits, the same one who Dad will feel misses his cancer years later – vague social friends who don't much like each other, beneath the veneer of occasional country dinner parties.

I make him food which he declares inedible, and we argue, then we hug. He cries a bit, which is something I haven't seen before, would not have imagined possible. I see a glimpse of a side of him he has worked hard to conceal.

The pain continues and the GP returns.

"I have a forty-eight-year-old male who really needs a hospital bed," he says, and Dad ends up back in Hereford hospital for a spell. He couldn't listen to the phone call, didn't want to be back in hospital; said he felt like he was being described as a thing, a specimen, rather than a person. It re-confirmed everything he thought about the GP, which seemed unfair to me, but he had to take his anger and his fear out on someone.

I visit him in the ward after one of my A level exams. Matt is doing his GCSEs. It had been thought that us both doing exams at the same time would create major stress, but that has been overshadowed by all of this.

When Dad comes out we walk in the grounds of the college in Hereford while Mum pops in for a staff meeting.

"It's been a bit of a time, but things will be better now," he says, as we turn slowly round the bright green lawns in brilliant sunshine. It is not really just his heart that he is talking about.

We had argued in previous months about what I should do at university, where I should go. I wanted to read history, but they both thought this would render me unemployable. I was pretty certain I would be that anyway, but their dire warnings did have an effect on me and I chose to do law. The college wanted me to try for Oxford but Dad did not.

I apply anyway and get an interview. My politics teacher has concluded I am a gifted soul who has the misfortune to be living with a lunatic, an idea I did not entirely plant but equally did not entirely disabuse him of either.

Two days at Wadham for interviews and exams. The exams are fine; the interviews are terrible. I feel that they ask me questions without giving me time to read the paper they are based on. They are polished and in control. I am tongue-tied and inarticulate. The green jacket I am wearing does not fit properly and I am far from comfortable in my own skin.

In the evening they take us all to a pub and then the cinema to watch *Aladdin*. "A whole new world," one of the characters sings. I meet someone there who I will meet again in a few different settings over the years. A few of us drink wine until late with some of the undergraduates. Everybody is really nice, but all possess an air of brilliance that I do not. I think it is called confidence, but I did not know that then. They do not offer me a place.

"Father will be pleased," my politics teacher says to Dad at a subsequent parents' evening. Mum says that Dad didn't catch his meaning, missed that this was a dig at him, at his lack of confidence in me. She said my father was just worried about whether I would cope at Oxford, but I resented both his lack of belief and him being proved right, although my real focus was more on my grades than where I went.

Mum said Dad had turned down a place at Oxford because it was for history and he wanted to read physics. He had been accepted into places I was not, and he had declined to go. Did that somehow sum up our relationship? Were we always secretly competing or, rather, was I always coming up short, without him even realising that this was all part of the game?

They were both pleased by my A level results and I could see they were proud I was going to Bristol, where of course you could have all the same conversations about which Oxbridge college you had applied for and how many As you had got in your A levels, as if you were there.

I think wherever I had gone I would have faced the same challenges. Not the work; I was conscientious, which was enough. I went to virtually all the lectures and tutorials and did the reading. I once skipped a lecture to go to the library which did rather seem to confirm certain things. The course interested me to a point. The trick was to stay on top of it. I did office hours, nine to five, with the occasional day off to nurse a hangover. It was fairly obvious it would be fine, if unspectacular.

The challenge was more everything else. In amongst the drinking and the table football and the nightclubs and the day trips to Weston-super-mare and the cricket and the late-night chats in people's rooms, which were earnest and deep and now forgotten, there were other difficulties.

I lost a lot of weight in my first year, as the food in Wills Hall was terrible, virtually inedible, and at eighteen my metabolism easily shrugged off alcohol and midnight pizzas. Things I made in my room were of questionable quality and nutritional value: pasta boiled in a kettle, Pot Noodles, peanut butter and crisps, possibly some liquorice.

You could see the bones of my ribcage more prominently than should have been the case. A house share that didn't work in the third year, a sense of not quite finding what I was looking for or knowing what I wanted to do afterwards.

I was quite awkward in a lot of ways. Bristol was never quite what I'd hoped it would be. I was never quite who I thought I might be. It was all more fragmented and transient than I had expected, but I left with good friends, a degree and a better understanding of myself.

Many of those I shared some wild times with I still see

at the occasional birthday or drinks party. Things seem easier and more comfortable now. We have all grown up. Solicitors, barristers, a regional television presenter, high-flying civil servants, other jobs that have been explained to me but which I do not fully understand, although they seem to be quite successful. Even the wild Irishman, whose only piece of writing in his final year was a short note he placed under his tutor's door to say that he was going nuts, is now a respected tennis coach.

I still played chess; I was the fifth best player in the university. But the best was an International Master and I was nowhere near his standard. It was like Keith Talent in *London Fields*. He gets to the darts final, but when he comes up against a real player he is shown up for what he is. It didn't shake my enthusiasm, but it did give me an insight into my limitations.

I had discovered books by this point. If I did stay in Bristol for the weekend, I would rarely work on a Friday, rather shut myself away to read: Miller, Camus, Sartre, Orwell, Byatt, Barnes, McEwan, Amis, Iain Banks. I was interested in artists and outsiders and societies breaking down, places where things happened at the margins. Worlds of which I knew little, as Martin might have said. I was also now open to the sorts of books my mother liked. *Wuthering Heights* sent a dark chill through me. Unquiet slumbers on Yorkshire moors indeed. William Blake. Innocence and experience; I was a mix of both by now, as well as of both my parents, even if I hadn't formed that thought back then. One early spring day, with pockets of melted snow still heaped in the corners of the quad, they came to visit me, the three of them: Mum, Dad and Martin. This a few months after Anna's death. Martin was determined that life had to go on.

"What other choice can you make?" he asked me once. I remembered the trip I had made to the Island for the funeral; part preoccupied by a phone call I needed to make that day, more rooted in my own world than I should have been. But now Martin was here in Bristol, to see me doing something he would have liked to have done, if things had been different for him, if it hadn't have been for the shop, his father, a hand he had dutifully made the best of even if he wouldn't quite have chosen it for himself. Not that he ever said any of this.

We sat in my room, which was numbered M12, and drank tea in freshly scrubbed cups that I could see they were all still doubtful of. The room had a wooden floor and gas fire, which none of them thought smelt quite right, so I had to turn it off. Wrapping paper and Oasis posters on the walls – perhaps in hindsight not the most original or coolest of looks. It wasn't en-suite, and the shower facilities were questionable in this, the old block of Bristol's grandest hall of residence.

Apparently the head of the hall liked law students from state schools and there were lots of us there, in amongst others whose parents owned half of Surrey. Not that it made much difference in the Wills Hall formals (bring your own bottle of wine), the alcohol being the only element of the meal that contained any nutrients. Then there were the discos that followed: Whigfield's

Saturday Night, Oasis, Pulp, Supergrass, and Take That, now fashionable again. One of the tutors had a printout on his door explaining why Alanis Morissette did not understand the meaning of the word ironic. Some of us thought he was trying too hard.

Nobody talked about Dad having been in hospital here in this city, not long ago. I have no idea what I told them about Bristol or whether I showed them around, where we ate or what we looked at. I don't remember Mum and Dad ever talking about the time when Mum lived in Bristol either. Certainly never about the letters that they wrote to each other back then. What it was like. Either then, or coming back. Perhaps they did. Perhaps these were things that were theirs to share with each other and no one else.

Autumn Harvest

Red streams the sunset on the hill tonight
And now, as woodsmoke drifts from cottage chimneys
It is the time and it is the season to mark
The turning year with Harvest Festival.
Rejoice in the time to reap and strew the church
With gaudy show of earth's fruit, all safely
Gathered in. Children bear baskets
In procession, following the pattern
Worn by countless footsteps on grey flags
Down so many long-forgotten years.
And they know, without the telling,
That it is right and fitting to give thanks,
Joining with past voices, as darkness slowly falls,
For centuries of praise still echo round these walls.

M. G.

Martin's Journal – Anna

Martin wrote about Anna in his journal, and Aunty Noreen (Martin's brother Hugh's wife) recorded the events around Anna's death in her diary. These accounts follow below, along with a letter Anna wrote soon after my father's heart surgery in 1994.

It seemed to me that Martin did not really say all that much about Anna in his journal. Perhaps he saw it as either too personal or too painful. How we choose to write about those who are closest to us is something I have also had to consider in writing about my family. What should be said, and when are things better left un-said? How do we balance the need to tell the story against the needs of those who are no longer in a position to determine how they are being given a voice? I have been less reticent than Martin was. It might be said that I appear to be more open than my own father was, although it is impossible to say if the course I have chosen is necessarily a better one.

* * *

I suppose you will be wondering why I have left my darling Anna until toward the end of these reflections.

I think it is mainly because I knew that thinking about her for these pages would sadden me. All those years when I and everyone else assumed that she would outlive me. It never occurred to anyone that she might go first, and as a consequence I was not prepared, if it is ever really possible to prepare for a loss like this, which I doubt. Many feel that they can draw strength from those they were close to after they are gone and whilst this is true, mostly I feel a sense of absence.

I wanted to focus more on the dead than the living in this work. Yet I do not feel that our stories are mine to tell; much of what went between us belongs just to the two of us. I still feel shaken by her final illness and that is certainly not something that I want to talk about. All marriages have their moments, but I would say in short that I was truly blessed.

It does not seem like it would be enough to leave it at that, so I thought, would share some stories from around the time of our marriage and my first meeting with her family. In doing this I did find myself thinking to a lot of people I have not thought to in a long time, and they are all still very real to me. There is hope that springs from that.

Before we were married, Anna had qualified as a senior nurse and left Ryde Hospital to work in Bournemouth, returning to Ryde as a staff nurse on the men's surgical ward, and deputy night sister after our wedding. For this responsible job she was paid £1.12 per week, which would have included board and lodging had she wanted it. The average wage for a man at this time was £3 per week. She felt, with the best will in the world, that she was a bit hard done by. After a month or two she heard that Cowes needed a nursing sister. Up to then they had relied solely on station ambulance men, but the regulations had now changed and this had created an opportunity.

Anna applied for this job, and cycled to Cowes to be interviewed. This being a management appointment, she had been told it came with a head-of-a-department title, a silver bag and a personal seat in the management canteen!

The MD said, "Well, you've got all the qualifications we need, but you are very young; you only look about sixteen to me." Anna was very much on her dignity, "Sixteen, for goodness sake! I am twenty-three and a married woman."

"Yes," the MD said, "that's just as well in view of the challenges you will have to deal with!" He was right! He said he would ring the hospital matron, and if she agreed Anna was up to the job it was hers. Anna then enquired about salary.

He said, "We thought £6 per week." We were on our way.

We had married in '42 without me ever having met a single member of Anna's Irish family. Her father had died in 1938 shortly before I met her, leaving her mother with eight children to look after, five of them still at school.

Originally she had been running two farms with the aid of Anna's elder brother, Michael; Anna's father, having been a colourful character, was involved in setting up a farmers' cooperative to operate a creamery in the nearby village. He was a JP and it appears that he had acquitted a member of the IRA (no connection with today's IRA), and my mother-in-law recalled the Black & Tans breaking down the door before storming into the house to shoot her husband. In true family fashion he talked his way out of that one.

Shortly after that, he heard that on a particular night the IRA were going to burn down the Shanagolden creamery. So, there he was with his fellow farmers, galloping around the countryside on his horse, shotgun in one hand, ready to rally to the defence of the creamery. Blasting away with their shotguns, they sent the IRA packing, never to return! It is extraordinary when I think to it, the experiences people have.

In '46, four years after we were married, we went together to Ireland for the first time. Having spent a night in London, we caught the steamer of course, to Holyhead, then the boat to Dublin where we were met by two of Anna's former colleagues. They had arranged lodgings for us.

Food in England was even more severely rationed than it had been during the war. We had a Labour government with a passion for controlling everything, but things were very different here and it was amazing to suddenly be able to eat as much of whatever you wanted again, as if stepping back into an earlier and more optimistic age.

So I met my extended family for the first time.

One of the family was Maurice, my brother-in-law. A humorous character, he looked, dreamed and sounded like a farmer, as he drove us around in the pony trap commenting on the crops and the cattle. However, appearances can be deceptive, and in point of fact he knew very little about farming, having spent most of his working life as a smartly dressed salesman in the menswear department of a large store.

After a special lunch at the Lake Hotel, we went out for a drive in a family car around the lake. The driver was busy pointing out legendary beauty spots, until interrupted by mother-in-law Lesley, a skilled driver.

"Young man, attend to your driving; if a horse comes down we shall all be killed."

"That wouldn't worry me at all, madam," he replied. "I know when I die I shall go straight to heaven, on account of the fact I've never done a wrong thing in my life!"

"I wouldn't count on it," commented mother-in-law drily. "You are a terrible liar, for a start." I did see some of Anna in her mother, it has to be said.

When it was time to return to England her whole family were in floods of tears; my bond with all of them had been formed and would endure.

It was when we were living at our old flat in Wood Street that Mary was born. We were overjoyed, and obviously there had never been such a baby before or since. We were also overwhelmed by the awesome responsibility of keeping this perfect expression of humanity alive.

Before long we were able to obtain a mortgage to build a pretty little house, with plenty of land for the children to play in. However, we were desperately hard-up. The business was not doing well. My father had run out of steam and times had changed. The things we had once done which were successful now were less so.

After my father's death, the business continued to go from bad to worse. I soon accepted an offer for our main premises from Boots the Chemist. The shoe shop was abandoned, and a smaller menswear shop opened in a property opposite Woolworths, now the Abbey National. The Shanklin shop we also sold, and not for a good price in hindsight. Later we became involved in the affairs of the Wight Starling & Piling Co – disastrous, best forgotten. It was a mixture of everything: changing circumstances, my lack of, I don't know what exactly, but something.

For all of the challenges, Anna was with me throughout, as a calming and supportive presence. She provided a wonderful environment for Mary and Mike to grow up in and we had so many happy years. I think that what I learnt is that money comes and goes and crises are generally survived. There are things that go deeper and these are what it is important to hold onto.

Introduction to
Aunty Noreen's Diary

Every year my mother gave my Aunty Noreen a copy of the *Good Housekeeping Diary and Account Book*, which was renamed the *Good Housekeeping Diary* in 2000, perhaps in commemoration of the millennium. Between 2001 and 2007 the series was renamed again as *Good Housekeeping Everyday*, and what happened to it after that I cannot say. Noreen started a 2008 diary but did not finish it, and it is now lost in any event.

My mother the diary giver outlived Noreen the diary writer by six short months in 2008. They had other connections too. Both were literate, and despaired when apostrophes were misused, as it was alleged Noreen's son Richard sometimes did when advertising potatoe's (sic) for sale at his pub. For many in the family the day they came to say goodbye to Noreen at her funeral was also the last day that they would see my mother.

The two of them were linked by the gift, the annual Christmas present that spanned all the way back to 1979. Noreen wrote an entry most days. I look at the volumes now as they are all laid out on her daughter Janet Morter's table, in her house on the Isle of Wight.

The covers are mainly dark blacks and browns, with a handful of bright red ones from 1981, 1982, 1986, 1987, 1988 and 1992. All are smooth to the touch, other than 2001 which is much rougher, although you can only tell this by actually stroking the cover. The silver lettering on blue background gives no hint of this difference from its siblings.

The books are a little smaller than A5. There are pages in the middle dedicated to a 'Guest Menu for August'. I did not know Noreen wrote a diary until, while on the Island for a family wedding, I mentioned to Janet that I was working on this book. A few weeks later I got up early one Sunday morning and drove to Portsmouth. I was due on the 10am, but managed to make it onto *St Clare* for the 9am crossing. It felt strange to be on the Solent by myself, with no family with me, even if this was all part of the exercise of trying to understand a bit better what had gone before, to find a way to share it in some way – a day as a detective, unsure what it was I might find.

Noreen's handwriting was better than Martin's, which was something, if not as good as Mum's. Certain themes emerged very quickly. She wrote a lot about the weather: high winds, and boats stopped by fog, and the lashing rain.

'Snow from Sat. night still V. thick + temps down to -5c, though wind dropped. J arrived from Yarmouth 3.30, & met by R after prolonged attempts to get home from Kim's. Colin forced to go back to Aldershot without M & the boys' was an entry from 1981.

Significant events were re-highlighted year on year: Hugh's broken leg in 1960, Richard in hospital in 1963.

Much later, the arrival of Sky television in 1996 was deemed worthy of repeating in future editions.

Birthdays were also recorded. In 1981, she wrote that I was six and she had sent me a Meccano tractor set. A few years later a £5 book token. Later still, rather than references to my birthday, that date came to feature repeat mentions of an upgrade to the toilet, which I tried not to take personally.

She had been a deputy head, and a formidable one at that. She wrote of somebody throwing a brick through her office window and how she essentially shrugged it off. I mentioned this to Janet who said Noreen would have been furious, but that didn't show in her writing. She wrote of dealing with drunken parents and psychotic pupils, managing school office politics, all with a steeliness and skill that she undoubtedly possessed. She was a magistrate too, but while she recorded when she was in court and when she finished, she never wrote of the cases she heard.

There were some entries about times in our own childhood that we had spent with her, such as this one from Sunday Dec 30th, 1979. 'Cleaned up kitchen floor & laid new tiles – v. pretty. Ben, Matthew came in pm & Mary and Colin for a meal in evening. M&C = 8 years.'

There were also some anecdotes from the parenting of her own children, in one of which she mentioned waiting up for Richard from 5.45am to 7.45am, desperate with worry, before it transpired that he had been sleeping at a friend's house.

I remember seeing her and Hugh when we were older children - picnics in the field, shooting with Hugh's guns.

She always had a certain intelligence and approachable grandness about her. In 1994 she had a stroke and her writing became unreadable for a while, before improving again. Her recovery was a long and slow one and she said it did change her attitude to things, but she managed to go forward.

Noreen's Diary – 1994

Monday 5th September –

What a day! It began normally and we got on with repainting the shed wall. After lunch, we went to the hospice to see Anna. Wonderful caring feel to it and Anna seemed bright despite a broken arm. Later we heard from Martin that there was no cure in prospect, so perhaps 2 weeks or a month, not much more.

Saturday 10th September –

Martin rang early to say Anna had settled into the hospice and we hope to see her tomorrow.

Sunday 11th September –

Saw Anna with H & Rich and it demanded a lot of self-control from me as she looked so frail and thin. Home to clean up in garden.

Tuesday 13th September –

Prepared soup for Anna who came out of the hospice this P.M. We ate in the garden.

Thursday 15th September –

H off early with ferrets so another early start. Martin here in evening for a rabbit casserole, so only a bit of gardening today.

Saturday 17th September –

Anna died at 7am – the end of a long association with many happy memories. May she rest in eternal peace. Day was confused by this news but I did my Chequers duties, came home for a snack lunch then to Janet's to help with the children. Anna is to be cremated on Friday.

Friday 23rd September –

What a day – the requiem mass, the get together at Michael's then the evening meal with Janet and Paul. In all the trauma, it was a wonderful day in Anna's memory.

A Letter from Anna – 1994

Carmel
Stonepitts Close
Ryde
Isle of Wight

My dear Colin,

We talk to Mary every day and it would seem that you are now making good progress.

Trying to sleep in a Hospital ward is no easy task as we can both testify.

We are sending you a small token which we hope you will spend on something you need.

It must have helped you having your family rally round in support.

Make the most of the rest and treatment. Concentrate on getting back to full strength as soon as possible.

The Summer has arrived today and hopefully we will have a long spell.

With love & best wishes for a speedy recovery.
Anna & Martin

Ghosts – 1995

"Of course they exist," says Martin. "How could they not? I'll never forget that house. Not ever. When I woke in the night there were figures around the bed, all looking at me, just looking at me," he pauses, the silence drawing me in closer. "I just kept the light on and read. What else could I do?" His face is frozen, his eyes somehow accentuated in the ensuing stillness. He delivers his lines with the air of an actor. It is a story he has told me before.

We are both comfortable in the silence, as we sit in the kitchen of his house in the late evening. A year on from Anna's death everything is as clean and tidy as it ever was but somehow more empty, more functional than when she was here. More of a house and less of a home. Something I think he senses too, but knows cannot be changed with her gone. Whilst not in the process of falling into the sea, like their last house, this one too has problems: set back from a main road, it has been burgled twice in recent years.

"I can't bear the thought of people looking at my things," said Anna at the time.

It's a dormer bungalow, with lots of internal glass, small kitchen, but bigger dining room and sitting room.

278

Royal blue carpets. The garden, with its elaborate fish ponds and greenhouse rammed with tomato plants, is a suntrap that smells of summer at its height.

Fixed to the wall of the stairway is a framed piece of writing in elaborate lettering that starts *Go placidly amid the noise and haste...* It speaks of your career, however humble, as a true possession in changing times, and a universe no doubt unfolding as it should – be careful, strive to be happy, that sort of thing. I would often read it if I went to the toilet in the night, which was not every night in those days. Sometimes, I would listen in the stillness, to the bleat of a ferry's horn on the Solent, the ticking of the clock on the landing, my father snoring upstairs.

Martin tells me about the hospice movement, for which he is now a fundraiser. A caricature of him in this role hangs in the hallway and will eventually find a new home in Mike's games room. The day before Anna died she had a beautiful haircut, he says.

There were no good choices toward the end. One of the few times I saw my mother cry was when she told me that Anna had said she had wished she had died the year before, on the operating table. Anna could remember her childhood but not much beyond, although she still knew who everybody was.

"When are we going home?" she would ask Martin.

"This is home," he would say.

"Yes, of course it is," she would reply.

He's long since moved from drinking half-milk, half-coffee to martinis. I'm drinking beer. Working in a holiday camp on the other side of the Island for the summer and staying with him while I do. He is easy to talk to in some ways. Roughly the same mass of contradictions as the rest of us. He has extreme views on law and order, but is a committed, and by all accounts popular, prison visitor. He thinks drug dealers should be shot, but when a family friend runs into completely unexpected difficulties, he is supportive. The key is to gently steer him off his soapbox. Perhaps that's the secret with all of us.

He has always been a good storyteller and, for years, telling me and Matt a bedtime story was a part of the summer holiday ritual. But his own attempts to write were a disappointment to him, although I remember one very good short story he wrote, now lost.

When we first moved to Hereford, we stayed with him and Anna while Mum and Dad sorted out the new house. There were fights with water pistols, games of swingball, which Anna was to ban in future years. As we got bigger it looked more inevitable that either I was going to decapitate Matt or, more likely, vice versa.

But the way my grandfather tells this, this thing about ghosts around his bed, does not feel like a story. He's too matter of fact, even if he does have a certain disposition to this sort of thing. I can almost sense what the figures might have looked like, even though he has not described them.

Though in many ways as different as two people could be, Martin and Theresa shared an interest in mediums and tarot cards, although I doubt they knew that they had this in common. Theresa said she and Dave had been to a séance in the 1970s. There were people milling around in the crowd to gain information before the event started, which she thought was a bit odd, but you know… She even mentioned Helen to one of them. But nothing. Nothing.

They went home and they wept.

Dad and Matt both say they saw Mum immediately after she died. I did not, and both resented it and hoped that they had seen her. It was something that could only be placed in the category of the unexplained. However, a few years previously, when the four of us were driving past Quarr Abbey very late one evening, something shrouded and luminous seemed to cross the road just in front of us, oblivious to all around it but clearly moving, then gone. "Did you see that?" Mum had said. My father and brother had not seen anything, but I had.

And perhaps if I had seen this figure at Quarr, then what my brother and father thought they saw might have been real too, and that would mean… I don't know… something… and in the absence of everything, sometimes something has to be enough. The slightest hint that there might be other things, other realms, other ways of being… that we cannot quite touch but might occasionally catch a glimpse of.

Bognor – 2000

I get the train from London and Dad picks me up at the station. "I'm sorry," I say and he nods. He pats me on the shoulder and Mum hugs me, saying that it wasn't the initial heart attack but the subsequent drugs they gave him at the hospital to prevent another one.

"It's rare, but he had a very bad reaction to them and died instantly."

Back at the flat, Theresa is shaken.

"He was just on the floor," she says. "He told me he had twenty pounds in his pocket that might be useful. I told him Matt was on his way and he nodded." I acknowledge the point, irrationally jealous that I was not mentioned in the interaction. "He was very calm and he didn't really say anything after that. He was just cleaning the bathroom this morning, so it doesn't make sense. We'd been watching television. Just the usual, you know."

The doctor arrives and Theresa embraces him. He is in his fifties I would guess, corpulent and stately, dishevelled in a vaguely patrician sort of way, with greying hair that need washing, rumpled shirt and protruding stomach.

Before he can speak, Theresa says, "What happened, what happened? He saw you last week and you said he was fine. How can this be? How can this be?"

She half hugs, half shakes him and he hugs her back, before wriggling free, much like we used to as children.

"I told him his life was not in immediate danger, in that moment, as we were talking. That's what I told him. I also told him that he was in the final stages of heart disease." He speaks with a certain gravitas that is both calming and somehow underscores the finality of the moment. There is compassion and a sense of empathy, but no surprise. The doctor has done all this many times before.

"He told me, you said he was fine," she says. "He was fine."

We sit quietly that evening, sometimes wandering out to stand on the balcony, breathing in the warm summer evening air. That everything looks the same is both extraordinary and entirely as it should be. It's just Dave; he can't see it anymore, unless of course he can.

I think that the day of my own death will be similar, as will the day of all our deaths: in a world where so many other things will be happening, and where the sky and the season will doubtless be unremarkable. Days will outrun us all.

We pause to peer at photographs on the sideboard as if looking at them for the first time, Theresa unusually quiet, knitting untouched.

"I was just talking to him," she says to herself.

"He wasn't meant to be here at all," Theresa says later, as the two of us stand on her tiny balcony.

I ask what she means.

She says that Dave's parents had fled Lithuania around

1900, before Dave was born, after the man who would have been his uncle had been murdered by two soldiers. He had been shot, seemingly randomly, outside his house.

Except it was not random.

"Anti-Semitism did not start with Hitler," she says with a sigh. "So they fled on a boat. They had booked their passage to America, but when they reached London they were told that they were in New York. How were they meant to know any different?

"That was when they changed their name to Graff. It had been Wengrow, but they wanted to make it sound more English. They did not really know what they were doing.

"Still, if the boat had gone to America, Dave would have been born there and we would never have met. None of this could have followed. Whoever cheated them out of America, I am grateful."

She turned and walked back into the flat and the moment was gone. It was the only time I would hear this story. I mentioned it to Dad once, but he shrugged and I could not tell whether he did not know it, was not interested, or if the shrug indicated something else, perhaps simply that it did not matter now, but his reticence might have run deeper than that. He was always wary of opening up the past. Whatever the truth, I never did learn more about this.

It will only take fourteen years for me to be the only one who was there that night to be left, looking back on a time when I marked the loss of my grandfather with others who are now also all gone.

That night we light candles. I sleep on the sofa, the flickering light keeping me awake, but blowing them out seems very wrong. In the morning it is clear that my grandmother forgot they were still burning, and blows them out as soon as she enters the room, with a slightly flustered look.

I don't even have a dark-coloured suit with me, but it doesn't seem to matter. We stand in the bleak cemetery of stone, which is on a vast scale beyond anything that comes to mind when you think to Christian churchyards. Huge slabs of marble, a special section for the Cohens, a stone that says the mother of a teenager who died in a car crash will be in anguish forever; these become lodged in my mind.

There are no flowers here. Jews believe that the living and the dead should be kept separate. Instead, rocks and pebbles have been placed by some of the graves. There is a tap to wash your hands on leaving, to symbolise life, but it conjures up other associations for me.

Mum says she doesn't know where she is going. Theresa tells her it will be alright. There is not quite a tension between them, but it is not quite a connection either.

"He's arrived, poor soul," my Mum will say as he reaches the cemetery. Again, it is all different from what we know. A simple car, a plain coffin placed on a cart to be moved inside for the service, and then onwards for the burial.

Dad says the Hebrew prayers fluently, which impresses everyone, death and endings bringing him back to his beginnings.

It is a long, solemn walk to the grave. Theresa is briefly furious that there is a slight gap between the hole that has been dug for his final resting place and Helen's grave, before Dad reminds her why this is, that the place she thought should be for Dave, is not, because one day it will be for her.

Theresa's brother Lesley, who was one of eight, and his partner Bernie are in among the mourners. Wise and sympathetic, we hardly know them really, but we are all joined together in this.

"Back then I didn't know he was gay," she has told us. Lesley was a ballet dancer and then a tailor and they lived in a house that was painted pink. But it was illegal in those days and people did not say.

Bernie cannot manage the walking and is driven on a buggy. He tells Theresa he feels breathless. She tells Mum that this does not sound good. Two weeks later, he is buried in the London clay of a neighbouring cemetery.

It is the Jewish tradition to literally bury your dead. The rabbi throws bags of sacred books into Dave's grave. We all appreciate the irony. Then, as he somehow moves a little further away from us and a little closer to Helen, the men pick up shovels and spoon the earth in over them, and over him.

'To know him was to love him' will be inscribed on his stone, which is similar to the inscription on Helen's grave. We will all be mentioned by name.

"Was he a believer?" our cousin Simon asks of Theresa. Simon had once been jailed for something to do with a chemist's that he used to own that no one ever elaborates on. He seems to have been rehabilitated these days.

"He said it was all fairy stories," she says.

Simon nods. "That's not nothing."

Martin's Journal –
Going Home – 2001

I think I have spent enough time looking back now and it is time to look forward again. Today is the last day of my treatment in this place and tomorrow I will be going home, to the house I once shared with Anna and now live in alone. There are things I am looking forward to: going to Rotary again, catching up on all the gossip, even if there will be more of it surrounding illnesses, and worse, than strictly speaking I care for. This is what happens when everybody gets old.

I want to go to the yacht club to drink a large gin and tonic whilst looking across the water to the ferries making their way in and out of the harbour. Water I have known since I was a boy, mainly in peacetime but also during war. I want to see Mike again and to stand with him in his house, which is on the site of my father's old place. The Holmeses have a lot of history here and more will follow.

There are roads I want to drive on, walks I want to take, many others I have not seen for too long who I will be catching up with. I have not flown a kite for nearly seventy years and I have resolved to buy one and to launch it on Fishbourne beach, on the strip of stone and sand in front of Coastguard Cottage. Mary will be coming at the weekend; no creatures on earth could be closer than we are and it will be lovely to see her, Colin and the boys. Simple things really, but they are what I want.

I will tell everyone that I am rested and feel better, and in that moment it will be the truth. I sense somehow though that it might not really be the case, however confident my assertions. Partly it is how my body feels: tired, less responsive; partly it is just a sense that this really is another phase ahead of me, and a more uncertain one at that.

Looking back to when I was young has reminded me that I no longer am. What I could do then is not what I can do now, and the fact that I know more does not fully compensate and is somehow double-edged in any event. My time is finite.

I miss all of those who have gone and they all remain very dear to me, especially Anna and my mother of course, but also him in his way. I have enjoyed spending time with all of them again whilst writing this, even if he was just as difficult as when he was alive and all the more authentic for that. But in the end you have to live with the living, just as they must do the same after I have gone.

They say that all lives are remarkable, and I do not know whether or not this is true. But I have found mine full and rewarding, if not without its challenges and disappointments. More normality, I think.

I have no final advice or words of wisdom as I close these pages. I hope the reader has enjoyed my stories. I have enjoyed speaking with you, making this connection or re-acquaintance, depending on who you are.

My bag is packed and the room in which I have been sleeping has now been de-personalised again, all ready for its next inhabitant. I wish whoever it is well, but beyond that I can do no more.

Rotary, the yacht club, a gin and tonic, these are my final thoughts for this journal, because they speak to my tomorrow. Tomorrow is all any of us ever has and it transpires that I do have a piece of final advice after all. You will have to forgive an old man for not getting as quickly from A to B as once he did.

Simply, make the most of it.

Mary's Journal – 2003-2004

Μy mother kept a journal for six months between 2003 and 2004. It was intended to focus on her teaching. However, it also captured a number of significant changes for the family, including one of her friends being quizzed (wrongly) as a murder suspect. The journal covers the period in which her first (and only at this point) grandchild Annabelle turned one. She would be six when her grandmother died. We have a photo of Annabelle sitting on her lap perhaps a year or so earlier, a link between the generations broken all too soon. Theresa is also in these pages, as is Flora, Katharine's grandmother.

What follows is an abridged version of Mary's journal.

* * *

3 September 2003

Term has begun. I intend to record key events of this teaching year. This may not give me something sensational to read on the train, but may help me remember exactly what the year was like. Time moves by so quickly and I thought this might prove a way of capturing some of what would otherwise be lost in a blur.

I was telling Ben the story about people always assuming that blind students will somehow be amazingly well behaved, as if their blindness in some way was part of a wider virtue. Of course, this is not the case. There is no link, the whole point is that people are people and all are different. Any assumptions that are based on someone acting or being a certain way because of this or any other condition always grate with me, even if they are generally born more from a lack of understanding and thought, rather than any real malevolence.

13 September

A full teaching week has now passed. The new AS Group has 10 students – my biggest ever group + not really feasible. Some may drop out, I suppose. They are a mixed bunch with a couple of really worrying conditions.

After I had explained that Shakespeare was censored in my day, Maria asked me if piano legs were covered then. I said I hoped I did not belong to the Victorian age, but when you are 17 the 60s obscenity trial of Lady Chatterley's Lover must seem pretty remote. I always feel my age when this happens!

17 September

A long gap, due to the usual pressure of the early days of term – it does not get any easier. I am only in my fifties, but I don't know what it is really. I feel I have less energy than I once did, need more recovery time. It happens to everyone I suppose, but it does weigh on my mind somewhat. I often get home exhausted & barely able to speak, aching all over. It's a horrid feeling, a kind of numbness & it often seems to happen when the day is too long, too taxing. I know I won't be able to do this indefinitely, yet I have a dread of giving up.

It is Annabelle's birthday today & I am so happy about her. She is so new and so perfect. So much ahead for her, I think to my parents Anna and Martin who would have loved to have seen her, to be a part of this. I feel them close when I hold her.

21 September

Annabelle's birthday lunch in Warwick Gates. She was so charming & had wonderful presents. It was good to see Ben & Matt & see everyone enjoying the gathering. Katharine's parents + Grandma were there. Grandma determined to come in spite of falling last week & knocking out her front teeth. Mat & Kate helped cook & Kate was a trooper in cleaning, washing up etc. A very happy day. Ben & K very proud of their little daughter understandably. Got home v. tired & not looking forward to work.

22 September

Hard times. AS group v. silly indeed. So much for the average 16-17 yr old today being mature in comparison with previous generations.

Colin working hard too, I worry that he does too much. Every day there seems to be some drama or big meeting. He is doing a lot of miles at the moment.

I worry that he doesn't think enough about what happened to him. Not that I would want him to dwell on it of course, but he does need to look after his heart and I am not sure he always does. That is what you are for, he will say.

25 September

A level group v. civilised & rational compared to the As group in the afternoon. M is particularly annoying, as she interrupts with inane comments about things that bear no relation to the text. Her loud voice is v. dominant & it took all my patience not to say something sarcastic. The irony of it is that I had her for a tutorial first thing in the morning & stressed the need to avoid speaking out of turn about irrelevancies. I suppose the time lag was too long for her to remember. Felt really fed up when I got home, esp. as will have to do all the homework as K. is sick.

27 September

Surprise visit from Ben, Katharine & Annabelle as Ben needed help with his stats for his MBA. Colin was v. tired but did his best, he hates stats. Annabelle slightly poorly – another cold. Good to see them though.

I did a roast and in the afternoon we all curled up in the sitting room. It is still funny to think of your children visiting with their children. It doesn't seem so long since, well, this is what time is and how it travels.

28 September

Arthritis so bad I had difficulty walking at all this am. A very bad night during which the pain stopped me sleeping, this cannot be right. Had a quiet day & felt better by the end. I'm dreading winter, as so much of this is caused by cold.

There is always the ideal of a country winter, brilliant snow and glowing log fires, but the reality is always different. I hate the journey to college in the dark and the bitterness in the air. My whole body seems to move more slowly, everything seems more difficult. Was it always like this? I think not. I have never liked winter, but I notice its challenges more than I once did.

2 October

As group particularly silly when asked to compose an alliterative couplet. Should not be surprised as students are horribly immature & love to shock. (W in particular.) Am delighted at prospect of weekend. On getting home find K had not been able to come to clean again. It feels the last straw after this grim week. Things which should not be getting on top of me somehow are.

5 October

Ben's birthday. Great news – Annabelle started walking this week. Colin has some amazing pictures of her birthday via his digital camera/new computer. It is quite something – though I have yet to get to grips with the computer as he spends hours on it.

He is always like this with a new gadget. I just want to know how something works, am most interested by the outputs (in this case the pictures) but he really wants to understand, to master all of it, to test things out, his scientific personality coming to the fore as it so often does.

12 October

Yet another fine weekend. The autumn has been unparalled after an amazing summer and the apple trees in the orchard are all red and gold. It all looks so perfect, the air so fresh, this time of year always speaks to newness for me. All that thing of going back to school in autumn months, which I have of course done for most of my life.

Ben phoned in the evening. He seemed reasonably cheerful. I got the sense that things were going quite well for him at work, that he was enjoying what he was doing. I think they are both also getting more sleep now, which has to help.

20 October

Latest College drama: 2 students from the As English group have been suspended. It appears that A was attacked by W, who struck him with his cane while J prevented him from leaving. Hitting someone with a brain tumour over the head is an appalling thing & they had to be suspended. This is the 1st time that anyone from an Eng. Group has been suspended, so I was really shocked. The group is easier to teach when it's a little smaller, but that is hardly the point.

Spoke to a BBC Radio 4 producer who wants to recruit students to keep an audio diary in the period leading up to A levels. Suggested, H, P and S. Have some concerns over D, but he is certainly a "different" character.

24-27 October

Embarked on trip to Dorset – Swanage – with Theresa. Long drive after collecting T who was v. pleased to see us. It did all feel like an adventure, but I always do a doubletake when we see her without Dave. She has coped admirably but it saddens me that she has to. Of course this is what happens, another reminder that time keeps moving.

We stayed at the Pines Hotel – a 3-star place with some somewhat depressing décor, but amazing sea views. I went for a walk on the sea wall with Colin before dinner, he was quiet, reflective. It is possible to know someone well and still not always know what they are thinking, I understand that now. Clocks change on Sat/Sun 25/26 but had some evening light tonight. Wonderful food at dinner – restaurant is excellent & looks out over the sea.

Amazing weather throughout stay. T. not able to walk far when we visited Corfe Castle, Lulworth Cove & Lulworth Castle. But she seemed to enjoy the expeditions, different places, doing things. Staff at hotel very friendly & helpful, whenever we stay anywhere I always think to *Fawlty Towers*, but fortunately it was nothing like that.

Colin took photos with new camera – he is v. thrilled with it. When we got home on Monday 27th (pm) after 7 hours of driving he went & printed a couple of his shots. I admire his energy levels, his enthusiasm. We were sorry to leave T. on her own, but she is v. independent & seems to cope. I think she very much has her own routine and was probably ready to get back into that.

28 October

An early phone call from Chris with shocking news that Liz's Jeremy has died suddenly when they were out in his boat. I do not know how things like this appear from nowhere, devoid of any sense of premonition or warning. As they were alone she had to try & recover him after he suddenly fell into the water, tying a rope around him + trying to resuscitate him before calling the emergency services. He is larger than her and you can only imagine the shock and the horror as well as the physical challenge, but she did get him back on the deck and did all she could for him.

They had to assess whether she had murdered him, which obviously was not the case. To see all her hopes for the future disappear and then be suspected of murder is just too horrible to contemplate. How a world can change forever in a moment. I phoned later & she was calm & glad of the support of J's friends with whom she was staying. I've always known that she has incredible strength and resilience and admire her for that.

Other than to be supportive and to pray for them both, there is nothing else that I can do. I think a little to other sudden deaths I have seen. Students at college particularly, all around us is more fragile and temporary than we know.

November–December

2nd half of term proved so tiring and I know I have neglected this journal as a result. The run up to Christmas: carol service, student crises, fallings out & so on left me worn down + hardly ready to embark on the prep work needed at home. Managed to get cards written, & Colin cleaned bedrooms over several weekends. We shopped together on Dec 12th, then we went to John Lewis in Solihull & then went to Warwick to Ben's to babysit for Annabelle. She has a fairy dress with little wings to wear to a party. Felt shattered afterwards, but it was good to see them all.

Colin has been utterly distraught in the pre-Christmas period over his boss' plan to swallow up his division & destroy everything he has worked for. I hate to see him like this & think boss is mad as everyone knows he's the only one making money at present. Is this what it comes to, that we spend our lives building things only to see them undone and taken away? Everything still matters for what it was in the moment.

Christmas 2003

Though this is supposed to be about work & college, family events have been looming large. Theresa came on the 21st to stay for the whole period, collected by Matt and Kate. We had a few days to get ready for the mass influx on Boxing Day. Ben, Katharine, Annabelle, Matt & Kate stayed – it was lovely to have them but I now have to confess that I found all the cooking etc v. tiring indeed. I have had a recurrence of problems with my neck & cannot see the osteopath as he is off sick. Visits to another acupuncturist have proved useless.

But through all that, Christmas is still Christmas, the pattern not so different to years gone by. Katharine, Kate and Annabelle now with us, Dave no longer, but we do the same things. A Christmas Eve meal in country pub, Carols from Kings on the radio, Church in the morning, lunch then presents. It does change though, with little Annabelle now at the centre. So loved and protected, with many more Christmases ahead of her than I will have. I expect we will see more grandchildren over the next few years. I just sense that we might have rather a lot one day and I feel blessed by that, even if my own frailty scares me sometimes.

As well as looking forward, I inevitably think back to my own childhood Christmases with Anna, Martin and Mike, Hugh, Noreen, Janet and Richard. We certainly knew how to celebrate. I remember also Colin's first Island Christmas and taking Ben and Matthew across the water when they were tiny. Neither remembers spending a Christmas on the Island, but I can remember it for them. It was not really so long ago.

28 December

Arrival of Mike, James & Francesca. Great to see them. We had a big dinner (11) in the evening. Lovely to all be round one table, but wondered how much longer I would be able to do this. Mike as ever working frantically hard on various projects. I know both that it stresses him and that he would not have it any other way. He has a kind of toughness and practicality that I have never had, an entrepreneurial spirit that has taken him far. It is good to see him relax and it is obvious how much he adores his children.

29 December

Ben + Katharine left today. Lunch out with Mike & co. Matt & Kate back to supper. That funny period between Christmas and New Year that is neither one thing nor the other, when you start to notice pine needles falling from the tree in greater numbers and everything has a somewhat uncertain air. One year nearly over, the next yet to begin.

Colin still pre-occupied by work and what is going on there, but not really keen to talk about it. He paces a lot and occasionally after he has gone for a solitary walk I can smell the hint of cigar smoke on him. I know he takes it all quite personally, finds it hard to get a perspective on it. I never know quite what I should say, to suggest it will all be alright is to be dismissive of the problems, to agree that it is all terrible hardly seems that it will help.

30 December

Mike & Co left. All planned to meet at Mike's on 3rd Jan. Our leg of the festivities now over, for which I feel relieved.

2004

3 January

Dropped Theresa then drove to Portsmouth. She was in good spirits, looking forward to seeing her friends again. She always enjoys this time of the year and I am glad that even without Dave that has still been the case, although I know how much she thinks to him.

4 January

We had a big party at Mike's for Noreen, Janet, Paul, Nick, Patrick, Richard, Sue, Mike & Sarah. They were absolutely stunned by the house which is huge & grand, almost unreal in its scope. The place is on four stories and I will try to describe it.

From the road it looks a bit like a wedding cake, given its different layers and it appears very grand. However, this is not how it is meant to be viewed. It has been designed such that its best view is from the water. It is built into the slope and is almost twice as tall when viewed from the garden, rather than the main road entrance. Of course, the garden ends where Wootton Creek begins, and Mike's boats are moored on his jetty.

There is a games room at the top with table tennis,

table football and a pool table. An amazing place for everyone to play, and we have already had a lot of fun up there. The next floor down sees the bedrooms which are all en-suite with wooden floors and luxurious fittings. Then there is the main grand hall with a huge chandelier (albeit some of the light bulbs need replacing), main sitting room with large log fire and a host of other rooms, including an eating area that looks out across the sea. There is a large roof terrace for summer barbeques. Finally, on the lowest level, is the indoor swimming pool, complete with Jacuzzi and changing area!

The party went very well and went on from 4–12 midnight. It was really good to see the other side of the family again. I thought to how many years it must have been since we first celebrated Christmas together with Anna and Martin, Noreen and Hugh. The year of all our births of course, so long ago and yet...

Further developments post-Christmas! Theresa has decided to move to Ledbury so have visited estate agents to check prospects – no good at present as nothing is available. It will be easier for her to be closer. The drive from Hereford to Bognor is not an easy one, and she feels that she needs a little more support now. I think this could all cause other challenges though. We will make it work.

23 Jan

Still no progress with estate agents. Matt's situation still the same, did not see him at all this weekend. Great news about Ben – a promotion. He's acting boss after his boss was seconded to another firm. He has that look about him I remember seeing in Colin toward the start of his career when finally things seemed to be moving in his direction.

Chess Stories –
Viktor and David – 2011

It is a soft meeting, an excuse to be in London during the day. To catch up with someone who used to work for me, but now does not and is leaving the business anyway. She had been in my team when my mother died, but this is another time, a different sort of conversation. We talk about her new job, what she wants to achieve, what might worry her, and then finally we say goodbye for what will be the last time and I cross the city to play chess. The London Chess Classic is taking place at the Olympia Conference Centre on Hammersmith Road, and I am due to take on one of the game's most famous players

Sitting on the tube, heading through London tunnels and then onto streets I do not know, I think to what will follow. It is called a simultaneous, where an elite Grandmaster takes on thirty mere mortals at once. A chance to actually play your heroes; few other games or sports could facilitate something like this.

The tables are set up in a horseshoe shape, such that the Grandmaster can make his way from board to board, game to game with ease. Like a doctor surveying a mystified patient, he knows in an instant what needs to be done. The chances are that his prognoses will most likely be more accurate than a doctor's. Julian Barnes once wrote something along the lines that for the protagonist a simultaneous was like brushing the sleep out of his eyes. I will be sat at one of these boards and my opponent will be Viktor Korchnoi, widely considered to be one of the strongest players in the history of the game never to have been World Champion.

He had been a slow developer in the scheme of things, only peaking in his forties – at a time in life when most elite players were well into their decline, he was just getting started. Perhaps it was the complexity of his style, which meant it took so long to hone. Many other world -class players acknowledged that they found it hard to understand his ideas. Perhaps it had taken him that extra time to tame those complex thoughts, to finally be all he could be, even if at one level it hadn't been quite enough. He had fallen agonisingly short, although things might have been different had the playing field not been tilted against him.

Three huge battles with Karpov for the world title in the 1970s and early '80s had captured the public imagination and left Korchnoi's followers distraught. During the first two he had come so close despite the huge Soviet backing for Karpov, the youngster who described his hobbies as Marxism and stamp collecting, the face the regime wanted to show the world. Karpov was certainly seen as the safer and better long-term bet for a Soviet chess establishment which had been rocked by the rise of the American Bobby Fischer and was now determined to reassert itself. The ageing and unpredictable Korchnoi simply did not fit the mould.

After the first of these matches Korchnoi defected to Switzerland. The Soviet press refused to print his name. His family was persecuted and denied leave to join him. A state attempt to ban him from future competitions was unsuccessful.

Their subsequent matches were amongst the bitterest in memory, mired in controversy over coloured yoghurts potentially containing coded messages, rejected handshakes, hypnotists' glasses, a wooden panel placed underneath the table to stop the two from kicking each other.

In 1978, in this an atmosphere of extreme hostility and suspicion, Korchnoi came back from 4-1 and 5-2 to 5-5 as Karpov tired, before going down 6-5. He might have been the older man, but Korchnoi had the greater stamina and it nearly paid off. His famous biography, *Chess Is My Life,* told the story of these matches and all he faced off the board, enshrining his place as a symbol of resistance against the Soviet regime.

By 1981, age had finally caught up with him and Karpov won their final match more comfortably. In 1983, at his final series run at the world title, Korchnoi was knocked out in the qualifying matches by the young pretender, and Karpov's ultimate usurper, Kasparov, though he did manage to win the first game. He remained one of the world's strongest players, the next level down so to speak, for a very long time after.

He once remarked that every time he won a tournament in advancing age, he despaired for the future of chess. Even now, in his early eighties, he had just beaten Fabiano Caruana, who would make number two in the world soon afterwards. His history was his main draw, but even in 2011 he clearly still had it.

Before any simultaneous, someone will come and talk the players through the rules. You can pass three times if you are not ready to move, but no more than that. You can only physically make your move when your opponent is at the board to see it.

Announcements such as these are generally quite routine information for the participants. I had played simuls before and knew the drill, but this one would prove to be a touch different.

"Viktor is a little prickly today," the organiser says, somewhat wistfully. "If you do happen to win, please don't ask him to sign your score sheet for you, as he almost certainly won't. In fact, if you do win, it is probably best to avoid talking to him at all."

There are wry smiles all round. It is not unheard of for a Grandmaster to lose a game in a simul. Indeed, an expected performance would probably be something like twenty-eight wins, a draw and a defeat. It is almost impossible in thirty games not to make a mistake somewhere, not to give a potential chance that could be seized upon by a competent player, if their luck holds. We all play these events in part because the chance is there, but none would think it in any way spoke to our strength relative to that of our opponent, but there we have it. Even here and now in this setting, at this advanced age, his ferocious competitiveness is undimmed.

Then he appears. An old man now and a little stooped, suit both clean and well worn. He wears a tie, perhaps draped a little loosely around his neck. Before he even reaches the tables, one of the players rushes up to him with a photograph he wants to share. Korchnoi is clearly irritated but listens whilst the guy explains that this was a picture taken actually playing Korchnoi in the 1970s.

Korchnoi makes little effort to hide his lack of interest. "Would you mind signing it for me?" he is asked. There is a pause and the organiser looks on from the edge of the room like a startled hare, unsure whether or not to run.

"I am here to play chess, not to sign things," Viktor says firmly. "Perhaps later," he adds, in a voice that makes it clear he will not.

The younger man's partner is also looking on. "Well, if he won't he won't," she whispers and gives a conspiratorial wink. The man smiles back at her and the room seems to breathe a sigh of relief. He has retained his dignity and Viktor has not walked out either, so we are good to go.

The organiser re-caps the rules again and explains about the three passes. Korchnoi shakes his head. "No passes. I'll say if people can pass later on." Everybody is happy to agree not to pass.

He sips from a plastic cup of water and finally we are off. I am on the sixth board of the thirty and I watch him start to move around the horseshoe. He pushes his king pawn up two squares on the first three boards, then his queen pawn in similar fashion on the next two.

Finally he is standing in front of me, both a colossus

of the modern game and a prickly eighty-year-old. There is nothing about his air or his mannerisms that remind me of either of my grandfathers. He shakes my hand and we look into each other's eyes for a moment, just as he has thousands of times before with everyone who is anyone in chess for the last seventy years. In that instance, it is just me and him and this is what I have come here for. I push my queen pawn up two, the most common response to his identical thrust, and he pushes his queen's bishop pawn to take us into the queen's gambit.

The hall is air-conditioned and cool. Other tournaments, including the London Classic main event, are going on in different parts of it. Occasionally a game will finish and we will hear a mutter of commiseration (rarely congratulation) and players will start to fiddle with the pieces, trying to appraise what should have happened, before they are shushed and pointed in the direction of the analysis room.

Disputes are not uncommon. Somebody touches a piece and then does not want to move it; that happens from time to time. A mobile phone going off results in an automatic forfeit, which always creates bad feeling. Once in a league match this happened to the most hapless of our first team stand ins. His ring tone announced "Peter, answer your phone", which made the crime difficult to deny.

This is all a long way removed from the atmosphere when I first played competitively as a kid. Then, smoking was not only allowed, it was virtually compulsory. You would look to make out the outlines of your pieces through the glooming, and by the time you had finished playing you would stink. In hindsight I was grateful that neither of my parents objected to the time I was spending in such an environment.

Both drove me miles along country roads to the points of civilisation where things like chess happened. The Hereford Congress always used to take place in the Royal College for the Blind where my mother taught. I think she used to like telling her colleagues that I was in it, even if I was not very successful in those early days.

"I am pleased to reach one out of three in such a big tournament," I wrote in my scorebook at the end of the Saturday of my debut, aged eleven, in the Hereford Minor. If it hadn't been for my somewhat unlikely knack of being able to look on the bright side when it came to chess, at least back then, I would probably have retired before I started.

Korchnoi plays down the main line of the Cambridge Springs. It is pretty solid, unspectacular stuff. The rule for the Grandmaster in these situations is to play carefully, not to commit. Wait for your opponent to show you why he is nowhere near your level. It is the same for all of us when faced with a weaker player. Show me, you think. But in the early stages of the game his approach means there are advantages for me too. I know the theory and do not have to think much about my responses. Everything that is unfolding is not too bad for Black.

Korchnoi plays slowly, taking his time as he moves from board to board. I think back to the first simul I ever played in as a child, organised by the Hereford Chess Association, a village hall somewhere, another Grandmaster, though a very different one: David Norwood. Young and charming, immaculately suited. As he was a long way removed from the normal greasy haired, carrier-bag hugging figure my mother had come to associate with the world of chess, she was clearly impressed by him. It was just before the 1992 general election and I had got Dad to place a bet for me on Party Politics in the Grand National, and I am thinking partly about this as we play.

David is very smiley, and very good. He will not reach Korchnoi's level and will semi-retire to make vast sums of money in the City soon afterwards. Our encounter is interesting but lacks intensity. He hangs a bishop, but I fail to spot it. You just aren't programmed to expect such a thing from a Grandmaster. He goes on to win, but so does Party Politics, and I do not mind too much. Only later do I start to see it as an opportunity missed.

We are into a complicated middle game now. The position is an interesting one and a handful of spectators are looking on. Adrian Walker is playing in a different event in the same hall and every so often he will come across and look at my position. He is my chess colleague in all this as well as my friend and I am pleased he is here with me in London. If I had thought, I would have asked him to take a photograph, but I didn't and he doesn't.

Other games are starting to finish already, though Korchnoi's simuls are known to generally last for a very long time. Perhaps it is age, but from what I remember reading about him I think not. Where most Grandmasters will whizz from board to board, barely stopping to look,

Korchnoi stoops to examine each position with extreme care. There are long moments where he stands in front of me, and for all the games he has played in the past, right now this is his focus.

Whenever you play chess you have to want to crush your opponent, to destroy him, to prove his worthlessness. But in the here and now all I want is not to annoy him and not embarrass myself. I could cope with most people's verdict on me, but to be condemned by a deity of chess would be something I would not find it easy to come back from; I would not have been able to shrug off him refusing to sign my picture as easily as the other guy seemed to.

I still understand this game, can see what is happening, but it is impossible for me to imagine what is going on in his brain as he looks down on these same lumps of plastic. Then finally we reach the crucial moment and I sense that he has made a mistake. Or is there a tactic I have missed? It is not clear to me what he is doing. It is now or never and I take the chance.

He pauses and frowns at the position for a long time. It is almost as if he had not considered that I would do this. Perhaps he instinctively knew that it did not quite work, without even having to consider it when he made his last move. He hesitates for a long time and then in response comes up with something I had not considered. As he plays, both I and the spectators recognise what he has done; my sense was that those watching weren't sure either during the wait, but we all are now.

Now there is no way back. A few moves later he plays

another good move and says politely in English still heavy with a Russian accent "… and you resign?", which I do.

He shakes my hand and smiles at me. I sense he appreciates the suit I am wearing (one of the few) and my sense of deference. Perhaps the game even interested him for a moment. Who can say?

Had my father been a chess player, he would not have cared what Korchnoi thought of him, would have been more ferocious in combat. If he was at my level technically I think he would have had a better chance of winning a game like this than I would. The result would have mattered more to him, the rest of it less so. It is all conjecture, but I suspect that it is true.

"Good effort," says the organiser, and I can sense his relief with the way things have turned out. A spectator introduces himself to me. He is a professional magician as well as a keen chess player and he gives me his email address so that I can send him a copy of the game, but unfortunately I lose his scrap of paper on the train.

I phone Dad and talk him through it. He sounds interested, but I am not entirely sure whether or not he knows who Korchnoi is, who back in the real world beyond the subculture of chess was still relatively obscure.

He certainly knew who Nigel Short was though. When Short had played Kasparov I used to make Mum drive us home from school as quickly as possible so that we could watch the match on Channel Four. Years later experts reckoned Short had got himself into better positions than most but ultimately was facing the greatest player of all time, probably at his absolute peak, and so was crushed. Short was rubbished in the media, disparaged as an Eddie the Eagle type figure, despite the fact that he had beaten everybody else on his route to the final.

I played him in a simul a year after Korchnoi and lost just as would be expected. A level endgame, the sort of position where a draw would be agreed against a player of similar strength, but inevitably I was overwhelmed by his endgame technique and lost a few moves on from my apparent equality.

It was shortly before Dad's diagnosis that I played my last simul during his lifetime. He almost came along. He was with us for the weekend and expressed an interest. It wasn't far from our house and I would have liked for him to see me play; it had been years since he had last peered over a board while waiting to drive me home.

In the end he chose the newspaper, and so after so many near and not so near misses he was not there to see me draw a complex knight endgame with Jon Nunn. A chess achievement that, even if it could rightly just be shrugged off as a simul performance, partially validated the time I spent on this impossible game.

It meant a lot to me and he was not there to see it. But if it hadn't have been for his teaching and his driving, and the previous experiences against Korchnoi, Short and thousands of others, there would not have been anything to witness.

As he sat on the sofa reading the paper while I sweated over the board I knew I was doing something that Dad had had a hand in.

Find Another Place –
August 2008

It was the only night of the year when we were all under the same roof at Mike's house on the Isle of Wight, on the site of his grandparents' house which had been the original Holmes dwelling. Mike and Rona had watched a film. We had turned in early, tired from the journey. Things could have been different that night, if only we had known.

Mum had not come downstairs when we arrived the day before. I sensed something might be wrong then, though not this, but relaxed once she had been to see the doctor. Dad drove her; a final trip. Her final outing. She had returned to a house for the last time; it was better that she did not know this.

Later, I looked in. She was sitting up in bed, reading a book about lay people spending time in a monastery. It was based on a television programme. Radio 4 on in the background. Normal.

She hadn't felt well for several days. A brief trip to the Ventnor Botanic Garden earlier in the day had been aborted. Now she worries that she won't be much use this holiday. I keep my distance, wary of germs. She has an infection of some sort.

I tell her it will be alright. I do not kiss her. When I leave the room, something will be over, but it would have been unbearable had we known that.

Standing at the kitchen sink in the early morning, making a cup of milk for Francesca, bright midsummer light streaming through the window. Even at this hour it is clear it is going to be a beautiful day. I am half-awake, which is as good as it gets with a battery powered two-year-old, especially in a house that for all its luxury does not have good blinds in the bedrooms.

But we are here, at the start of our first full day, and everything is as it should be. Except, unbeknown to me as I apply the lid to a bright green beaker, it already is not. Everything has changed forever, even if not for me for another moment or so.

I had spoken to my mother a few days earlier on the phone. A week before that, we got stuck in traffic on a long trip back from Cornwall and stayed the night with them. A chance meet-up, the last proper one, another hot day. "Kicking off the summer," someone said. We drank juice in the garden, read newspapers, splashed with the children in the paddling pool. Another normal day. Dad bronzed by the sun. Time somehow stilled in the heat. The year at its peak; no hint as to the rapidness of the descent about to follow.

Mum had phoned the day before we set off for the Island. I was out at a work dinner. Team building: watching my boss play footsie under the table with his secretary and hearing her ask whether her toothbrush was in his car. So it *was* true.

Katharine said that Mum had sounded slightly confused on the phone. A warning that might have been heeded, perhaps; but, equally, how could it have been? It might not have been linked at all. I don't know. I would have phoned back, but it was late.

Now here on this morning, in Mike's kitchen, I feel a presence and turn to see Rachel, my sister-in-law. "Mary's dead," she says and walks away, giving me the space to think.

This piece of information cannot be right. It has no place here and can surely be rationalised away if I can only focus on it for a moment. There has to be a solution.

I hear noises; people are congregating in Mum and Dad's bedroom. He is trying to rouse her. He shakes her but it is as if he is shaking a rag doll, and I can see by his expression that he knows that it is hopeless.

It all starts to move, in wave after futile wave. The screech of sirens, police and paramedics, the crunch of feet on gravel; it is all much too late. The look in the policeman's eye, that this might be something interesting. To him, at first, in among the money and the heat, but it is just as quickly obvious from his subsequent expression that he can see that there is no story. Not one that he will remember or tell.

"There are no vital signs," a paramedic says, confirming what we already know, but it still feels like a verdict being rendered.

Emergency vehicles stand idle on the drive, lights flashing but no sound; it is somehow all half-hearted. No urgency now. Wailings on arrival have faded to nothing; just mechanics and paperwork, routine questions.

I tell Katharine while she is in the shower and she takes the children out of the house, away from the melee. "The longest ever day on Appley Beach," she will tell me later. I want them anywhere but here.

Matt leaves to tell Theresa. "Is it Mary or Colin?" she will ask.

They are only three weeks back from their holiday in Greece. "It was nice, but he didn't think the food was great," she had told me. There are photos of her swimming and looking at Dad across restaurant tables.

All so normal.

We had been responsible for Theresa in their absence and she had fallen when we went out for lunch, blood running down her leg in a pub restaurant, other patrons pretending not to notice. A trip to Worcester hospital, a wheelchair she would not use. Farce, then sorted.

"An adventure," she says, with a huge smile.

We had taken her back to her flat and re-stocked the cupboards with food within its sell-by date. I had driven back up the motorway eating a packet of Hula Hoops with one hand, which Katharine said was dangerous.

"You did very well, but we are back now, so we can take over," Mum had promised. A fortnight ago, that was all.

A priest arrives and says some prayers, at peace with himself, his aura of calm somehow soothing.

Dad and Mike talk to the police in the lounge. The

things that need to happen are being taken care of. The professionals know their roles and give a structure for the rest of us to cling to. This has happened before, except it hasn't, not exactly. Not to her. Not to us.

A year and two days on from her sixtieth birthday party in this same house, her body is taken away in a red bag.

"They won't let her stay here," Mike has said.

I will see the paramedics carry her down the stairs, under the chandelier and through the front door to the ambulance. Natural causes, the post-mortem will decide.

We light candles at Quarr Abbey. Mike and Dad attend a service.

"That's the worse news," my boss will say when I tell him. My deputy (neither of our choices) will text on the day of the funeral – All Our Thoughts Are With You.

I will keep the text.

The Royal National College for the Blind website is soon alight with tributes. They radiate shock. A year on from retirement, Mum knows most of those still there, many she has known for years. Knew, I suppose.

The principal, who is widely seen as a disaster for the college, by Mum and all her friends, writes a nice letter. Shortly she too will die unexpectedly.

In the weeks that follow we will be overwhelmed with letters and cards. Could it have been other? Had Dad missed a clue in the night? He always says not. Should the GP who saw Mum that last evening have suspected something apart from the kidney infection, accurately diagnosed? Seen beyond the obvious?

Maddie asks why Grandpa is sad. She says he should forget about her and waves her hand dismissively. She is four and is trying to help. He does not react. She shares a birthday with her grandmother. Last year they had a joint party. The final party they will share. They blew out candles on a cake together.

Later in the funeral home, Theresa will ask Mum to give a sign and generally goes completely crazy. They will play an Enya tape that Dad hurries to switch off. There are booklets in the waiting room about surviving a murder, coping with suicide. A poem on the wall says that whatever I was to you, doubtless I still am. I visit twice and she is less present on each occasion. I doubt I will go to a funeral home again. I hope not.

"You are braver than I am," Mike says when I tell him about the visits. On the way to the funeral itself, Theresa complains about the slowness of the car and urges that more speed should be utilised at her own funeral, when the time comes.

"She was always fragile," she will say to Dad.

"She wasn't. She just got arthritis. OK?" For once his irritation with her feels well placed.

Then, in a service that starts in rain and ends in sunshine, the church filled to overflowing, we will say something. Not goodbye. It's not that.

"You have to find another place for her," the counsellor will tell me. That is what I am destined to keep looking for.

Dad's Other Women

"I thought he was very handsome," Mum smiled, her first reflection back to when they met. I am not sure what he would have said had I asked him what his sense had been when he had first met Mum. None of your business, probably. Perhaps it wasn't surprising, given she married him and all. What did surprise me was how often other people said the same thing. Old friends from back when they first got together: "Very handsome," or "He was so tall and handsome," and "Very dark and masculine." He certainly had some appeal. There was a presence: six feet tall, jet black hair, solid build, and outward confidence, that when blended with his enigmatic nature seemed to present an intriguing proposition. Mum was not the only one to think so, although I never saw any hint of an affair.

After she died there were at least two years in which he could not contemplate anything, let alone another relationship. No Christmas tree or decorations. Trips out rarely worked, such as a time at Center Parcs where he broke down and cried while we ate at the sports café. Loud music banging, a waiter asking if he was alright and being reassured he was fine. It was all very British and a long way from where he wanted to be.

In the end we encouraged him to think about meeting somebody else. Not a replacement, nothing like that. I told him that I didn't think he was very good on his own, and surprisingly he agreed with me.

So began a slightly bizarre period of watching my father's internet dating career.

"Why do they always use out of date photos?" he would ask me with a sigh. There was a reason, and I assumed he would figure it out for himself.

He was surprisingly open, in his more familiar not entirely open way, about what he was up to. We would get snippets of updates. Occasionally he would pop in at our house with somebody for cups of tea, when they had happened to be in the area. A slightly random phone call, such as you might get from a teenager: "Are you around, because we are?"

One Christmas Eve he phoned to say he would be bringing a guest, somebody we had not met before. She was to form the subject of much discussion when we went out for a Christmas Eve meal.

"Who is coming tomorrow?" one of the waitresses asked.

"Grandpa's girlfriend," Francesca replied to much laughter from her sisters.

According to the stories, one was beautiful but crazy, another just crazy. He met a whole host of other characters along the way. He was always struck by how many had been abandoned by their husbands and left with nothing but still managed to keep going, looking forward, making new plans. None of this was what he would have chosen, but in the end what could he do?

"You have to make the most of things," he said quietly, as if to convince himself as much, slowly nodding his head and looking straight at me. Not aggressive, but rather as if he had learnt to come to terms with something hard, with a truth that could not be changed, or at least with the fact that he was not going to come to terms with it, but there were still things he was going to do.

He dated the widow of a famous sports star for a while.

"I'm not being funny, Dad, but if he was her type, what does she see in you?" I said.

"Well," he said, "I often wonder the same thing myself."

For whatever reason, they drifted apart on good terms, and then he met Sheila and it seemed that things were coming together. Sadly this was not too long before his diagnosis, and everything was cut short by that.

Beginnings and endings can be one and the same, and this one was all the more brutal for it. Sheila had already lost one partner and now had to go through it all again.

At the wake after the service another lady came up to me and said that if Colin had not become ill he would have been with her instead of Sheila.

Even after the end they all thought he was very handsome.

New Year

Dad had come up for Christmas too. We had eaten lunch quite early. Francesca was given a skateboard that we went out to test, watching her skate past windows through which people with paper crowns were still eating. Katharine drank too much and fell asleep. Gabriella toddled.

He was relatively relaxed, at least for him. The fact that it was all more chaotic and alcoholic than it would have been during our childhood Christmases did not seem to trouble him. He had learned to let some things go, to live in the moment a little more, even if that was not always easy. Things did not have to be perfect. Nothing ever is, I had said to him, not even back then and he knows it.

Then back for New Year's Eve, with Katharine's parents, Anne and Roger. Not as good as the neighbours' party, is Annabelle's verdict, but not bad. We played party games: Charades, Jenga; lots of buffet food and alcohol. Prosecco. Maddie made sure there were no nuts.

Sitting on the black leather sofas we watch the countdown to 2014 on the television. Fireworks flash across the Thames. Gary Barlow. "You are the best audience I've had all year!" he shouts.

They say it can be a melancholy time, but it wasn't. Not really. Just the normal sense of time passing, as the family followed a recognisable variation on the usual rituals. No more than that. The end of one season, the start of another. We weren't a big New Year family. There was nothing to suggest that there was anything particular about this one that it would be the last Dad would see.

I remember him marking the millennium in Bosbury in The Bell. "Grab a table and it's every man for himself," he said enthusiastically on the phone, when he talked about his plans. But they had arrived too early and ended up going back home to return later.

Mum said he used to go to Trafalgar Square when he was younger. Something I did once too. I remember battling the crowds, and the bustling in the freezing London air that fogged with cigarette smoke and alcohol, wanting the night to be over. All those stories you could only part guess at. Once was enough for me, but I think he did it more than that. Those were different times and different Londons. But we must have stood on roughly the same patch of concrete, in the same chill air.

I thought getting through 2013 unscathed was a relief. A ridiculous superstition perhaps, but 14 felt like a much better number. Luckier. He was more settled. Not over anything, but his grief felt less raw. He was coping better six years on.

The Christmas where we argued at Mum's grave seemed a long time passed now. I had only just passed my driving test at that point and was meant to be driving him up to our house for Christmas, as a seizure had temporarily meant that he was not allowed to drive himself. He had wanted to go to Ledbury to buy flowers and to go to the grave, which we did, but I was nervous; the radio had said that this was the worst day of the year for travelling, and I thought that the longer we waited, the more difficult the journey would get. He did not realise that that was why I wanted to keep moving and we clashed. He thought I was just rushing him or had no interest in being at my mother's grave, and eventually we drove to my house in a silence that extended for several further hours.

He was still not busy enough. A governor at our old school. Playing bridge. Some astronomy. Meals out. Buying two more cars than it was strictly necessary for one person to need. Perhaps lacking the big project.

Mum had said to me years ago that the trouble with life was that it was easy to be too busy or not busy enough, but getting the balance right was much harder. Dad hadn't wanted a big project after his job, but maybe he needed one. There was a slight rootlessness to his retirement. Of course, it would have been different if Mum had been there.

He could be dismissive of both people and ideas. Sometimes he didn't seem able to tolerate bright people particularly well, fools even less so. He could put up barriers without being aware that he had, and would then be surprised that others could not reach through them. But on that New Year's Eve, many of these challenges were less visible. His more playful side, often to the fore at this time of year, was so once again.

None of us, least of all he himself, knew that as we watched the fireworks and drank the Prosecco he was already terminally ill.

2014
PART 3

Endings

Every bit of news had been worse than the last, and it was terrible to start with. Those few months from which there was no escape, or rather there was but it was not the escape he would have wanted.

Bowel cancer, in the liver, in the lungs. Perhaps not bowel cancer – primary site not obvious, the outside of the bowel perhaps. Unfortunately, it makes no difference.

"It is not uncommon not to find the primary," the consultant says. But it is not in the lower bowel, we know that much. A nurse examines this a few weeks in and tells him it is clear.

"All I can tell you is that there is no cancer here," she says.

He goes home and drinks wine to celebrate with Sheila. The last glass he will drink, I would guess. They have danced down the hospital corridor together, literally apparently.

He phoned me with the news while I was driving to him and I have to pull over to think. Torn, I had adjusted to one thing, in a way, and this is now different. I should be delighted, but I know it can't be right, that a mistake has been made somewhere. Something has been misunderstood or miscommunicated, and so it proves. The nurse is an idiot. The cancer is not in the lower bowel, but it is everywhere else. "Someone should speak to her," he says, shaking his head as another door closes.

All of this was only weeks ago but it has already taken on the aura of a distant memory; it has no relation or relevance to the here and now. On this autumn night through which the elements are pointing toward winter we are together in his house and I am his sole carer.

"Don't leave me here by myself," he says, which frustrates me. I have sat on the bed with him before, to be told that he is tired and needs some peace to sleep.

It is hard to guess at what he might want. I am not really the answer. He would want it to be Mum, but that is not possible. So many other things no longer are either.

"I like the sound of the rain on the roof," he says. "It's soothing. All these years I've lived here and I had never really listened to it until the last few months. You know?"

I am still surprised by any display of openness, even if it is only about the weather and how it makes him feel. A slight chink, that in many ways does not bode well, but the connection counts for something.

His world has receded. He is more of this house than he has ever been, no longer really awaiting news of men and great events.

It started raining when I was a few miles from the village and it is heavier now. I hold his hand on the bed. It feels thin and warm. There are pins and needles in my wrist, which is rare but does happen from time to time. He smiles at me.

"Well, here we are, then," he says. "We should probably pass on the drinking and the nightclubbing tonight."

"Maybe just a quiet one," I offer, and he smiles again, then he sighs.

"What a life," he says, shaking his head.

"It's been good, Dad, hasn't it," I say, not really as a question.

He rolls his eyes and he grins. This is what we have come to. Even if he does try to open things up, I close them down again, the alternative too scary. It is almost automatic, a well-trodden groove for us both, but for all that, there is a closeness now.

Helen, then Mum, his parents gone, working his way up, getting fired, falling out with the neighbours, meeting Sheila, getting cancer. It is a life that has been lived with its share of happiness and sadness, disappointments and setbacks, but it must be the richer for that, just not necessarily any easier.

"You boys are everything," he said once in a hospital ward or corridor, I can't remember where exactly. Perhaps there was more intimacy and openness than I thought, much like when Martin's father told him once that he only felt safe when he was around.

Yet, for all that, I wanted more, more than was going to be possible, checking myself because I did not want to make things difficult for him, was scared of where openness might lead.

The Macmillan nurse said that we had to respect how he was going to do this. She had him sussed after one cup of tea at the dining room table, at least insofar as a cancer nurse does when categorising her patients by type.

He probably wasn't going to open up much, she said. Not really. Who he was and how he was. It was not that unusual for someone in his position to still be focussed on getting better.

"We often see this," she said in a voice devoid of any judgement. A lot of people want to do what they always did.

Why wouldn't they? I read on the internet that the majority of terminally ill people never fully accept that this is what they are.

The clock has run down as we have watched *Match of the Day* and *The Big Bang Theory*. If there are things you want to do, let's do them now, I would say. "Just this," was always his answer.

For all that, there have been lots of visitors over the last few months. Mike has been twice, his ex-wife Janet and their daughter Francesca.

"He hasn't got long," Janet warns me, "two weeks at most."

A former neighbour has popped in and they work on a jigsaw puzzle together, both engrossed in the task. His only concern in the moment separating out the edges and looking for shapes that fit, bringing order to chaos. Friends from work also visit; he has told me who I should phone to organise that group, when the time comes.

But this is not where we are at this moment, as I sit on his bed holding his hand as we listen to the rain.

"Just be with me," he says again and I am, but in some ways I am not. He is terminally ill, I am not. I feel both guilt and relief, mainly guilt, which in part stems from a sense that I am somehow strengthened by his weakness, if also diminished; much of what is in the house and around him only means something because he is here. At one level it is impossible for anyone to be with him, to really experience what this must feel like, to fix it. I've told him that anything can happen. None of us know for sure. He might outlive me yet.

"You are not going anywhere," he has said with a confidence that surprises me. He has gone, in a few months, from well, to not being well, to dying. But some certainties remain, at least for him.

In the summer the thought of him making it to Christmas had seemed implausible. Then things had changed. Palliative chemo was a borderline call that made a difference.

"It's up to you," the consultant in Cheltenham had said. "If you are going to start this, you need to do so today, right away." It was all about trade-offs between time and wellness.

"I just hope it doesn't make things worse," the consultant says. Could it be worse?

"What do you think I should do?" he asks us in the waiting room, once he has finished writing Sheila a large cheque, now he knows the best guess is weeks. That was how he was with money, always generous, always wanting to share it with those around him. I knew in many ways he was a more generous person than I am.

He knows what he wants to do; it isn't really a question. He wants to try. Finally, he is being offered something: a concrete plan, a way forward, steps away from his current predicament. It would be impossible to say anything other than "let's go for it", to support him in his choice, one of the few still open to him, one of the few gifts left that we could give him. He had seemed better almost immediately.

The week in Cheltenham was followed by day patient treatment in Hereford. You have to phone up and confirm you are coming in on the morning of your treatment as the toxins are too expensive to make up for people who don't show.

It was more than a placebo effect. The data showed the cancer receding in some places. The consultant was pleased.

In early October, things seemed possible that had not before. But even in the brief Indian summer there were warning signs. He struggled to urinate. He tried wearing a catheter and not wearing a catheter. It is not the cancer but a prostate problem. He explores having it fixed. It is difficult for him to hear the explanation as to why this is not possible; some test results on his heart have come back. He is told they are not good.

"I can't take more bad news," he says and won't pick them up. We have permission to talk to his doctors about everything else, but he doesn't want us to talk about this, twenty years on from his by-pass. He feels less well and agrees to a break in the chemo, just to get his strength back.

As we sit on the bed, he tells me that he can't eat anymore, but dreams of food. Even sweets and Rennies make him gag now, jelly a thing of the past, and he has dropped the pretence of even playing with toast and cereal.

Increasingly I notice that he seems to be drinking less too and will yell in pain when he does, though he pretends he has not reacted at all.

He will not consider being anywhere but home. He is going to manage this his way, on his terms. I try, not for the first time, to coax him to go into a hospice.

"Just to get checked out, to see if there is anything there that might help you. What harm can it do? You don't have to stay there or anything." He is sixty-eight. He was young until a few months ago. A hospice was not a part of his thinking.

He surprises me again, saying that he *will* go, just for a day. The last plan we will form, never to be executed. He feels ill and I help him manage the bathroom.

"You are a good lad," he says with a grin that speaks to a different him. Not acting, not so guarded, more at ease, no pretence.

His glasses glint against the fluorescent light and his face for a moment looks younger, fuller. His accent with a stronger trace of cockney than normal, which is to say just a little. For a flash I see him as his parents might once have looked at him, and then the moment passes.

"I need to sleep," he says and I help him into bed, Radio 5 on in the background, as it always is. The last night either of us will spend in this house, even if we don't yet know it.

"Call me if you need anything," I say.

"Look in on me in the night," he says, something he must have done for me so many times when I was young.

I go into my old bedroom to sleep, phoning Katharine to say I think he is struggling. We are struggling. I am surprised by both my stress levels and the wave of tiredness that now comes over me. More care is needed. We are not winning but we must make this work. The hospice will help and finally he has agreed to go. Just to get checked out. In the night I look in several times and he is sleeping peacefully.

In the morning, I go in again and he is awake. He drinks some water and winces. His stomach is a problem. He tells me he feels 'very odd.' We agree he should rest in my bedroom and he puts his arm around me as we cross the hallway very slowly. But he is smiling, jocular almost; this is not a difficult moment. He leans some of his weight against me but he is steady. There is no hint that these will be his last steps. At the edge of the bed, he slips to his knees.

I say, "Just take a minute and we will get you up. Tell me when you are ready." He nods. There is no problem if we don't admit to one, but the longer he takes to move, the more I begin to fear that there might really be a problem. Yet he is still communicating normally. He is worried about the bed sheets in his room, and asks me to take them to the utility while he gets his breath.

"It's fine," he says. I take the sheets downstairs,

marking the stairway wall as they brush against it in my haste, making a mess.

I feel a sense of panic rising.

He is less calm when I get back to the bedroom. He says he can't move. He yells for me to get Jane and I call her. These will be the last words he ever speaks.

She is round in minutes. He just looks at me, right at me.

"Dad," I say, "Dad." But he doesn't answer, just goes on looking.

I don't know whether he can hear me or not anymore. I don't think to ask him whether he can squeeze my hand. A year or so later it will occur to me that that is what I should have asked him to do. I don't know the precise moment when he drifts out of consciousness as he wedged kneeling by the bed.

Jane phones an ambulance. We struggle to lift him from his knees and onto the floor. He is heavy and it is not easy, for all his thinness. We have to wrestle to break him free, to get him on his back on the bedroom floor.

Over the phone we are instructed how to do CPR. Very calm, as if they are in the room with us, which in a way they are. I push at his chest, and again.

A helicopter lands in the field and a team is here. They are young, accomplished looking; they are his best chance. I notice how much more forcefully they press than I had. He is more alive than when the emergency team had arrived for Mum. There is considerably more activity, if not any more hope. Not really.

We go downstairs whilst they work. Matt is here too

now. I know it is the end, that all of the effort upstairs is an illusion. I know how this will end. The terminally ill rarely survive a heart attack, I have heard somebody say before. The medics emerge eventually to tell us that they had got a trace on his heart. But it was just their equipment.

They could take him away to the hospital to keep going but they didn't think it would help. What did we want to do?

There was nothing left to do. A Chinese doctor came later in the day to issue the death certificate. It made me think that for all of us there will be people who enter our lives just after the point at which, for us, it ends. In some way I was strangely comforted by this. A part of how things are, people with us even after we are gone. Then the undertakers arrive. Big men in formalwear. Black gloves. They take his rings off. Matt puts one on, me the other. Unlike Mum, they make sure we don't see him being carried down the stairs.

We burn his sheets and his mattress in the garden, his ruined pyjamas. Think how to make the house secure, now that he can no longer protect it. Automatic pilot or whatever kicks in. But there, standing by the fire, his body on its way to the funeral parlour, I thought there might have been a moment I had missed, had forgotten to mark, where he crossed over from us back to Mum. There are always other journeys, both real and imagined, either side of death.

The priest, who soon concludes that we are a bunch of heathens, implies as much in his funeral sermon. "When I met Colin, it was too late to talk to him about God, but who knows what reflections he might have had at the end?"

It doesn't matter. We say the things about him that need to be said. The priest has allowed him to be buried with Mum and we have done the necessary to facilitate this. You could have got long odds at the outset, for the final resting place of this London-born Jew.

Winter Church

This is your element, this cold and dark
This grey day, sharp frost, chill wind
And absence of all cheer. Snow dusts
The churchyard evergreens and ridges the tower
Bleak and uncompromising, the east wind blows
Through draughty walls? Shrieking & creaking,
The arched roof timbers echo and shift.
Such sounds in a place so aged disturb
Uneasy prayer. And yet this is your time
Of triumph. No lush greenery distracts
From your presence. Seen for so many miles,
Dominating this landscape, telling of another,
Can it be you shall lose hold on men's minds
When still within your greyness God's light shines?

M.G.

342

Maddie's Memories – Sponge Cake and Wheeler Dealers

We are on the Island, at The Crown, near Sharwell. It has a stream that runs though it which is filled with large trout. They have swum here for as long as we have been coming, which is since childhood. We always do the same thing: a meal here and an afternoon at the beach under a beating sun. As we walk through the gate I can see all of them. Martin ordering a seafood platter, expertly breaking up pieces of lobster that have been mixed with prawns, Anna sipping on half a cider. Mum and Dad fussing at the menu. None of them are with us now, except in my memory.

I ask Maddie if she will write something for this book and she sits on the swing and texts me her thoughts. Later, after a kick goes wrong, Francesca will have to rescue her football from the stream, and then there is a near miss when walking from our car to the beach. Gabriella will want an ice cream and we will calculate how much insulin this will take. Normal things really, another day at The Crown to add to the memories, but Maddie's reflections are what will stay with me most.

One of my memories from Herefordshire was when Annabelle, Reuben my cousin, and I were together in Grandpa's field which is next to his house. We were just chilling when Basil the really cute dog came to join us and we played with him for a while. All of a sudden the neighbour's horses, Teddy and Solomon, came rushing in from the other side of the field with a person riding each one of them. Then, someone's quad bike came into the field and started riding around really fast. The horses were going crazy being chased by this machine and running super-fast around the field. Of course, Basil joined in. Reuben, Annabelle and I were still in the field trying to run away but kept nearly getting hit by the horses or run over by the quad bike. When we finally did get out, we got shouted at like it was our fault by Reuben's mum, but oh well. It's funny now looking back on that memory because of how much fun it was.

I also remember the last time I saw Grandpa. It was just me and my dad going down to visit him for the last time as he had severe bowel cancer. I remember giving him a hug as I came in, but a little too hard as I remember it hurting him as I was only waist high. I remember talking about old memories like his old flying toy bat with glowing red eyes we would all pester for him to get out. I remember that I brought this bag with me with lots of designs on, which was made out of special material that was blank that I coloured in with these special pens while watching TV with my dad and Grandpa. I remember that we always used to watch a programme called Wheeler Dealers which was about fixing up cars and selling them. We all loved the programme and we watched so many episodes before bed.

I miss my Grandpa and was really upset when my dad came home one day and said that he had passed away. It was really upsetting for all of us, which is understandable, but we will never forget him.

I also haven't forgotten his wife Mary. I always loved her because we shared the same birthday of August the 2nd and she always made the best Victoria sponge cakes. Even though I had just turned four and she had just turned sixty-one when she died, I still remember her so well. She's included in some of my earliest memories. I only remember snippets of her being around but that's enough for me.

Both of them are in our thoughts and prayers, and we will never forget them. My dad's doing OK now though. I mean, he has five girls and way too many pets in the house to keep him happy, after all. He just needs to protect his debit card and he's all good.

Francesca's Memories –
Christmas, Secret Sweets and
Steep Hills

Then a few weeks later, Francesca and Annabelle wrote some words on the same day. Francesca while we waited for Maddie at a Playbox rehearsal over Saturday lunchtime. She ate a ham and chese toasty and I had a cheese and cucumber sandwich. In between trips back up to the hatch for crisps, Diet Coke and sweets, she started to type her piece and then I typed while she dictated. I do not believe she could really have remembered the sponge cake, but I liked that the story of it was within her.

* * *

The first thing I remember about my grandma is when she always made her delicious Victoria sponge cakes… yum … I never knew her that much because when she sadly passed away I was only two years old.

I remember more about my grandpa because I was only seven when he passed away (I'm eleven now). He used to call me Chessy. He always gave us chocolate Santas every Christmas but he secretly gave me wiggly sweetie worms.

He gave me a drum set one year. It was the biggest present there and when I opened it I was shocked and I played it straight away. One Christmas we went to The Leopard. The waitress said, "Who is coming down the chimney?" and I said Grandpa's girlfriend, because we were meeting her for the first time and that was what I was thinking about.

Grandpa always gave us a Sunday dinner because we always used to come on Sunday. It was so good. My grandpa always had a snooker table, so my family and I always had a game, and if we didn't I kept on pestering them to play because I loved pool.

His drive had a hill, so every time I was on his tricycle I always went down his hill. Once I went over a bump I had not seen and went flying through the air. Every time I had a race I always had first dibs on the tricycle because it was the fastest thing there. I always used to win, and one day I did not have the tricycle so I lost.

In his conservatory I always used to play my favourite games with him: fishing the duck and the car racing game and mini table football. I liked the table football the best. It was sometimes a draw and sometimes a win for me, but sometimes I lost. He always had a smile on his face when he won, and when I won. But more of a bigger smile when he won!

Sometimes my cousins would come over. Reuben and I would play football against the adults and we would win. Grandpa had a treehouse we would go in with the cousins. It was very creepy as there were lots of cobwebs and Reuben would always pretend he had a spider in his hands and pretend to throw it at me. I always used to throw the apples that had fallen off Grandpa's apple tree back at him, and I always tried to play dodgeball with him.

One time my family came over, it was pouring with rain but that didn't stop me from going outside. He had a massive field, and my dad and I walked in his field. It was raining, however, and I got stuck in the mud and when my dad tried to pull me out my welly boot fell off, but my dad fished it out eventually. There was a dog who lived next door. I always used to play fetch with him. He was a very obedient dog.

He was the most secretive grandparent ever because he always gave me sweets. I will always miss him, and her.

Annabelle's Memories – Final Visit and More Sponge Cakes

Annabelle wrote her words in her bedroom. Where else would she write than the somewhat dark teenage cavern from which she emerges sometimes, blinking into the light. I was not allowed to read her writing with her present and I make no further observation on the sponge cakes other than that of all of them, Annabelle was the one most likely to remember. My mum had always pointed to her experience with older children and said that she would come into her own with them as they grew. Alas it was not to be, but she left enough.

* * *

I miss my grandparents a lot. One of my favourite memories of my grandma was her sponge cake; it was so delicious, the highlight of my Sunday afternoons. I vaguely remember the day she died; we were on the Isle of Wight at my uncle's house. I just remember lots of crying, not really knowing what was going on, wanting to see her, asking my mum why I couldn't go and see her.

I loved my grandpa so much; he never failed to make me smile with his weird bat toy and when he tickled me until I cried with laughter. I loved going in his paddling pool in the summer and in his treehouse where we tried to hide from the adults. His greenhouse with the tomatoes, and his orchard with the hundreds of apples and pears, were so fun to explore. The last time I saw him was the last time I got to pick some apples from his garden.

I remember going to see him, knowing that it could be the last time. I was quite apprehensive if I'm honest, I didn't know what to expect, I hadn't seen him for months and didn't know what he'd look like due to his illness. When I saw him I was quite taken aback: he was so thin, so pale, his face so gaunt. I tried to hug him as gently as I could; we then continued to play Scrabble which I was awful at. I'm pretty sure he won by miles. My dad and I let him have a rest and went and picked apples and stroked the horses in his field, Solomon and Teddy.

I miss them both a lot; there are so many more memories they made, so many little things that remind me of them, like a good old Victoria sponge or even just an apple tree; Rest in peace, you're both missed by so many.

The Kindest and
Most Loving of Fathers

Charmian had first met my mother when they taught together, before I was born. She is mentioned in Anna's letter from 1975, and she and her husband Tim were in touch with my parents until their deaths. My father last went to see them at their beautiful house in Yorkshire early in 2014, for a dinner that he much enjoyed. He told me he had sat next to a high court judge and was very impressed by the sharpness of his intellect, the way he dissected the issues. I would have remembered this anyway as it was unusual for him to be so effusive, but the memory is heightened because it is the last formal social gathering he ever told me about. Perhaps it was the last one that he ever went to.

We talked a little about the fact that judges generally were quite clever and I said that I had sometimes seen the judgements I studied at Bristol as being literature's best kept secret; albeit the fact that Lord Denning upheld the rights of an Englishman to pepper his neighbour with cricket balls if they happened to live next to a cricket ground, meant this was probably not much consolation for those affected.

Charmian and Tim had now moved to Oxford to be near their daughter, Francis Larson, an anthropologist and historian, and author of the books *Severed* and *An Infinity of Things*. We had not spoken for some time, until in the summer of 2017 I received a card through the post inviting me to meet up with them both, together with another old friend who also taught with my mum, Rosemary Chambers. I drove along country lanes that increasingly reminded me of those around Bosbury, more remote still in some ways. Visiting people who had known my parents when young was to take a bridge to a world that could still be travelled, but only just.

We talked about books and memories, families, stories. Tim said that when I was younger I had looked like my mother, but that now I had more of the look of my father about me. I knew that this was so.

Charmian and Rosemary talked about teaching with my mother. A production of a play she had directed that had been really good, still remembered by both of them, its energy not yet entirely stilled. In amongst the food and the warmth of the conversation, time seemed to press, my parents' absence a marker that nobody in the room was still young.

I thanked Charmian for the beautiful letter she had written to me after my father's death. That letter is reproduced below.

A Letter from Charmian

6th November 2014

Dear Ben,

*The shock and sadness of the death of your father –
surely one of the kindest and most loved of fathers – has
in the last week released a flood of memories, of how
Mary and Colin were when Tim and I first knew them.*

*Mary, as you know, was my colleague at work, and it
was one of those partnerships where work and pleasure
exactly balance – a rare privilege. Imagine us acting in
Twelfth Night which Mary produced at Alton leading a
cast of 6th formers, with me as Viola and Mary as Olivia!*

*Your parents, as you know, were a strikingly attractive
couple, and I was deeply impressed by the Romeo + Juliet
story of how they had overcome their parents' opposition
to what was then so feared – a "mixed" marriage. (It
strikes me that in general the better the mixture, the
better the marriage.) I knew then that this was a special
couple with a special love for each other – and so it
has always proved. I put that together with a moment
that stays with me, for some reason, from their last visit
to Yorkshire together. They came for a weekend a few*

years ago, and we went to the theatre in Leeds. Tim and I crossed a road, in this night time city of bright lights and heavy traffic. As I turned, the traffic parted, and I saw Colin arm in arm with Mary, escorting her carefully across the road. I will remember it.

There is a saying that "the good die young" – as a consolation it seems pretty useless, and of course it's not always true. But it's true in this case. Your parents will always be young – if there's a consolation, at least they saw their children's children.

And, in the encounters we had with them more recently – sadly so few – their love for you all has glowed as brightly as their love for one another always did. So full of interests and activities, so highly valued at work and by their friends, their later life, despite their troubles, has been as successful as their early days. But nothing has lit it up for them the way their children and their grandchildren have. It's unbelievably hard for you – but they will always live in your hearts.

Love from Charmian

Afterword

A handful of letters from the 1970s, Martin's journal, Noreen's diary, some poems, work-based assessments and references, memories of holidays and Christmases and normal goings-on, some happy, some less so. All of it marked by too many deaths and everyday disasters. I do not think it joins perfectly, but in that sense it mirrors life generally, and family life in particular.

I hope this story at least preserves a small part of what is now passed and that it speaks as much to life as it does to death. Some things that were in danger of being forgotten or lost, now at least recorded. I think to the Dylan Thomas line *Though I sang in my chains like the sea.* Perhaps that is what all of them were doing, what all of us are destined ever to do. Making plans. Falling in love, often with the right people, if not always. Building careers, teaching, managing business ventures that grow then falter. Things that work out and things that do not, when you look back a certain arbitrariness between the two. Many games of all sorts played along the way.

I wanted to record the big events, particularly around some of the endings, but I did not want this to be a book just about death. Endings can be just that; it is not true that they are always beginnings too. Capturing perspectives of the everyday, through different eyes and different lenses, was what this was meant to be about.

Relationships within families are a little like sailing on a ferry in choppy waters, with the end destination uncertain. The vessel might bob and sway, the contours of land difficult to decipher, while in the wheelhouse different views as to how to proceed are probably not unknown. Yet, through it all, the journey is still one that is taken together, there is a common purpose to it all, even if some crew members have further left to sail than others. Fathers and sons. Arthur and Martin, Colin and I. Fathers and daughters too; none of it is easy. Yet as I write I think to the poster a colleague displays in her work cubicle. It says that boats are safe in a harbour, but this is not what boats are made for.

I have been grateful to have the opportunity to think about it all.

I have shared some of the things that worry me, the fear that patterns repeat. I have come to notice that there are many ways in which my father parented better than I do, and that there are things that can still be changed, that I can work on. I hope that my own daughters will one day reach the same conclusion in relation to me, that it was probably all alright and that they were happy when they were young. I know that there is nothing else that is really worth hoping for. We are all part of the same pattern after all.

It was certainly a sense that time was passing that finally compelled me to write all of this down, after many years of avoiding writing anything. I had to write and now finally, thanks to them all, I have, such as it is. Through these stories, I do feel that I have drawn closer to all of them. It has triggered memories I had not thought of for a long time. It has prompted me to think of things anew. I hope to go on to write other stories.

They say that a marriage can only be really understood by the two people in it. A family on a wider scale is similar. Except even the thing about a marriage is only a partial truth. We all understand these things, our relationships, as best we can. Our information set is not complete. A family multiplies the scope for misunderstanding. Who knows what anybody else really thinks? What they show and don't show. In many of these chapters I remember my parents as old, but they were younger than I am now. They experienced all of these things from different vantage points to my own. It is either like poker or chess. In poker you can't see all the cards in your opponent's hands. In chess you see all the pieces, yet the plays are so complex they can only be deciphered to a point.

Were they happy?

Mum fulfilled her vocation as a gifted teacher who touched many lives. We were overwhelmed by the number of people who told us how much she had helped them, going back over years. She worried about a lot of things and was deeply concerned at the way the college was being run in her final years. A worry, I think looking back on it, that I did not take seriously enough.

As I said at her funeral, "Successive governments' education policies were a disappointment to her," which made people laugh, though it was not a subject she looked on with benign amusement.

Where Dad is concerned, who knows? He seemed to do responsible jobs that won the respect of others. He had a powerful intellect that he got to use. He had a lot of interests, even if they did not fully occupy him, and a reluctance to commit to structured activities in retirement sometimes left him isolated, that, if truth be told, *too often* left him isolated.

He loved his family, but some of the pain from Helen and Mum's deaths could never be assuaged and left him guarded, difficult to read. I do not think he was happy during his final illness. Why would he have been? But, taken as a whole, there was a lot of happiness in his life, and even on that final night he had been smiling in spite of it all. This is what people do. He could be very difficult. There is no shame in saying this and it does not equate to a definitive verdict but is rather to acknowledge a reality.

For Theresa and Dave, the question is easier and not. They overcame the greatest tragedy parents can face: the death of a child. They kept her memory and all that was good about Helen alive for the rest of their lives. They were not conventionally successful in their jobs, but that was not what drove them, it was never about that, so it does not form a measure. Their vocation was each other. Dave could not have survived without her. Theresa summoned up the strength to carry on without him, at least for a while. As with all these things we do not have the counterfactual. What would they have done differently had Helen lived? What they did was enough, and the obvious happiness in their relationship after all those years was something very rare.

Anna always seemed to me to be where she wanted

to be, but I thought that before I knew of her depression, and now I am not sure. She was a nurse by vocation, most comfortable with her family around her. Her own final illness was challenging, but it seemed to me that whatever difficulties she faced she was equal to them.

Martin is the hardest to know because he was the one of them most like me, and I know that no one could answer this question on my behalf. In truth, I am impertinent to try and do so for any of them, I know that. He was more sociable and more of an extrovert than I am, with fewer opportunities to study. Both of us did jobs that probably weren't entirely what we would have wanted. Both of us wanted to write, and ultimately both of us did. This in part written now because I did not want to be desperately trying to get it all down in my eighties, as I had seen him do. My guess is that he was happy, whatever that actually means. His youthful spark and sense of adventure undimmed. But to be human is to also have disappointment, and that of course goes for all of us.

I have to think about ending this now. The stories have been told, the letters and poems shared. One day soon, there will be a neatly typed up version of this manuscript, a book hopefully, that I will give to the children. It could be a moment that they remember. Annabelle, Madeleine, Francesca and Gabriella. They might read it, they might not. Is it possible all of this will be forgotten and then re-remembered like Martin's journal?

There will be a copy for Katharine and for my Uncle Mike and my brother Matthew, his children Reuben and Evie too. If nothing else, it will not be like *Bleeding*. I have written about the people that I know and the things that I can see. I hope that the sense of all that was good in Mary and Colin, Theresa and Dave, Anna and Martin is just as clear to the reader.

My children are all still children, and any illusion they still might have that I am all-seeing will be lost if they read these words, perhaps replaced at least with the notion that I am trying to see, however imperfectly, to find my way and that none of these things are easy. I am hopeful that any such thoughts this reveals to them about my own many inadequacies will be displaced by a game of Monopoly or some football in the garden. Perhaps my solutions to things that might be difficult are not so different from my father's after all.

When I am gone, will they think my life was more about me than them? If they do, on this they will be wrong, just as I knew, when my father said, "You boys are everything," that he was telling the truth. If there was to be one thing that remained, I would want it to be that the girls knew they were everything to me. There might still be a myriad of other disappointments and missed expectations, perhaps some that are entirely unknown to me but matter to them. The history of my relationship with my father tells me that this might be so. It also gives me hope that it will not be the whole story.

In the end, Annabelle, Francesca, Maddie and Gabriella will write their own chapters, whether on paper or in other ways that matter more, and I will have to be content that I told my side whilst I still could.

Epilogue – Last Journey

There is one last journey left to make. Annabelle and Francesca are coming with me as we leave Warwick on a summer morning which has just a trace of autumn in the air, a quiet whisper that the season has already peaked. My back feels fragile, it gives me more warnings than once it did, but we have a plan for today and that matters more. Maddie is staying at home with Katharine and Gabriella to do some baking; we have been promised cakes on our return.

Down the motorway we go, teenage music blaring out as we make good progress. The roadworks that used to shape this journey have long since been completed, and today there is no trace of the bollards and average speed cameras that used to mark this route. Annabelle and Francesca squabble benignly, but mainly there is calm. I think to the drive on the day before my father died and it feels both vivid and distant. A long time ago and not so long, even if he was alive then and is dead now, today is better. What we will face is more certain; some things if not all have been resolved. I am not making the trip alone.

Eventually we divert to go through Malvern rather than straight onto what had once been my parents' house.

We talk about Francesca's latest football trial and then the play that Maddie and Gabriella will both soon be in. Annabelle shares a plan to dye her hair silver.

Finally we are there and we walk down the steep hill and stand before the grave which is still and peaceful in the delicate summer breeze. The children now quiet, thoughtful, and just as I never knew what he was thinking when he stood here, now I cannot read them.

I have not been here for a long time and we clear some weeds and lay fresh flowers, just as my father used to do in the six years between my mother's burial and his joining her in this place. He was the custodian for such a short space of time; how can any of us be other? I resolve to come more often.

I remember again her funeral, in the sun, rain, then sun again. Arguing with him at the graveside a few months later, the packed church at his funeral, which first impressed and then just saddened me. Earlier happier memories here: Matt and Rachel's wedding, Reuben's christening; they are all part of the same cycle, the same patterns.

Annabelle is thoughtful and does not say much. Francesca talks a little more and holds my hand. None of us are quite sure what we are doing, but we are going to make this work. We stand for a while and in the end it is Francesca who tells us that it is time to go, that we still have things to do. Her grandparents will still be here whenever we want to come back.

We drive on to their old house, twenty minutes or so away, and park at the top of the small private road. The drive is smooth now, but other than the fresh tarmac it looks much as it did when I saw it for the first time nearly thirty-five years ago. It is likely it will look the same to others many more years on from this, further than the three of us can go. All of us are part of something that will transcend us all, even the children, whether we like it or not. Mum and Dad were Anna and Martin's, Dave and Theresa's children, once. My children are never allowed to die.

I can feel a tingle in my back and in my leg, but here today, as on so many previous days, it means very little. The new owners are friendly and would doubtless invite us in if they knew we were here, but we have no desire to intrude. The physical place is not ours now, but some of its past surely still is.

I tell Annabelle again about the bike races down the drive and skating on the duck pond in winter. She has heard these stories before but listens politely.

Everything might look the same but nothing really is. I remind Francesca of the time we picked apples in the orchard, just before the house was sold. She remembers. I start to tell her some of the stories I have been writing about. Their great great grandfather riding a motorcycle in World War One, Martin in the fire service in World War Two, the chess, and some of the other games that have been played.

I notice I avoid telling them about how writing all of this made me think, about me and about them. Perhaps I keep the same things from them as Dad did from me. I am my father's son. They both nod politely and I know these should be the last stories for today.

In the morning we are heading to Uncle Mike's and we will be on the Isle of Wight once more. That is still part of our present in a way that the house is not.

We will bring Maddie and Gabriella's cakes with us. Francesca will bring her football.

Finally Annabelle looks at me.

"Let's go home, Dad."

Traveller's Joy

Deep in the dark time of the year
Remember one who came so quietly
The outsider unremarked save by a few
Travelling men. Shepherds and stable beasts-
Not momentous, as first impressions go.
But this is why, for near two thousand years.
The greyest days are lit with candle flame
As green-black holly gleams,
Sharp and redly-berried, cut from
Three trees on a hill, which do not yet
Cast shadows. Against all judgement
It is again the season for a journey,
A time for fond reunion, joy and light,
For Christ has rescued us from depths of night.

M.G.

Acknowledgements

Find Another Place would not have been possible without the help and support of many others.

If it had not been for my grandfather Martin Holmes's journal there would be no book. He might not have become the writer he wanted to be, but hopefully in some small way this book showcases both his talent and his story. I am also grateful to Kelly Stevens, for her expertise in deciphering Martin's handwriting, without which I do not think his journal could have been rescued.

The letters from my parents Mary and Colin Graff and my mother's poems are equally integral to this book. It still moves me to read stories of their beginnings at a time when their lives are both over. As so often with these things, the best moment to say thank you to them both is past, but I want to take this opportunity to place on record my thanks for everything they did for me. I will always miss them.

I would like to thank the other contributors to *Find Another Place*. In particular my daughters Annabelle, Madeleine and Francesca for their passages and my youngest Gabriella who helped her sisters with these. I am also grateful to Madeleine for taking a photograph one Christmas Eve, back on the Isle of Wight where so much of this book is set, that formed the basis for Dave Hillsarts cover design.

Janet Morter very kindly let me use her mother Noreen (my great aunt's) diary and her encouragement and support for this project was very much appreciated. Charmian Knight graciously let me use one of her letters. As a lifelong friend of both my parents, her enthusiasm for this project meant a great deal to me and helped to set my mind at rest that this book should be written.

The role that first readers play in helping to shape a book is something I have come to more fully appreciate during the writing process. My editor Gary Dalkin helped me to better navigate this story than I could have done alone. His care and precision have played a big part in making *Find Another Place* all that it can be. I am grateful for his friendship.

The professionalism of the team at Matador has also made a big difference. I am sure there are many others, but I would like to particularly thank Lauren Bailey, Heidi Hurst and Emily Castledine.

Finally and most importantly I would like to thank my wife Katharine. Without her encouragement and patience *Find Another Place* would still be nothing more than an idea. Here is to many more stories…

Ben Graff - January 2018